THE CONCEPT OF UNITY IN PUBLIC INTERNATIONAL LAW

'Fragmentation' has become a defining, albeit controversial, metaphor of international law scholarship in the era of globalisation. Some scholars see it as a new development, others as history repeating itself; some approach it as a technical issue and some as the reflection of deeper political struggles. But there is near-consensus about the fact that the established vision of international law as a unitary whole is under threat. At the core of the fragmentation debate lies the concept of unity, but this is hardly ever rationalised and is more assumed than explained. Its meaning remains vague and intuitive. The Concept of Unity in Public International Law attempts to dispel that vagueness by exploring the various possible meanings of the concept of unity in international law. However, eschewing one grand theory of unity, it identifies and compares five candidates. Intentionally pluralistic in its outlook, the book does not engage in normative arguments about whether international law is or should be unitary but seeks to show instead that the concept of unity is contested and that discourses on fragmentation are necessarily contingent.

The thesis on which the book is based won the 2009 Prize for best doctoral thesis from the Association des professeurs de droit du Québec.

Volume 7 in the series Hart Monographs in Transnational and International Law

Hart Monographs in Transnational and International Law

Series Editor: Craig Scott, Professor of Law, Osgoode Hall Law School of York University, Toronto

The objective of this series is to publish high-quality scholarship in public international law and private international law, as well as work that adopts 'transnational law' as its thematic, theoretical or doctrinal focus. The series strives to be a leading venue for work of the following sort:

* critical reappraisals of foundational concepts and core doctrinal principles of both public and private international law, and their operation in practice, including insights drawn from general legal theory;

* analysis and development of conceptions of 'transnational law', including in relation to the role of unofficial law and informal processes in transnational regulation and in relation to theories and studies of 'governance' in transnational spheres; and

* empirical studies of the emergence, evolution and transformation of international and/or transnational legal orders, including accounts and explanations of how law is constructed within different communities of interpretation and practice.

The series will also be home to monographs that explore the interactions between the ever-integrating fields of public and private international law. Of special interest are explorations of the extent to which these interactions are structured by higher-order principles and policies, on the one hand, and by politics and the exercise of various forms of power, on the other hand.

The series is open to work not only by law scholars but also by scholars from cognate disciplines.

Recent titles in this series

Volume 4 Between Governing and Governance: On the Emergence, Function and Form of Europe's Post-National Constellation
Poul Kjaer

Volume 5 Rough Consensus and Running Code: A Theory of Transnational Private Law
Gralf-Peter Calliess and Peer Zumbansen

Volume 6 The Payment Order of Antiquity and the Middle Ages: A Legal History
Benjamin Geva

Volume 7 The Concept of Unity in Public International Law
Mario Prost

For the complete list of titles in this series, see
'Hart Monographs in Transnational and International Law' link at
www.hartpub.co.uk/books/series.asp

The Concept of Unity in Public International Law

Mario Prost

·HART·
PUBLISHING

OXFORD AND PORTLAND OREGON
2012

Published in the United Kingdom by Hart Publishing Ltd
16C Worcester Place, Oxford, OX1 2JW
Telephone: +44 (0)1865 517530
Fax: +44 (0)1865 510710
E-mail: mail@hartpub.co.uk
Website: http://www.hartpub.co.uk

Published in North America (US and Canada) by
Hart Publishing
c/o International Specialized Book Services
920 NE 58th Avenue, Suite 300
Portland, OR 97213-3786
USA
Tel: +1 503 287 3093 or toll-free: (1) 800 944 6190
Fax: +1 503 280 8832
E-mail: orders@isbs.com
Website: http://www.isbs.com

British Library Cataloguing in Publication Data
Data Available

ISBN: 978-1-84946-043-9

Typeset by Hope Services, Abingdon
Printed and bound in Great Britain by
Lightning Source UK Ltd

Table of Contents

1

Introduction

THERE IS SOMETHING peculiar about international law. Ever since its emergence as an autonomous professional discipline, international law has been a contested object. For how can law exist – let alone rule – among sovereign nations that recognise no authority beyond their own? What can be the significance of a legal system in which juridical subjects themselves, and most notably powerful ones, control the meaning and enforcement of legal rules? In any case, should one really speak of 'international' law when, historically, this law has been created by and for European nations? Although at the turn of the twentieth century international law has consolidated its position within the academy, through the creation of new chairs, learned societies and scientific publications, scepticism remains high. International law is too different from the familiar forms and techniques of municipal law. It seems primitive, weak and under-elaborated. Above all, international law is accused of being either too philosophical or too political.[1]

Faced with scepticism, early international lawyers have had to spend considerable energy defending their project and proving the autonomy and positivity of their law. The strategies and arguments used to legitimise international law in this foundational period were diverse. Some were merely rhetorical ('international law is not primitive, it is simply different'). Others were more pragmatic ('international law exists: states speak its language and use its processes in their dealing with one another'). Most arguments, however, were analogical or comparative. Despite appearances, it was claimed, international law is not so different from domestic law. States can be construed as legal subjects possessing property (territory) and negotiating contracts (treaties). More importantly, international law was defended as being just as complex, technical and sophisticated as municipal law. Hersch Lauterpacht, who was typical of this way of thinking about international law, considered for example that the whole of international law could be read as the rough equivalent on the international plane of rules, categories and institutions of private law (contract law, tort law, property law, law of succession, rules of evidence and procedure and so on).[2]

[1] Martti Koskenniemi, 'The Fate of Public International Law: Between Technique and Politics' (2007) 70 *Modern Law Review* 1, 1ff.

[2] Hersch Lauterpacht, *Private Law Sources and Analogies of International Law* (London, Longman, 1927).

Whilst these strategies were quite successful in the inter-war period, the Second World War prompted a new cycle of existential angst and questioning. International law's failure to prevent the war and the Holocaust plunged the discipline into a period of metaphysical turmoil. International lawyers, yet again, had to face criticism, not only from within the legal discipline, but this time also from without, most notably from the discipline of international relations, where realists depicted international law as utopian, irrelevant or at best peripheral, a mere continuation of politics through other means.[3] Post-war international lawyers were therefore compelled to resume the self-justificatory enterprise started by their predecessors. Though the tone and vocabulary were different – for one does not speak about international law in the same way before and after the Holocaust – the themes and strategies remained essentially the same. Whilst admitting that international law had its limits and specificities, international lawyers continued to fight to prove its reality, its positivity and its materiality.[4]

Two decades after the War, however, these various strategies seemed to bear fruit – if only internally – and international law entered a period of relative self-confidence. The discipline, it seemed, no longer felt compelled to prove the existence and relevance of its object. In 1966, Ian Brownlie published the first edition of his *Principles of Public International Law*.[5] The book, which quickly became a standard text, marked a significant change of style. The tone was resolutely anti-apologetic. Brownlie wanted to write a textbook on the substance, the methods and the techniques of international law in very much the same way one would write a textbook on domestic law subjects like contract or criminal law. Brownlie saw international law as an established field of law and saw no need to venture into ontological questions about the basis of obligation or the legal nature of international law.[6] The book thus featured 12 chapters on 12 substantive areas of positive law, but no introduction on definitional and foundational issues. These questions, the author wrote in his preface, 'belong to books on legal theory'.[7]

Brownlie, of course, was a product of his time. From 1958 to 1969, international law underwent a series of decisive developments, including the adoption of the four Geneva Conventions on the law of the sea, the Convention on diplomatic and consular relations, and the two Vienna Conventions on the law of treaties. This 'golden decade of codification' bred new confidence in interna-

[3] See especially Hans Morgenthau, *Politics Among Nations* (New York, Knopf, 1947).

[4] See, eg, Richard Falk, 'The Reality of International Law' (1962) 14 *World Politics* 353; Wolfgang Friedman, 'The Reality of International Law – A Reappraisal' (1971) 10 *Columbia Journal of Transnational Law* 46; Anthony D'Amato, 'Is International Law Really Law' (1984) 79 *Northwestern University Law Review* 1293.

[5] Ian Brownlie, *Principles of International Law* (Oxford, Oxford University Press, 1966).

[6] Although he did write on these issues on other occasions. See, eg, Ian Brownlie, 'The Reality and Efficacy of International Law' (1981) 52 *British Yearbook of International Law* 1.

[7] Brownlie, *Principles*, above n 5 at v.

tional law. The momentum was largely confirmed in the 1970s and 1980s, both on the diplomatic plane – with the adoption of treaties like the Law of the Sea Convention – and on the judicial plane – with a succession of seminal decisions such as the *Nicaragua* judgment which marked the victory, in a court of law, of a small nation against the great superpower of the day. Following the fall of the Berlin wall, the General Assembly even proclaimed the period 1990–99 as the 'United Nations Decade of International Law'.[8]

In the early 1990s, the mood was resolutely optimistic. International lawyers were well aware that the post-Cold War era offered as many challenges as opportunities. But the discipline seemed to have rid itself of its existential predicament. International law, some said, had entered a 'post-ontological era' in which lawyers had become emancipated from the constraints of defensive ontology and were free to end the cycle of doubt and introspection that had for so long inhibited their discipline.[9] Around the same time, some scholars even started speaking of the 'constitutionalisation' of international law, a term that seems to suggest that international law may have reached a degree of maturity and complexity comparable to that of domestic legal systems.[10]

Despite this renewed confidence and the post-Cold War optimism, however, the 1990s were a rather paradoxical period for international law. Just as the discipline seemed to be overcoming its metaphysical malaise, growing numbers of international lawyers started expressing concerns over a new peril: the so-called fragmentation phenomenon. International law, it was said, was developing too fast and in too many directions. There were too many rules and too many regimes, and too little normative and institutional glue to hold the system together. International law's unity may be in danger and, without reform, the system may slowly descend into chaos. Between 1998 and 2000, three successive Presidents of the International Court of Justice spoke publicly against the dangers of fragmentation, most notably before the UN General Assembly.[11] The latter, convinced of the seriousness of the situation, even decided to put the matter to the International Law Commission which, in 2006, issued a 'toolbox'

[8] GA Res 44/23 17 November 1989.

[9] Thomas Franck, *Fairness in International Law and Institutions* (New York, Oxford University Press, 1995) 6.

[10] See, eg, Richard Falk et al (eds), *The Constitutional Foundations of World Peace* (Albany, SUNY Press, 1993); Bruno Simma, 'From Bilateralism to Community Interest in International Law' (1994) 250 *Collected Courses* 217, 256–84; Bardo Fassbender, 'The United Nations Charter as Constitution of the International Community' (1998) 529 *Columbia Journal of Transnational Law* 558.

[11] Robert Jennings, 'The Role of the International Court of Justice' (1997) 68 *British Yearbook of International Law* 1; Address to the Plenary session of the General Assembly of the United Nations by Judge Stephen M Schebel, 26 October 1999: www.icj-cij.org/court/index.php?pr=87&pt=3&p1=1&p2=3&p3=1; Address by HE Judge Gilbert Guillaume, President of the International Court of Justice, to the United Nations General Assembly, 26 October 2000: www.icj-cij.org/court/index.php?pr=84&pt=3&p1=1&p2=3&p3=1; Gilbert Guillaume, 'La Cour internationale de Justice – Quelques propositions concrètes à l'occasion du cinquantenaire' (1996) 100 *Revue Générale de Droit International Public* 323.

to deal with issues of fragmentation.[12] Everything happened as if international lawyers, busy as they had long been with dealing with ontological questions, were suddenly caught up in an acceleration of historical time and were seized by a sort of 'postmodern anxiety'.[13] But what, exactly, are the causes of this new anxiety?

I. THE ROOTS OF A POSTMODERN ANXIETY

The fragmentation anxiety stems, first of all, from the material expansion and densification of international law, that is, the spreading of international legal activity into new fields and the diversification of its objects and techniques. Traditionally, the ambit of international law was rather limited. In fact, until the end of the nineteenth century, international law was primarily concerned with two questions: the limits to state jurisdiction and the conduct of diplomatic relations. Since the end of the Second World War, however, and more so since the end of the Cold War, international law has spread far and wide into virtually all areas of human activity – from trade, transport, telecommunications and finance to health, human rights, the environment, terrorism, culture and so on.[14] Even in the discipline of international relations – where the mainstream has long played down the importance of international law – this transformation has been recognised, with some scholars now speaking of the 'legalisation' of world politics.[15]

At a different level, the fragmentation anxiety can be explained by the broadening of the international legal community. Historically, international law has been an instrument of domination of a handful of European nations over the rest of the world. The international legal community has long remained an exclusive 'club' of Western powers, in which non-Western societies were not admitted.[16] International law, however, has progressively abandoned the degree

[12] *Fragmentation of International Law: Difficulties Arising from the Diversification and Expansion of International Law – Report of the Study Group of the International Law Commission* (finalised by Martti Koskenniemi), UN Doc A/CN.4/L.682 (2006) (ILC Fragmentation Report). See also *Conclusions of the Work of the Study Group on the Fragmentation of International Law: Difficulties Arising from the Diversification and Expansion of International Law*, UN Doc A/61/10 (2006) (ILC Fragmentation Conclusions). The final conclusions were adopted collectively by the study group as a whole and represent a condensed version – or 'executive summary' – of the larger analytical study.

[13] Martti Koskenniemi and Paivi Leino, 'Fragmentation of International Law? Postmodern Anxieties' (2005) 15 *Leiden Journal of International Law* 553. The idea that fragmentation is a new concern in international law scholarship is contested by some authors who see in the modern rhetoric of fragmentation a mere revival of past anxieties over the state and direction of international law. See, eg, Anne-Charlotte Martineau, 'The Rhetoric of Fragmentation: Fear and Faith in International Law' (2009) 22 *Leiden Journal of International Law* 1.

[14] Oscar Schachter, *International Law in Theory and Practice* (Dordrecht, Martinus Nijhoff, 1991) 1–3.

[15] See Judith Goldstein et al, 'Legalization and World Politics' (2000) 54 *International Organizations* 385.

[16] On the role of international law as an instrument of Western hegemony, see especially Anthony Anghie, *Imperialism, Sovereignty and the Making of International Law* (Cambridge, Cambridge University Press, 2005).

of civilisation (at least in its classical form) as a membership criterion. It has become, if only on the surface, a truly universal law which in theory applies equally to all nations, big and small, rich and poor, old and new. Following decolonisation, the international legal community has grown dramatically from about 40 recognised state actors in 1920 to nearly 200 today.

The change is not only quantitative, however. It is qualitative too. The international community has become an 'outer-less community', that is, a community without 'barbarians'. Without barbarians does not mean without barbarism. The twentieth century has had its share of genocides, committed by civilised and barbaric nations alike. International law, however, has slowly abandoned the civilised/barbarian opposition as a structuring dialectic. International law no longer defines itself in relation to its enemies from without. There remain rogue, undesirable or untouchable subjects (terrorists, unlawful combatants, refugees, etc) within the international community and these continue to be used to construct an image of international law's self as a progressive force in a savage and violent world.[17] But the fantasised figure of the barbarian 'other', which is excluded *ab initio* from the community of civilised nations, has largely disappeared from international law discourse.[18]

Whilst barbarians have formally disappeared as a legal category, new speaking subjects have emerged, however, which also contribute to the perceived loss of coherence in international law. For most of its existence, international law has been the exclusive preserve of states. To international lawyers, the state has been a familiar face, a reassuring voice, a firm ground on which to base their theories of law, obligation and justice. Yet again, this is no longer the case today. It has become practically impossible to understand international legal matters in relation to states alone. Individuals, who were once considered mere objects of international law, are now the holders of international rights that are actionable in court, including against their own state, and can be held personally responsible for violating international criminal law.[19] Multinational corporations have become regular interlocutors in the governance of transnational problems. For example, the *Global Compact* is a strategic partnership between the UN and the business sector aimed at promoting compliance with universally accepted principles in the areas of human rights, labour, environment and anticorruption.[20] Major cities have even started acting as global players and stakeholders in the areas of trade, finance, human rights or sustainable development.[21]

[17] See Anne Orford (ed), *International Law and Its Others* (Cambridge, Cambridge University Press, 2006).

[18] On this theme, see Mireille Delmas-Marty, *L'adieu aux barbares* (Laval, Presses de L'université Laval, 2007).

[19] See Andrew Clapham, 'The Role of the Individual in International Law' (2010) 21 *European Journal of International Law* 25.

[20] See Andreas Rasche and Georg Kell (eds), *The United Nations Global Compact – Achievements, Trends and Challenges* (Cambridge, Cambridge University Press, 2010).

[21] See Paul Knox and Peter Taylor, *World Cities in a World System* (Cambridge, Cambridge University Press, 1995).

In the United States, for instance, a vanguard of large cities representing more than 30 million people has taken upon itself to drive the country forward in the fight against climate change, signing up to the Kyoto protocol and committing to its greenhouse gas emissions targets.[22]

The rapid development of international organisations, both intergovernmental (IOs) and non-governmental (NGOs), has also played a major role in the transformation of the familiar state-centred international law landscape. IOs, which were almost non-existent in the early twentieth century, now outnumber states in a three to one ratio.[23] Whether as law-makers, law shapers or dispute settlers, IOs have significantly changed the way in which international laws are made, implemented and enforced, as well as becoming forums in which state sovereignty is regularly defined, exercised and contested.[24] NGOs, for their part, number in the tens of thousands. Though they lack international legal personality in the traditional sense, their influence on the formation and implementation of international norms is now well documented and hardly contested.[25]

A final well-recognised mutation in modern international law concerns the emergence of juridical 'monsters', that is, of unfamiliar forms, objects and processes that do not easily fit into the classical categories of public international law. There are, first of all, new forms of normativity such as 'soft law' or 'unofficial law', a term coined to describe new forms of transnational regulation developed directly by private operators, without the state, in specific economic sectors (*lex mercatoria, lex sportiva, lex electronica* and so on).[26] New kinds of institutions also appear, which are neither strictly national nor strictly international. The European Union is a prime example of this sort of 'unidentified legal object', located somewhere between an international organisation and a pre-federal state.[27] More recently, 'mixed' and 'hybrid' jurisdictions have been established in the field of investment disputes (ICSID) and international criminal justice (special tribunals for Sierra Leone, Cambodia, Lebanon, etc), which are composed of both domestic and international judges and apply a blend of

[22] Paul Brown, 'US Cities Snub Bush and Sign Up to Kyoto' *The Guardian* (London, 17 May 2005).

[23] The number of IOs varies according to the criteria employed. The figure for public international organisations, however, is almost certainly over 500 and probably under 700. See Chittharanjan Amerasinghe, *Principles of the Institutional Law of International Organisations* (Cambridge, Cambridge University Press, 2005) 6. On the multiplication of international organisations, see Mario Prost and Paul Clark, 'Unity, Diversity and the Fragmentation of International Law: How Much Does the Multiplication of International Organizations Really Matter? (2006) 5 *Chinese Journal of International Law* 341.

[24] See especially Jose Alvarez, *International Organisations as Law-Makers* (Oxford, Oxford University Press, 2005) and Dan Sarooshi, *International Organizations and their Exercise of Sovereign Powers* (Oxford, Oxford University Press, 2005).

[25] See Steve Charnovitz, 'Nongovernmental Organizations and International Law' (2006) 100 *American Journal of International Law* 348 and Gaëlle Breton-Le Goff, *L'influence des organisations non gouvernementales sur la négociation de quelques instruments internationaux* (Brussels, Bruylant, 2001).

[26] See in particular Gunther Teubner, *Global Law Without a State* (Aldershot, Dartmouth, 1997).

[27] On the 'European monster', see Mireille Delmas-Marty, *Les forces imaginantes du droit III – La refondation des pouvoirs* (Paris, Seuil, 2007) 102–10.

local and international law.[28] More unusual still is the Caribbean Court of Justice, a dual-function institution that operates as a regional court of justice, applying rules of international law in respect of the interpretation and application of the Treaty Establishing the Caribbean Community, as well as a final court of appeal for all members of the Community in civil and criminal matters. Unique among its kind, the Caribbean Court of Justice is thus both a municipal supreme court and an international tribunal.[29]

'Material expansion', 'widening international legal community', 'proliferation of speaking subjects', 'diversification of sources' and emergence of 'juridical monsters': these developments, taken together, work to produce in the discipline of international law a feeling of dispersion and dissolution. With the propagation of international law in new spaces, with uncertain boundaries, many international lawyers fear a loss of control and meaning.[30] The old image of the Westphalian legal order, with its clear separation between domestic and international levels of governance, slowly gives way to the image of a complex 'disorder of normative orders',[31] a system where frames and margins are blurred, where legal spaces overlap and conflict with each other, a network with a plurality of voices, lacking a master plan or blueprint.[32]

Needless to say, things do not change from one day to the next in the 1990s. But a succession of important developments precipitates the emergence of this feeling of dispersion and dissolution. First is the deepening and consolidation of a series of special regimes: the establishment of a new European Union, the creation of NAFTA, the joint adoption at the Rio Summit of the Framework Convention on Climate Change and of the Convention to Combat Desertification, the constitution of the World Trade Organization, the entry into force of the UN Convention on the Law of the Sea, the adoption of the Rome Statute on the International Criminal Court and so on. Whilst the 1960s represented the era of 'general' international law (law of treaties, diplomatic and consular relations, etc), the 1990s are clearly the decade of 'special' international law.

Around the same time, a number of important decisions are issued by special courts and tribunals, which either depart from well-established principles of international law or interpret their own body of law in isolation from other branches of international law, that is, in relative ignorance of legislative and institutional activities in adjoining fields. The WTO Appellate Body, in its

[28] Lindsey Raub, 'Positioning Hybrid Tribunals in International Criminal Justice' (2009) 41 *New York University Journal of International Law and Politics* 1013.

[29] David Simmons, 'The Caribbean Court of Justice: A Unique Institution of Caribbean Creativity' (2004) 29 *Nova Law Review* 171.

[30] Slim Laghmani, 'Le phenomène de perte de sens en droit international' in Rafâa Ben Achour and Slim Laghmani (eds) *Harmonie et contradiction en droit international: Rencontres internationales de la Faculté des sciences juridiques, politiques et sociales de Tunis* (Paris, Pedone, 1996).

[31] Neil Walker, 'Beyond Boundary Disputes and Basic Grids: Mapping the Global Disorder of Normative Orders' (2008) 6 *International Journal of Constitutional Law* 373.

[32] On the paradigmatic shift from the hierarchical 'pyramid' to the heterarchical 'network', see Francois Ost and Michel Van de Kerchove, *De la pyramide au réseau? Pour une théorie dialectique du droit* (Brussels, Publications des Facultés Universitaires Saint Louis, 2002).

Shrimp-Turtle jurisprudence, struggles to look beyond trade rules and consider their interaction with multilateral environmental agreements.[33] The European Court of Human Rights, in *Belilos* and *Loizidou*, reverses the long tradition of judicial deference towards reservations and holds them inadmissible, *ex hypothesi*, in relation to human rights treaties.[34] The International Criminal Tribunal for the former Yugoslavia (ICTY), in the *Tadic* case, rejects the International Court of Justice's interpretation of certain rules of state responsibility.[35]

For all of these reasons, a shift occurs at some point in the 1990s. For nearly a century, international lawyers have been preoccupied with the under-development of their law. They have sought to shed light on international law's complexities, on its many ramifications and sophistications, to show that international law is not as weak and primitive as many would have it. Then the movement reverses. Norms and regimes multiply. Conflicts emerge between institutions with overlapping jurisdictions, ambiguous boundaries, different worldviews and preferences. The canonical oppositions that have traditionally structured the discipline (civilised/barbarian, public/private, national/international, law/non-law) are contested and challenged. As a result, international lawyers start looking behind the proliferation of forms, norms, regimes and institutions for new theories, but also for principles of coherence and unity. The discipline has moved from an ontological obsession with scarcity (of legitimacy and recognition) to a perplexity with excess.

II. FROM TOO LITTLE TO TOO MUCH LAW: MAPPING THE FRAGMENTATION DEBATE

It is in this context that the debate on the unity/fragmentation of international law has emerged and crystallised. Initially the marginal concern of a closed group of professionals, fragmentation has progressively gone mainstream, becoming the object of countless conferences and a great favourite in the legal literature.[36] No longer the sole concern of generalist international lawyers,

[33] For a recent analysis, see Erich Vranes, *Trade and the Environment – Fundamental Issues in International and WTO Law* (Oxford, Oxford University Press, 2009).

[34] Susan Marks, 'Reservations Unhinged: The Belilos Case Before the European Court of Human Rights' (1990) 39 *International and Comparative Law Quarterly* 300.

[35] See the section on the *Tadic* case in my general conclusion.

[36] See, eg, 'Symposium Issue: The Proliferation of International Tribunals: Piecing Together the Puzzle' (1999) 31 *New York University Journal of International Law and Politics*; 'Diversity or Cacophony: New Sources of Norms in International Law Symposium' (2004) 25 *Michigan Journal of International Law* 845; *Fragmentation: Diversification and Expansion of International Law: Proceedings of the 34th Annual Conference of the Canadian Council of International Law*, (Ottawa, Canadian Council of International Law, 2006); Karel Wellens and Rosario Vinaxia (eds), *L'Influence des sources sur l'unité et la fragmentation du droit international: travaux du séminaire tenu à Palma, les 20–21 mai 2005* (Brussels, Bruylant, 2006); Andreas Zimmermann and Rainer Hofmann (eds), *Unity and Diversity in International Law: Proceedings of an International Symposium of the Kiel Walther Schücking Institute of International Law* (Berlin, Duncker & Humblot, 2006); Matthew Craven, 'Unity, Diversity, and the Fragmentation of International Law'

fragmentation has spread far and wide across the discipline. Each branch of the law, each special regime has started debating its own fragmentation.[37] Fragmentation, as noted by one of its prime theorists, has become the 'doctrinal debate *par excellence* in the globalisation era'.[38]

The purpose of this book is to engage critically with this doctrinal debate. Before laying out my main argument, however, I must say a few words about the structure of the fragmentation debate, as well as some of its gaps and silences. Fragmentation, as we shall see in the rest of this book, raises a host of important questions, of a legal, political, technical and ideological nature. The literature on fragmentation is not only abundant: it is also extremely dense, diverse, complex and – in its own way – fragmented. In order to make sense of this broad and multifaceted debate, it may be useful to think of it as having developed in two distinct periods, two waves of doctrinal controversy.

The first generation of fragmentation debates has focused primarily on two questions: the functional autonomisation of special regimes and the multiplication of international tribunals. On both questions, opinions diverge widely.

On the question of special regimes, international lawyers are split into two camps. On the one hand are those who believe that, as soon as a special regime is equipped with a comprehensive system of secondary norms – that is, with its own sources and its own regime of responsibility – it becomes 'self-contained', that is, it is uncoupled – and works independently – from 'general' international law. Advocates of the self-containment thesis argue that, beyond a certain degree of autonomisation, a special regime becomes entirely efficacious and self-sufficient. It is a complete and closed sub-system of international law with its own secondary rules, tailored to its own characteristics, and it need no longer rely on general rules of public international law in order to ascertain, interpret and implement its substantive norms.[39] On the other hand are those who argue

(2005) 14 *Finnish Yearbook of International Law* 3; *Benedetto Conforti,* 'Unité et fragmentation du droit international: "Glissez, mortels, n'appuyez pas!"' (2007) 111 *Revue Générale de Droit International Public* 5; Eyal Benvenisti and George Downs, 'The Empire's New Clothes: Political Economy and the Fragmentation of International Law' (2007) 60 *Stanford Law Review* 1; Pierre-Marie Dupuy, 'L'unité de l'ordre juridique international' (2002) 297 *Collected Courses of the Hague Academy of International Law* 9.

[37] Alexander Orakhelashvili, 'The Interaction between Human Rights and Humanitarian Law: Fragmentation, Conflict, Parallelism, or Convergence?' (2008) 19 *European Journal of International Law* 161; Anthony Cassimatis, 'International Humanitarian Law, International Human Rights Law, and Fragmentation of International Law' (2007) 56 *International and Comparative Law Quarterly* 623; Tim Stephens, 'Multiple International Courts and the "Fragmentation" of International Environmental Law' (2006) 25 *Australian Yearbook of International Law* 227; Alan Boyle, 'Dispute Settlement and the Law of the Sea Convention: Problems of Fragmentation and Jurisdiction' (1997) 46 *International and Comparative Law Quarterly* 37.

[38] Pierre-Marie Dupuy, 'A Doctrinal Debate in the Globalisation Era: On the "Fragmentation" of International Law' (2007) 1 *European Journal of Legal Studies* 1.

[39] Willem Riphagen, 'Third Report on the Content, Forms and Degrees of International Responsibility' (1982) II *Yearbook of the International Law Commission* 22; Willem Riphagen, 'State Responsibility: New Theories of Obligation in Interstate Relations' in Ronald Macdonald and Douglas Johnston (eds), *The Structure and Process of International Law: Essays in Legal Philosophy, Doctrine and Theory* (The Hague, Martinus Nijhoff, 1983). See also *United States*

that the autonomisation of special regimes is never absolute. No regime, they claim, is ever fully self-sufficient. The establishment of a genuinely self-contained regime is not a realistic possibility. A regime is always situated, if only minimally, within the parameters of public international law. Even the most tightly integrated and autonomous regime will occasionally need to draw upon general international law, if only as a measure of last resort, whenever secondary rules are inexistent or ineffective.[40] On this issue, the International Law Commission, in its final fragmentation report, sided with the second camp, holding that 'no regime is a closed legal circuit'.[41] Although special regimes may be better suited to deal with specific problems, and states may opt out of certain aspects of general international law, no regime can ever be completely isolated from general law: 'a regime can receive . . . legally binding force ('validity') only be reference to . . . rules and principles *outside it*'.[42] In the Commission's view, even in the case of well-developed or 'thick' regimes, general laws always fulfil, at minimum, a subsidiary function, whether it is that of governing matters not regulated by the special law (gap-filling) or that of stepping in when the special regime fails to function properly (regime failure).

On the issue of the proliferation of international tribunals, the views are perhaps not as clearly demarcated. But international law doctrine oscillates between two extremes. At one end are those who consider that the multiplication of international tribunals is already creating problems of overlapping and conflicting jurisprudence in a way that undermines the coherence, foreseeability and efficacy of the international legal order. To these scholars, the multiplicity of judicial voices – absent an institutional hierarchy – means cacophony, disorder and, *in fine*, the loss of a global perspective on international law.[43] At the other end of the doctrinal spectrum are authors who consider the problem to be largely theoretical. These scholars observe that international tribunals are

Diplomatic and Consular Staff in Tehran (United States of America v Iran) 24 May 1980, ICJ Reports (1980) 3, para 86: 'The rules of diplomatic law constitute a self-contained régime which, on the one hand, lays down obligations regarding the facilities, privileges and immunities [of] diplomatic missions and, on the other, foresees their possible abuse by members of the mission and specifies the means to counter such abuses. These means are, by their nature, entirely efficacious'; as well as *Prosecutor v Dusko Tadic (decision on the defence motion for interlocutory appeal on jurisdiction)*, Case No IT-94-1, Appeals Chamber of the ICTY, 2 October 1995, para 11: 'In international law, every tribunal is a self-contained regime (unless otherwise provided)'.

[40] See especially Bruno Simma and Dirk Pulkowski, 'Of Planets and the Universe: Self-Contained Regimes in International Law' (2006) 17 *European Journal of International Law* 483; Anja Lindroos and Michael Mehling, 'Dispelling the Chimera of Self-Contained Regimes: International Law and the WTO' (2005) 16 *European Journal of International Law* 857.

[41] ILC Fragmentation Report, above n 12 at para 152.

[42] Ibid at para 193.

[43] See, eg, Gilbert Guillaume, 'The Future of International Judicial Institutions' (1995) 44 *International and Comparative Law Quarterly* 848; Pierre-Marie Dupuy, 'The Danger of Fragmentation or Unification of the International Legal System and the International Court of Justice' (1998) 31 *New York University Journal of International Law & Politics* 791; Shane Spelliscy, 'The Proliferation of International Tribunals' (2001) 40 *Columbia Journal of Transnational Law* 143; Christian Leathley, 'An Institutional Hierarchy to Combat the Fragmentation of International Law' (2007) 40 *New York University Journal of International Law & Politics* 259.

engaged in a robust transnational judicial dialogue which – by and large – maintains the integrity of international law and of its general principles.[44] Often, these authors view the proliferation of tribunals as merely reflecting a post-modern social world marked by functional differentiation or, better yet, as healthy pluralism. More tribunals means wider access to justice and more accountability. It also means creative diversity, the potential for cross-fertilisation of ideas, and a chance to see established categories, preferences and hierarchies challenged or revisited.[45]

On this question, the International Law Commission adopted a middle-of-the-road position. Whilst refusing to arbitrate issues of institutional overlap, but instead deciding to focus on the substantive aspects of fragmentation, the Commission took the view that the multiplication of rule-complexes and tribunals has both negative and positive effects. On the one hand, says the Commission, this phenomenon creates the danger of conflicting rules and institutional practices, and the unity of the law may suffer as a consequence. On the other hand, proliferation and fragmentation are responses to new technical and functional requirements in particular problem areas. They are manifestations of a pluralistic society in which different actors pursue different projects using different principles and techniques, each particular field becoming increasingly professionalised, institutionalised and autonomous. In other words, proliferation and fragmentation reflect rather than create the sociological reality of late international modernity.[46]

A second generation of doctrinal debates about fragmentation has recently emerged, which is less interested in empirical or normative questions than technical considerations. In this second period of the fragmentation literature, the question is no longer whether, and to what extent, international law is fragmenting, nor whether this is desirable or undesirable. Rather, starting from the assumption that coherence and unity are legitimate goals, the question becomes that of 'ordering pluralism', that is, finding principles, methods and techniques that can be used to put the pieces of the puzzle together and bring order to multiplicity.[47] This pragmatic and technical turn in the fragmentation debate – which essentially coincides with the publication of the ILC report – has given

[44] See, eg, Jonathan Charney, 'Is International Law Threatened by Multiple International Tribunals?' (1998) 271 *Collected Courses* 101; Rosalyn Higgins, 'The ICJ, the ECJ, and the Integrity of International Law' (2003) 52 *International and Comparative Law Quarterly* 1; William Burke-White, 'International Legal Pluralism' (2004) 25 *Michigan Journal of International Law* 963.

[45] See, eg, Koskenniemi and Leino, 'Postmodern Anxieties', above n 13; Bruno Simma, 'Fragmentation in a Positive Light' (2003) 25 *Michigan Journal of International Law* 845; Andreas Fischer-Lescano and Gunther Teubner, 'Regime-Collisions: The Vain Search for Legal Unity in the Fragmentation of Global Law' (2004) 25 *Michigan Journal of International Law* 999.

[46] ILC Fragmentation Report, above n 12 at paras 14–16.

[47] Mireille Delmas-Marty, *Ordering Pluralism: A Conceptual Framework for Understanding the Transnational Legal World* (Oxford, Hart Publishing, 2009). For an argument that ontological or normative questions about fragmentation are 'overrated' and that fragmentation is better understood as a technical problem of conflict of norms or conflict of laws, see Ralf Michaels and Joost Pauwelyn, 'Conflict of Norms or Conflict of Laws? Different Techniques in the Fragmentation of International Law' (2010) 9 *Duke Law Working Papers* 1.

birth to a burgeoning literature on the rules of treaty interpretation, and in particular on the so-called principle of 'systemic integration' under article 31(3)(c) of the Vienna Convention on the Law of Treaties (VCLT).[48] Similarly, the principles of *lex specialis* and *lex posterior* have attracted much attention as possible tools for resolving tensions between parallel or conflicting treaty obligations.[49] Even the notion of *jus cogens*, which had remained dormant for some time, re-emerged as a possible solution for creating hierarchies and imposing order among competing norms.[50]

What all of the above demonstrates is that the interest in issues of fragmentation has not faded away. Fragmentation, it seems, is here to stay. More than simply a term of art, it has become a powerful and defining metaphor of modern international law scholarship. But while fragmentation seems to be on everyone's mind, one thing is missing. For all the talk about fragmentation – its sources, its consequences and its remedies – the concept of unity is hardly ever mentioned, let alone theorised. This is remarkable, since fragmentation necessarily presupposes unity, either as something that once was and has since been lost, or as a programmatic objective. Either way, speaking about fragmentation is meaningless unless we can articulate some notion of unity. It would be like speaking about shadows without reference to light.

This theoretical gap is apparent, first of all, with regard to the *problematique* of unity. We have seen that there are many different views on fragmentation. Some see it as a threat. Others consider the danger overstated and merely theoretical. Yet others insist that its benefits outweigh its costs and potential hazards. But little is said about why unity matters in the first place. Often, law's unity is taken to be a regulative idea that is so evident – some even say tautological[51] –

[48] See, eg, Jan Klabbers, 'Reluctant "Grundnormen": Article 31(3)(c) and 42 of the Vienna Convention on the Law of Treaties and the Fragmentation of International Law' in Matthew Craven and Malgosia Fitzmaurice (eds), *Time, History and International Law* (Leiden, Martinus Nijhoff, 2007); Panos Merkouris, 'Debating the Ouroboros of International Law: The Drafting History of Article 31(3)(c)' (2007) 9 *International Community Law Review* 1; Campbell McLachlan, 'The Principle of Systemic Integration and Article 31(3)(c) of the Vienna Convention' (2005) 54 *International and Comparative Law Quarterly* 279.

[49] See, eg, Anja Lindroos, 'Addressing Norm Conflicts in a Fragmented Legal System: The Doctrine of Lex Specialis' (2005) 74 *Nordic Journal of International Law* 27; Erich Vranes, 'Lex Superior, Lex Specialis, Lex Posterior: Zur Rechtsnature der "Konfliktlösungsregeln"' (2005) 65 *Heidelberg Journal of International Law* 391; William Schabas, 'Lex Specialis? Belt and Suspenders? The Parallel Operation of Human Rights Law and the Law of Armed Conflict, and the Conundrum of Jus Ad Bellum' (2007) 40 *Israel Law Review* 592; Amna Guellali, 'Lex Specialis, droit international humanitaire et droits de l'homme: leur interaction dans les nouveaux conflits armés' (2007) 111 *Revue Générale de Droit International Public* 539.

[50] See, eg, Andreas Paulus, 'Jus Cogens in a Time of Hegemony and Fragmentation – An Attempt at a Re-appraisal' (2005) 74 *Nordic Journal of International Law* 297; Christian Tomuschat and Jean-Marc Thouvenin (eds), *The Fundamental Rules of the International Legal Order: Jus Cogens and Obligations Erga Omnes* (Leiden, Martinus Nijhoff, 2006).

[51] Georges Vedel, 'Aspects généraux et théoriques' in Jean-Bernard Auby et al (eds) *L'unité du droit: Mélanges en hommage à Roland Drago* (Paris, Economica, 1996) 5: 'le droit . . . est justiciable d'unité. Cette affirmation est à peine démontrable car elle est d'abord tautologique' ('law . . . is unitary. This assertion is hardly demonstrable as it is above all a tautology').

that to put it into question is unnecessary, useless and inappropriate.[52] Where the justification of unity is addressed, mention is made – generally in passing – to problems of predictability, security, reliability and consistency.[53] While these considerations are by no means irrelevant, much remains to be said, however, about why the monistic conception of law as a unified and coherent system should be deemed more rational as a theoretical preference than that, say, of legal pluralism. We are thus in a situation where unity, as one legal theorist puts it, is treated by lawyers as a basic assumption, similar to the assumption of causality in the natural sciences.[54]

What is true of the 'ethos' of unity applies equally to the very concept of unity.[55] As a rule, the notion of unity is more assumed than explained. In fact, most discussions about unity/fragmentation provide no definition at all. Often, unity and fragmentation are simply presented as opposite theoretical positions. But their meaning remains rather vague and intuitive. We are thus in a paradoxical situation where the fragmentation rhetoric is omnipresent but where unity – its *sine qua non* condition – remains entirely under-theorised. To be sure, this problem is not exclusive to international legal theory. In reality, the concept of unity remains under-theorised in analytical jurisprudence at large. Niklas Luhmann, writing in 1987 about the unity of legal systems, noted this fact:

> [T]he unity of the system is usually tacitly assumed . . . and no thought is given to the question of how the system acquires this unity. This is an unsatisfactory state of affairs. It seems to lead to a situation where sociologists leave to jurists and jurists leave it to sociologists to formulate theories on the unity of law.[56]

[52] Benedetto Conforti, 'Unité et fragmentation du droit international: "Glissez, mortels, n'appuyez pas!"' (2007) 111 *Revue Générale de Droit International Public* 5, 7: 'mettre en question l'unité ou la nature juridique de l'ordre international est tout à fait inutile et déplacé' ('to question the unity or the legal nature of the international order is most definitely useless and out of place').

[53] See, eg, Pierre-Marie Dupuy, 'Fragmentation du droit international ou des perceptions qu'on en a?' in Rosario Huesa Vinaixa and Karel Wellens (eds), *L'influence des sources sur l'unité et la fragmentation du droit international* (Brussels, Bruylant, 2006) v, xvi: 'c'est la sécurité même des rapports réglés par le droit international, donc l'efficacité de celui-ci, qui serait remise en cause [par la fragmentation]. L'unité d'application du droit international est un condition de son efficacité donc aussi de sa survie' ('it is the very security of international legal relations, and hence their efficacy, that would be impaired [by fragmentation]. The unity of application of international law is . . . a condition of its efficacy and therefore of its survival'). See also ILC Fragmentation Report, above n 12 at para 491: 'fragmentation puts to question the coherence of international law. Coherence is valued positively owing to the connection it has with predictability and legal security'.

[54] Aleksander Peczenik, 'Law, Morality, Coherence and Truth' (1994) 7 *Ratio Juris* 146, 154.

[55] I use the term 'ethos' here to underline that debates about unity/fragmentation are not merely about diverging legal theories but, more fundamentally, about competing ethical and ideological perspectives on law and social order. On unity and pluralism as 'ethos', see Margaret Davies, 'The Ethos of Pluralism' (2005) 27 *Sydney Law Review* 87. On the notion that discourses about fragmentation are predetermined by particular legal ideologies, see Mario Prost, 'Discours sur le fondement, l'unité et la fragmentation du droit international: à propos d'une utopie paresseuse' (2006) 39 *Revue Belge de Droit International* 621.

[56] Niklas Luhmann, 'The Unity of the Legal System' in Gunther Teubner (ed), *Autopoietic Law: A New Approach to Law and Society* (Berlin, Walter de Gruyter, 1987) 13.

To this day, this gap remains unaddressed. Moreover, despite the proliferation of fragmentation discourse, one simple question is yet to be answered: regardless of whether it is good or bad, possible or utopian, a mere postulate or an actual fact, what does the 'unity' of international law actually mean? What does this taken-for-granted concept entail in theory and in practice?

III. TOWARDS AN EXPLORATORY PHILOSOPHY OF UNITY

It is this critical but essentially uncharted question that constitutes the subject of the present work. The basic assumption of this book is that there can be no serious or effective debate about fragmentation without some preliminary understanding of the concept of unity, a concept that is deceptively simple and that requires sustained critical analysis. What follows is thus an invitation to suspend the mainstream discourse on fragmentation and to put unity into question. This does not mean rebutting or eliminating it. Rather, it means questioning its use as an undisputed assumption, unsettling the usage of this taken-for-granted concept, showing that it is not self-evident and that unity may not necessarily be what we thought it was.

Thinking about unity, needless to say, is an old and vast project. Unity is among the ideas that have occupied a constant and prominent place in the history of philosophy, and in the history of thought more generally. In fact, metaphysical thought, from Parmenides and Aristotle to Heidegger, can be interpreted as a long quest for unity, that is, a deliberate attempt to overcome phenomenal multiplicity by unveiling foundational grounds, underlying forms of oneness, or what Jaspers calls 'the encompassing' or 'the comprehensive', that which transcends diversity and difference in everyday existence.[57] Defining unity is thus not an easy thing to do, for unity is not a 'thing', but rather an instinct or – as Camus would say – a form of nostalgia.[58] Even if unity is something that is capable of definition and which can be the object of rational knowledge, many will question whether it can be essentialised and captured in a stable concept or idea.

Although thinking about unity is not an easy thing to do, it is nonetheless necessary. Short of a minimal common understanding of unity, there can be no meaningful debate about fragmentation. Disagreements over issues of fragmentation may merely reflect deeper but unrevealed disagreements over the meaning of unity. Similarly, false or superficial agreements may be formed over fragmentation issues, because of some conceptual vagueness concerning the premise of

[57] Karl Jaspers, *Way to Wisdom: An Introduction to Philosophy*, 2nd edn (Yale, Yale University Press, 2003) 28–30.

[58] What Camus calls the 'nostalgia of unity' is man's natural and, in his view, absurd obsession with totality, oneness and the absolute. See Albert Camus, *Le mythe de Sisyphe* (Paris, Gallimard, 1942) 34–35.

unity. Any argument on fragmentation begins from a predetermined position on unity. Without explicitly theorising this position, international lawyers may be debating very different things without even knowing it. *Meaningful* agreement or disagreement requires some understanding of what the agreement/disagreement is actually about.

Finding a common frame of understanding does not require complete agreement over the meaning, form and content of unity. One can debate fragmentation without an *a priori* consensus on the 'correct' interpretation of unity. After all, lawyers speak about international law all the time without sharing a universal conception of law. But finding a common frame of understanding involves at the very least some consideration of the conceptual space within which the discussion is situated. It means being 'in tune' with other participants and calibrating one's instruments (in our case conceptual instruments) according to accepted standards. Just like in an orchestra, this 'tuning' exercise is what allows the different participants to listen to each other and play their individual parts together, in the same space, without the music turning into a cacophony of out-of-synch voices. Unity must therefore be theorised. Without a preliminary understanding of what unity might mean, the fragmentation debate may turn out to be no more than a series of unrelated propositions, a concert of disjointed voices in which arguments seemingly respond to each other but never really meet up on the same epistemological terrain.

Having said this, the unity of international law can be approached and theorised from a great many perspectives. The descriptive approach, for instance, would endeavour to show the extent to which unity exists, in some real sociological sense, as a matter of 'positive' international law. The normative approach would have us evaluate unity against possible alternatives (for example, pluralism) as a paradigm of law. The genealogical approach, for its part, would search for the causes of unity and would seek to identify the circumstances under which the 'law-as-unity' postulate emerged as a condition of legal thought.

Although it contains elements of these various approaches, the present book is of a rather different genre. What follows is fundamentally a work of legal philosophy. The term is not used here in the Kantian sense, that is, as a set of normative or evaluative inquiries into the nature of law and justice. Rather, philosophy is taken here in its Deleuzian sense, as a creative mode of thought that seeks to construct and develop concepts. Deleuze sees philosophy as the art of acquiring 'competent intimacy' with conceptual personae and objects, that is, giving life to their intensive multiplicity without ever reducing them to finite, stable or definitive categories.[59] In this broad Deleuzian perspective, the present book 'does' legal philosophy by dealing with the rudimentary and under-theorised concept of unity, and exploring its various possible forms, shapes and meanings in the context of international law.

[59] See especially Gilles Deleuze and Félix Guattari, *Qu'est-ce que la philosophie?* (Paris, Les Editions de Minuit, 1991).

This philosophy of unity, as will become clear, is merely exploratory. What follows is not an attempt to definitively establish the concept of unity. Neither is it a comprehensive and self-standing theory of international law's unity, a ready-made model that can be used to define, describe and interpret the legal world around us. This book only aims to *make a start*. It seeks to explore the possibility of discourse about international law's unity, by identifying and comparing various candidate conceptions of unity, without engaging in arguments about their respective merits. In other works, I have found certain perspectives to be preferable, from a descriptive or a normative point of view, but this book remains primarily an exercise in scene-setting. Its principal objective is to infuse theoretical life into an embryonic notion, and to expose unity for what it really is: an ambivalent, complex and fundamentally contested concept.

This exploratory philosophy is also a pluralist philosophy, though perhaps again not in a conventional sense. In the roughly 30 years in which it has been used in legal and social scientific writings, the concept of legal pluralism has generally been understood in two different ways. Pluralism as fact refers to the observation and designation of an empirical state of affairs, that is, the existence of a plurality of laws – or normative orders – within a given social arena. To be a legal pluralist in this first sense is to see – or be prepared to see – different types of law operating simultaneously in a particular social environment. This is pluralism about the sources of law (state law, customs, folk law, religious norms, private regulations and so on) and about the spaces in which they operate (nation-states, the international community, villages, families, churches, industries, schools and so on). Pluralism as (counter)ideology, on the other hand, refers to the intellectual move against the ideology of legal centralism, that is, the claim that law is and should only be understood as official state law. To be a pluralist in this second sense is to rebut the notion that the state is the sole relevant source of authority, and to understand the category 'law' as including non-state legal forms.[60]

This book is not strictly speaking pluralist in either of these two conventional ways. At work in what follows is pluralism as a mindset, rather than as fact or ideology. This version of legal pluralism is a looser form of pluralism, which attaches to the way we think about the legal. It is pluralism about the concept of law. In examining the concept of unity in international law, I do not advocate or adhere to one single concept of law. Instead, I adopt a relaxed attitude towards law's many faces and dimensions. International law is examined *tour à tour* as substantive rules, as a system of norm-generation and norm-interpretation, as an intellectual project, as a form of argument and as a value system. It is mainly in this sense that this work can be labelled as a pluralist philosophy of international law.[61]

[60] For a discussion of the different versions of legal pluralism, see Gordon Woodman, 'Ideological Combat and Social Observation: Recent Debate About Legal Pluralism' (1998) 43 *Journal of Legal Pluralism* 21; as well as Brian Tamanaha, 'Understanding Legal Pluralism: Past to Present, Local to Global' (2008) 30 *Sydney Law Review* 375.

[61] This way of thinking about legal pluralism is taken from Craig Scott, '"Transnational Law" as Proto-Concept: Three Conceptions' (2009) 10 *German Law Journal* 860.

IV. OUTLINE OF THE BOOK

The main thesis of this book is that unity is not – as is generally assumed in the fragmentation literature – self-evident, stable and unequivocal. Unity is, on the contrary, a graded and dynamic concept. It is a graded concept, for it can be taken from different angles and standpoints, and it possesses various 'semantic layers'. It is also a dynamic concept, for unity always rests on a complex of forces in tension, sometimes compatible and sometimes at odds with one another.

The argument is set out in six chapters, forming three broad analytical moves. The first part of the analysis serves to define, delimit and problematise the object of the study. Chapter two constitutes an *entrée en matière* through the history of ideas, and in particular the history of philosophy. It seems inconceivable to engage in a theoretical elaboration of unity without mentioning – if only by way of introduction – the long tradition of philosophical thinking on the issue of unity. From its inception, philosophy has been interested in the question of the one and the many, and in the relations of part to whole, so much so that it has become the object of a separate branch or tradition known as 'mereology'. Mereology, needless to say, does not provide definitive and linear answers to the question of international law's unity. It is, however, useful in at least two ways. First, mereology provides conceptual tools that are used in the rest of the study, such as the concepts of part, whole, categorial predicates, causation relationship, foundation, form and so on. Second, mereology is useful for what it suggests about the nature of unity. Philosophers have long formed the conviction that unity is never a pure and objective given, but rather something that always requires a certain degree of construction and interpretation. In this process of construction, the role of the observing subject is key. This conviction, as will become clear, very much underpins the whole of this book.

In chapter three, I define the scope of inquiry and explain what is *not* being addressed in the book. This chapter sets out a series of key distinctions, such as that between the question of unity and the related – but nonetheless distinct – questions of unification and universality of the law. This will hopefully serve to avoid analytical confusion in a debate that sometimes lacks clarity and precision.

The second part of the analysis features an 'internal' critique of the conventional discourse on international law's unity. The purpose here is to break down the rather vague and indistinguishable notions of unity generally found in the literature and to show that, behind these simplifying – and at times simplistic – discourses, lies a wide range of complex questions that are commonly overlooked. With regard to 'material' unity, for instance, I show that most lawyers discuss conflicts of norms as if the notion of conflict was semantically settled. In response to this rather ambiguous use of the term conflict, I show that 'norm conflict' is a polysemic and controversial notion, that no less than three definitions for this notion are available, and that depending on which definition is used, international law will look more or less unitary (chapter four).

Similarly, with regard to 'formal' unity, I show that the ordering of norms into a coherent system can be understood in various ways, which involve different logics and organisational laws. The conventional discourse on unity tends to understand formal unity as a monocausal phenomenon, that is, something that answers to a single 'law of arrangement'. A number of scholars, for instance, understand formal unity as having to do solely with the presence in the system of 'secondary norms'. Against these rather simplistic perspectives, I seek to diversify and complexify the analysis by identifying other dynamics – in particular institutional and hermeneutic dynamics (chapter five).

This first level of critique is 'internal' in the sense that it responds to conventional doctrines of unity on their own terrain. To this day, the fragmentation debate has for the most part limited itself to considerations of norm conflict and secondary rules, and the discussion has essentially been located within positivist frameworks. I have thought it necessary and interesting first to take stock of the conventional discourse on unity within these parameters, before considering non-positivist approaches to international law's unity. This is why, for instance, an entire section is dedicated to Hart's theory of the legal system, which today informs most discussions on 'formal' unity. I show that international lawyers often misunderstand or misuse Hart's theory and that, if one were to take Hart seriously, a number of highly problematic (and neglected) questions would arise, such as those of the determinacy and uniform acceptance of secondary norms.

The third and last part of the book considers what it means to think of international law's unity from a non-positivist standpoint. This is an 'external' critique in the sense that it does not respond to conventional doctrines of unity on their own terms. Instead, it seeks to articulate new visions of unity, the source of which does not reside strictly in positive law or in the interaction between legal norms. Two perspectives are considered, one called 'cultural' (chapter six) and the other 'logical' (chapter seven). In the first instance, international law is approached not as an organised set of rules, but rather as an intellectual discipline and discursive formation. Cultural unity, from this point of view, has very little to do with conflicts of norms or formal legal arrangements. Instead, it involves thinking about the mental and grammatical structures which frame international law as a social field and professional language, that is, as a space for the production and circulation of legal arguments. In the case of 'logical' unity, the unity of international law stems not from the compatibility between legal norms but rather from elements of transcendence of positive rules. This can be a rational and abstract transcendence, postulated *a priori* by the legal theorist or interpreter (what I call *epitesmo*-logical unity). Or this can be material transcendence, that is, the super-determination of legal norms by values or value-systems (what I call *axio*-logical unity). In either case, to think of international law's unity from these points of view becomes something radically different, which involves new objects, new forms and new criteria of unity.

V. SOME CAVEATS AND CLARIFICATIONS

Thus far, I have described the background, purpose and main argument of this book. Some caveats are in order at this point. First, a word on the scope of the inquiry. This book is primarily concerned with the concept of unity in the field of *public* international law. Whilst I am well aware that 'public international law' is increasingly contested as a category, the present work is only marginally interested in debates that have taken place in other disciplines, most notably questions of unification in private international law. This is not to say that these questions are uninteresting or bear no relation to our subject but they *are* of a very different nature and, for the sake of clarity, they have been left out of this work.

Neither is this a book about legal pluralism. In the process of writing this book, I was often asked – and indeed I often asked myself – about its relation to legal pluralism. Initially, I found this question rather puzzling and challenging. Isn't saying something about legal unity necessarily saying something about legal pluralism? Are unity and pluralism simply two sides of the same coin? Eventually, however, I realised that this book is not directly concerned with legal pluralism. As mentioned above, although my approach can be described as loosely pluralistic, since it explores a multiplicity of conceptual perspectives, my argument is not. I am not interested in showing that international law is unitary or plural in any sociological sense. Neither do I argue that unity is superior to pluralism as a paradigm for understanding law. At the risk of repeating myself, this book is neither descriptive nor evaluative, in the way that the tradition of legal pluralism can be. The present work is mostly conceptual, and starts from the assumption that there can be no meaningful debate about norm conflict, fragmentation, or indeed legal pluralism, without some prior consideration of what it means to say that there is unity in the law. This book is therefore interested in a different set of questions than the literature on legal pluralism. It follows, in other words, a different epistemological agenda.

In describing the approach of this book, I have used some rather contested notions. I have, in particular, called my work a 'philosophy' of international law and a 'critique' of dominant discourses on fragmentation. Both notions require clarification. First, I must say something about my use of philosophy. To specialist philosophers, some of what follows may appear impure, wrong, or perhaps even heretical. They may dispute my handling of certain concepts and ideas, and consider that I have taken liberties with established theories, vocabularies or traditions. They may, to some extent, be right. I should describe myself as an amateur rather than professional philosopher. I have borrowed from philosophy that which I have found useful in thinking about the unity of international law. But this remains a book written by an international lawyer and principally for international lawyers. I accept that, in this process of borrowing, some concepts and categories will have lost some of their initial meaning from the 'source' discipline of philosophy. I have, however, tried to be fair to the original context of philosophical ideas. If I have misconstrued them, I must ask for the indulgence of the professional philosophers. In any event, I take comfort in the fact that Deleuze himself, whose approach to philosophy has very much influenced this work, recognised the value of profane or 'non-philosophical' uses of philosophy, and in fact celebrated the resonance that his concept of 'the fold' had had in a society of paper-folders and in a group of surfers . . .[62]

The term 'critique', which I use to describe my main argument, is also far from unproblematic. Critique means different things to different people. The term 'critical' can be used to mark one's belonging to a particular school or movement, like the 'crits' movement. Or it can be used simply to signify a particular way of thinking about accepted wisdom. It is in this second sense that the term critique is used here. This book is critical not because it is part of a recognisable intellectual tradition or 'brand' of critique, but because it calls into question established methods and epistemologies. My aim here is to make explicit that which is often implicit in the fragmentation discourse, to map the ways in which the concept of unity is used in the literature, and to identify some gaps and problems along the way. Put simply, I seek to explain the existing tradition, and then critique it.

Something remains to be said about one important question that this book does not directly address. The main contribution of this book is to give shape to a concept that is used more intuitively than consciously by most people, to show what unity *can look like* in the context of international law, and to compare various possible conceptions of unity. However, this book does not elaborate on the way these different versions of unity interact. I do not argue that these different types of unity are either compatible or competing, only that they *are* different and that this difference matters for our understanding of international law and fragmentation. This approach may seem unsatisfactory or incoherent to those who see conceptual analysis as the art of turning fuzzy knowledge into stable conceptual constructs. I can only respond that conceptual analysis is *also* the art of picking concepts apart, attending to the vast diversity of meaning and suggesting possible models of reasoning. It is in this spirit that I have written this book. My project is not to provide the reader with a single and definitive vision of unity, but only to initiate analytical momentum and open the door to a richer, more complex and thicker theorisation of unity in international law. No sound or correct ideas then. Just ideas, and a few anchoring points, to get started, and 'zigzag' – as Deleuze might have said – between potential unities.[63]

[62] 'C comme Culture' in Gilles Deleuze, *L'abécédaire de Gilles Deleuze*, a series of video interviews with Claire Parnet, published in CD-Rom by Vidéo Editions Montparnasse (2003).

[63] Ibid, 'Z comme Zigzag'.

2

Of Unity, Perspective and Perception: An Ontological Preamble

> 'I realised that only superficial and defective observation attaches all importance to the object, when the mind is everything'
>
> Marcel Proust, *The Past Recaptured*[1]

A RETROSPECTIVE VIEW of the thinkers of unity and diversity takes us far back in history, to the pre-Socratics, five centuries before our era. Empedocles, in his philosophical poems, already pondered about the unity of the universe:

> [A]t one time there grew to be a single One out of Many; at another time it grew apart so as to be Many out of One – Fire and Water and Earth and the boundless height of Air . . . And these elements never cease their continuous exchange, sometimes uniting under the influence of Love, so that all become One, at other times again each moving apart through the hostile force of Hate. These in so far as they have the power to grow into One out of Many, and again, when the One grows apart and Many are formed, in this sense they come into being and have no stable life; but in so far as they never cease their continuous exchange, in this sense they remain always unmoved as they follow the cyclic process[2]

It would be wrong to see this as simple and primitive thinking. Empedocles, in a few sentences, constructs a sophisticated and complex dialectic of the One and the Many. Here, unity is understood as a perpetual oscillation, between unification and disaggregation. It springs from the tension between four fundamental elements, and two basic forces.

More recently, the philosophy of Leibniz – a mathematician, a metaphysician, but also a lawyer – is noteworthy. The thought of Leibniz is interesting for a number of reasons. Leibniz lived and worked at the junction of two great periods of European intellectual history. Largely influenced by late medieval culture, Leibniz became one of the leading figures of the early modern era. As a

[1] Marcel Proust, *The Past Recaptured* (New York, The Modern Library, 1959) 244.

[2] Empedocles, *Fragments* in Kathleen Freeman (trans), *Ancilla to Pre-Socratic Philosophers* (Cambridge, Harvard University Press, 1983) 53.

jurist, he took an active role in the movement for the unification of German law. He also had an interest in international law, having published a *Codex Juris Gentium Diplomaticus*, in which he attempted to order the mass of international treaties and the practice of nations.

Leibniz, like many thinkers of his time, had a passion for unity. Law presented itself to him in such complexity and multiplicity – German law at the time consisting of a blend of Roman law, traditional Germanic common law, local customs and municipal statutes – that the question of law's unity occupied his thinking for the rest of his life. Very early in his career, Leibniz developed a project of 'reordering' law and jurisprudence. In his doctoral dissertation, Leibniz addressed the issue of normative conflicts and antinomies. He sought to demonstrate that these could be resolved by the use of the scientific method. Starting from the medieval notion that law is a language, Leibniz argued that lawyers could solve complex or perplexing cases by resorting to rational principles of division and classification. He took the view that logic and well-designed scientific theorems should resolve antinomies independent of historical and political contingencies.[3]

This effort to unify law through *ratio juris* generated an interesting debate among lawyers and philosophers at the time. Some argued that, save for a few very general principles of natural law, no single legislation could govern all peoples, especially in the realm of private transactions. Leibniz, however, responded with a surprising suggestion, for which he is perhaps best known. He argued that it is logically possible to combine law's rational and argumentative unity with its normative diversity, what he would later call, in his general discourse on metaphysics, 'the simplicity of the means and the richness of effects'.[4] Leibniz then decided to suspend his work on judicial reform for a time and to look – beyond the law – for the principles of a general mathesis that would permit the unification of the One and the Many. It is on this occasion that Leibniz produced an astounding philosophical work – the monadology – in which he presented an idea that would allow him to sustain his theory of law's unity: it is not in the 'Whole' that the unity of the world must be found, but rather in each of its parts, in each atom or monad, which contains in itself the totality of the universe.[5]

More than 20 centuries separate Empedocles and Leibniz. And yet, despite the differences in their poetic, metaphysical and legal projects, their works feature a similar vision of unity as movement and tension between a plurality of causes and organisational laws: composition between Fire, Water, Earth and Air; tension between Love and Hate; balance between the simplicity of means

[3] See Arnould Bayart, 'Leibniz et les antinomies en droit' (1966) 20 *Revue Internationale de Philosophie* 257.

[4] Gottfried Wilhelm Leibniz, *Discourse on Metaphysics and the Monadology* (New York, Cosimo Classics, 2008) 8.

[5] Gottfried Wilhelm Leibniz, *Monadology and Other Philosophical Essays* (London, Macmillan, 1965).

and the richness of effects. These themes, it seems, spring from a common intuition: unity is not a given and unchanging fact. On the contrary – it is a conjugation, a conjunction, a multilayered and multidirectional construct.

This chapter begins our examination of international law's unity by exploring this intuition. It considers how the notions of multilayered and multicausal unity have been developed since Leibniz, in particular within the discipline of mereology, a branch of ontology which deals exclusively with the question of the relation of parts to a whole.[6] Mereology is a technical and at times thorny discipline, which draws upon metaphysics, arithmetics, axiomatic logic and set theory. But if this work employs a non-philosophical use of philosophy, at the same time it employs a non-mereological use of mereology. This brief detour into formal ontology is only meant to evoke a few lines of thinking about the nature of unity and about the different ways of being 'one'.

Let us turn, then, to one of the central questions of mereology: when, and under what conditions, is it possible to say that a thing – or an object – constitutes a unitary whole? This seemingly elementary question calls for terminological and conceptual clarification. One useful way to get started, which Edmund Husserl prescribes in his *Logical Investigations*, is to distinguish between simple and complex objects.[7]

I. FROM THE SIMPLE TO THE COMPLEX: ELEMENTARY UNITY AND UNITY BY COMPOSITION

Simple objects, Leibniz's 'monads',[8] are objects which have no parts, or which cannot be decomposed or 'cut up' into a plurality of distinguishable parts. A stone is a simple object. So are a wooden board and a cement slab. These objects, of course, can be 'broken down' or 'partitioned': the wooden board can be sawed in two, and the cement slab jack-hammered. But by doing so, one only obtains fragments which, but for their size, are indistinguishable from the original object. When sawn in half, a wooden board merely splits into two smaller boards that possess the same essence as the earlier object.

In mereology, these objects are called 'atoms', not in the physical sense – for physical atoms can be decomposed into protons, neutrons and electrons – but in the ontological sense of that which has no 'proper parts', or whose only 'improper'

[6] For a general introduction to mereology, see 'Mereology' in Robert Audi (ed), *The Cambridge Dictionary of Philosophy* (Cambridge, Cambridge University Press, 1995); 'Mereology' in Ted Honderich (ed), *The Oxford Companion to Philosophy* (Oxford, Oxford University Press, 1995). For a more in depth approach, see, eg, Peter Simons, *Parts – A Study in Ontology* (Oxford, Oxford University Press, 1987); Ariel Meirav, *Wholes, Sums and Unities* (Dordrecht, Kluwer Academic Publishers, 2003); Barry Sminth (ed), *Parts and Moments – Studies in Logic and Formal Ontology* (Munich, Philosophia Verlag, 1982).

[7] Edmund Husserl, *The Shorter Logical Investigations* (London, Routledge, 2001) 164–65.

[8] Leibniz, *Discourse on Metaphysics and the Monadology*, above n 4 at 67: 'the Monad . . . is nothing else than a simple substance, which goes to make up composites; by simple, we mean without parts'.

part is the object itself.[9] Unity, in relation to these atomic objects, simply means indivisibility, that is, to quote from Aristotle, the situation where there can be no 'qualitative alteration in the substance of the object' or in the 'being of the thing'.[10] Let us call this type of unity *elementary* unity.

Unity, however, becomes significantly more controversial in relation to complex objects whose disjointed parts are distinct, in form and substance, from the whole of which they are a constituent element. Since the whole can hardly be said to be simply the sum or aggregate of its parts,[11] the unity of complex objects necessarily involves some form of composition between the parts, and between them and the whole which they compose. This relation of composition can be of an infinite variety, however, and the ensuing unity can take on many different forms and shapes.

Complex objects can be 'one', first of all, by reason of a natural continuity between their constituent parts, that is, some form of physical connection which is not imposed externally. Aristotle speaks of that which is one in its own right, 'by nature and not by constraint (like things which are joined by glue or nails or by being tied together)'.[12] Similarly, Husserl speaks of connections 'in the narrowest sense of the term', that is, genuine relations of dependence between 'interpenetrating' parts.[13] This form of unity is found, in particular, in living organisms, whether vegetable or animal. One can say, for instance, that a tree is a unitary whole in the sense that its roots, trunk, branches and foliage are naturally attached to one another. Let us call this type of unity *natural* unity.

On the other hand, there are situations when the connection between the constituent parts of an object is not natural. Such is the case when the continuity between the parts is real but does not arise spontaneously from the very essence of the object. The object, in such a situation, is not 'one' in its own right. Unity rests on an external element of composition, on some form of added value (the glue or the nail of Aristotle). A house, a car, or a book are not intrinsically one. Their unity stems from the fact that their different parts have been brought together and arranged in a particular order. They have, in other words, been bundled, bound or fastened to one another.[14] Unity thus becomes *accidental* or *coincidental*, in the Aristotelian sense of that which is one by art rather than by nature.[15]

Less natural or obvious still is the kind of unity that rests not on a real and physical continuity between the constituent parts of an object but rather on a

[9] See Simons, *Parts – A Study in Ontology*, above n 6 at 41–45.

[10] Aristotle, *Metaphysics – Vol I* (Cambridge, Harvard University Press, 1933) 231.

[11] See, on this basic mereological assumption, Théodore Scaltsas, 'Is a Whole Identical to its Parts?' (1990) 99 *Mind* 583; Ernest Nagel, 'Wholes, Sums, and Organic Unities' (1952) 3 *Philosophical Studies* 17.

[12] Aristotle, *Metaphysics – Vol II* (Cambridge, Harvard University Press, 1935) 3.

[13] Husserl, *Logical Investigations*, above n 7 at 164.

[14] On this notion of 'bonding' or 'fastening' as a mode of composition in complex objects, see Peter van Inwagen, *Material Beings* (Ithaca, Cornell University Press, 1990) 56–58.

[15] Aristotle, *Metaphysics*, above n 10 at 230.

mere spatio-temporal coincidence, that is, on the proximity of the parts and on the relative stability of the arrangement. For instance, one could say that a heap of stones forms a unitary whole because the stones are arranged in a particular way and because this arrangement is, subject to the laws of gravity, relatively stable.[16] In this scenario, juxtaposition in space and persistence in time are constitutive of a looser form of unity by *superposition*.

Let us note here that this form of unity does not necessarily involve physical contact between the constituent parts of the whole. A flock of birds, for instance, can be apprehended as a whole inasmuch as the birds that form the flock are flying together in collective motion. The birds are not 'juxtaposed' or 'superimposed' in the previous sense. And yet, an observer will spontaneously perceive the flock, not the individual birds. The side-by-sideness of the birds produces a form of unity by *proximity* or *adjacency*.[17]

Whether it is natural, coincidental, or by superposition, proximity or adjacency, the unity of complex objects, as becomes clear from the above, always necessitates some form of connection or *rapport* between the constituent parts. There must exist a certain 'structure' in the object, that is, a mutual connection between its different parts that makes it possible to perceive it as unitary whole. This is what Aristotle means when he states that a whole is one by reason of its form: 'if we saw the parts of a shoe put together anyhow, we should not say that they were one . . . but only if they were so put together as to be a shoe, and to possess already some one form'.[18] A complex object, in other words, gains perceptible unity through the formal relationship that unites its constituent parts.

II. IN FLESH AND IDEAS: UNITY AS INTERPRETATION

Although necessary, this form of connection between parts of a complex object is rarely sufficient. Often, the unity of the object will requires something more than mere continuity between the constituent parts. It is questionable, for instance, that two friends who shake hands become one single object simply by virtue of being physically in contact with one another. Similarly, as I am writing this book, my fingers are in contact with my keyboard, and my eyes with my computer screen. This form of connection alone can hardly justify calling me and my computer a unitary whole.[19]

To understand this better, let us modify the scenario slightly and consider two adults – the Bukowskis – walking in a park, holding their son Charles by the

[16] On persistence as a possible condition of unity in complex objects, see Eli Hirsch, *The Persistence of Objects* (Philadelphia, Philosophical Monographs, 1976) 38–44.

[17] This example is taken from Dominique Pradelle, *L'archéologie du monde – Constitution de l'espace, idéalisme et intuitionnisme chez Husserl* (Dordrecht, Kluwer Academic Publishers, 2000) 222–23.

[18] Aristotle, *Metaphysics*, above n 10 at 233.

[19] However, some authors do defend the idea that contact alone generates unity. For an explanation and repudiation of this view, see Van Inwagen, *Material Beings*, above n 14 at 33–37.

hand. The physical connection between the Bukowskis is identical to the previous scenario. And yet, although it seems unlikely that the two friends shaking hands form a unitary whole, most of us will have no difficulty seeing the Bukowskis as a family unit. The reason for this is that there exists, in relation to the family, what Husserl calls an '*a priori* law of meaning', that is, a law which defines, in advance, a form, not of physical, but of ontological dependence between certain types of objects. The Bukowskis can be regarded as a family unit because we have internalised a law of organisation – the unitary concept of the family – as part of our common sense.

The example of the family is interesting since, the family being a fundamental group unit of society, the *a priori* law of organisation has become a truly *legal* law. Although the family exists to some extent as a 'natural' unit – through blood, emotions and other bonds – family relationships are heavily regulated by law. Law controls the definition of the family (what kind of relationship 'counts' as a family), the ways in which it comes into being and disappears (marriage, civil partnership, parenthood, divorce and so on), as well as the obligations of family members to one another (obligations of husband and wife, care and control of children, allocation of property entitlements following termination of the relationship, etc). The family, in other words, is a juridical institution *par excellence*. It is constructed and constituted through law.

The extent to which the family exists outside of the law is beyond the scope of this study. The point here is simply that the apprehension and comprehension of the family – a complex mereological object by definition – as a coherent and unitary whole, presupposes the existence of certain social conventions (if only, at minimal, certain linguistic conventions). The Bukowskis, when they are holding hands, give their family an empirically perceptible reality. But what constitutes the family as a unity is a logical fiction or, to use Husserl's terminology, a 'categorial predicate', that is, a postulate which determines, in advance, relations of dependence between certain categories of objects (in our case, a set of laws creating legal ties of dependence among the Bukowskis).[20]

Let us note – to come closer to the subject of law's unity – that although this 'postulated' dimension of unity is important in relation to material objects (that is, objects which occupy space, have a mass and surface and are made of certain materials),[21] it becomes absolutely crucial in relation to immaterial ones. To be sure, immaterial things are real and are susceptible of experience (think of fear, power or gravity). They can have a value (the price of a service) and indeed a face (the Antichrist is the face of evil, the Supreme Court the face of judicial power, and Newton's apple the face of gravity). Yet these objects, and their unity, are by definition devoid of tangible materiality and thus can only possess unity as a matter of idea, not as a matter of flesh and bones. Without any observable connection between their constituent parts, the unity of immaterial

[20] Husserl, *Logical Investigations*, above n 7 at 144.
[21] See Van Inwagen, *Material Beings*, above n 14 at 17.

objects can only exist in thought. It then becomes unity by *intention* or *interpretation.*

The intentional dimension of unity, it is worth stressing, is key even where there is a clear and obvious connection – albeit a non-material one – between the different parts of an object. Such is the case, for instance, with the unity of an *oeuvre*. Foucault makes this point very powerfully in his *Archaeology of Knowledge*.[22] At first glance, he notes, this unity seems self-evident: the unity of an *oeuvre* is established 'by attributing a certain number of texts to an author'.[23] But this apparent simplicity masks a number of complex questions: does the name of an author designate in the same way texts published under his name and texts presented under a pseudonym? Should texts found after the author's death, or notes and other 'jottings' be included? What status should be given to sketches, corrections, deletions, letters and other communications? The establishment of an *oeuvre*, as this makes clear, presupposes a series of difficult choices. It becomes apparent, says Foucault, that the unity of an *oeuvre,* 'far from being given immediately, is the result of an operation; that this operation is interpretative (since it deciphers, in the text, the transcription of something that it both conceals and manifests); and [that] when one speaks of an *oeuvre*, in each case one is using the word in a different sense. The *oeuvre* can be regarded neither as an immediate unity, nor as a certain unity'.[24]

Establishing the unity of immaterial objects – such as law – always seems to involve an element of discretionary judgement. Whether unity is mental, intentional, fictitious or constructed, however, this judgement cannot be purely arbitrary. To 'find' unity in an immaterial thing, there must exist between its constituent parts some causal link that justifies the categorial synthesis. A group of individuals, actions or discourses cannot be perceived as a unitary whole without an underlying cause, a form of ontological interdependence between them. This underlying cause can take on many different forms.

III. MULTI-CAUSATIONAL UNITY

First, the underlying cause of unity can be a relation of kinship, that is, in the broadest sense of the term, the fact that different (mereological) objects are of the same kind or genre. Aristotle, among others, regards this as one possible source of unity: 'things are said to be one whose genus is one'.[25] He considers, for instance, that 'horse, man and dog are in a sense one, because they are all animals'.[26] Similarly, Aristotle regards isosceles and equilateral triangles as one and the same figure, for they are both triangles. This sort of *generic unity* relates

[22] Michel Foucault, *The Archaeology of Knowledge* (London, Routledge, 2002).
[23] Ibid at 26.
[24] Ibid at 27.
[25] Aristotle, *Metaphysics*, above n 10 at 231.
[26] Ibid.

to the existence, beyond particularisms and singularities, of common traits and fundamental affinities that define a species (the existence of three sides defining, for instance, the geometrical species of the triangle).[27]

Unity can find its source, second of all, in a commonality of function or purpose. Things that have the same *raison d'être* can be regarded as bound in *teleological unity*. Consider, for instance, the digestive system. The digestive system is composed of a long list of separate organs: tongue, salivary glands, oesophagus, liver, gallbladder, stomach and so on. Yet these organs are considered parts of a same systemic whole by reason of the fact that they all perform the same biological function, ie the breakdown of large food molecules into smaller components that are more easily absorbed.

Another underlying cause of unity can be a community of ideas, values, beliefs or intentions. Consider a few hundred people walking on one of Paris' *grandes avenues* on a Sunday morning. In and of itself, this group of people does not constitute a unity. If, however, these people have gathered to express their opposition to racism, war or their government's policies, then this grouping becomes something very different: it is a demonstration, whose unity is constituted by the fact that demonstrators have come together to work on a common endeavour. Similarly, it is the common belief in a set of dogmas, myths, superstitions, values, traditions and rites – in other words in a set of orthodoxies and orthopraxis – which gives religions their identity and their unity. This community of moral beliefs is constitutive of a sort of *axiological* unity.

The final underlying cause of unity can lie in what Husserl calls 'a relation of foundation', that is, the fact for a variety of independent objects to have a common basis or origin, or to be founded on one another.[28] It has been argued, for instance, that the unity of political obligation (understood here as the duty of the individual to obey the laws of the community) lies in the fact that, in every society and in all situations, it springs from a common source. There has been much debate, of course, about the nature of this source. Some have given political obligation a mystical foundation, in which the authority of the state and other forms of institutionalised power is understood to emanate from God. Others, in the liberal tradition, see the basis of political obligation in contract and popular consent. But in any case, the underlying assumption is that political obligation is one by reason of its being rooted in a common will, whether divine or human.[29]

[27] On generic unity generally, see William James, *Pragmatism* (New York, Dover Publications, 1994) 53–54.

[28] Husserl, *Logical Investigations*, above n 7 at 179.

[29] On this point, see Georges Davy, 'L'unité de fondement de l'obligation politique' (1931) 1 *Archives de Philosophie du Droit* 87.

IV. UNITY AND THE LAWS OF PERSPECTIVE

Elementary or by composition, natural or accidental, in flesh or in ideas: unity is evidently a versatile and multifaceted concept. Unity can be viewed from different angles, at different levels, and in varying degrees. This is true most of all of the unity of immaterial objects, like law, which are devoid of perceptible materiality and are 'one' only insofar as the observing subject 'finds' in them some form of ontological interdependence which justifies their categorial synthesis. Unity, in this case, is not given, immediately and with certainty. It is produced by a meaning-giving act. It becomes a matter of perspective and therefore involves an element of subjective evaluation or interpretation.

Depending on one's point of view, the same object may appear at once one and many, no perspective being intrinsically or objectively 'truer' than the other. Whilst looking at an object – let us say a copse of trees or a company of soldiers – one can say with equal truth 'it is a copse' and 'it is five trees', or 'here is a company' and 'here are 500 men'.[30] Equally, one can say that 'France is more unitary than Canada' from a political or linguistic point of view. Or, from a territorial or geographic point of view, one can argue that 'Canada is more unitary than France' (France having many overseas territories). What changes from one judgement to the other is not the 'objective' quality of the object, but rather the point from which unity is measured.

Unity, subject as it is to the laws of perspective, may thus be perceived in various degrees – the object being more or less unitary depending on the criteria and the perspective used to gauge its unity – but also at different levels – one and the same object being simultaneously a whole in itself and the constituent part of another whole. A finger is both a whole – composed of different parts (phalanges) – and a part of the hand. The hand, in turn, is a whole in itself – a unity composed of five fingers – as well as a constituent part of the arm. And this can go on almost indefinitely: the arm is part of an individual, who is part of a family, which is part of a tribe, a society, a nation, etc. Leibniz expressed this idea in his own colourful vocabulary: 'each portion of matter may be conceived as like a garden full of plants and like a pond full of fishes. But each branch of every plant, each member of every animal, each drop of its liquid parts is also some such garden or pond'.[31] The point here is that, when considering the unity of a thing or object, the choice of a given perspective or level of analysis is critical.

[30] This classical example is taken from Gottlob Frege, *The Foundations of Arithmetic: A Logico-Mathematical Enquiry Into the Concept of Number* (New York, Harper, 1960) 59.

[31] Leibniz, *Discourse on Metaphysics and the Monadology*, above n 4 at 82.

V. INTERMEDIATE CONCLUSIONS: UNITY, CHOICE AND RUSE

This brief ontological detour, albeit superficial, has shown that there is no absolute or ideal-type of unity. Instead, there are various ways to be 'one', several sorts of unity, all of which have their own truth and integrity. This does not mean that there can be no debate about the unity of a thing like international law, or that one cannot prefer one perspective over another. What it means, however, is that no perspective is self-evident or intrinsically right and that an element of choice is always involved in dealing with unity. This may be the choice of a level of interpretation, or the choice of a criterion of unity. This choice may be made consciously or unconsciously. But a choice is always present.

The Palestinian poet Mahmoud Darwish has nicely brought out the importance of choice – he even speaks of ruse – in any account that seeks to present an object (in his case a poetic work) as a synthetic and unitary whole. In the preface to one of his anthologies, he writes: 'every anthology is, to me, tantamount to a ruse, for whoever compiles it can do whatever he sees fit with his poet: put aside the dark sides of his *oeuvre* and retain the bright ones only; isolate one poem at the expense of its position within the *oeuvre*; keep in a poem only the prosaic path to poetry; insist on images, metaphors or on an atmosphere that sustain a certain approach and, following these subjective processes, turn an average poet into an outstanding one, or the opposite'.[32]

The fundamental intuition of the present study is that one cannot completely ignore this element of doubt and construction when speaking about the unity of international law. To paraphrase Darwish, any account of international law as unity is potentially a ruse, for whoever writes it can do whatever he or she wants of this law: retain only the clear and coherent aspects of the legal order; isolate a principle at the expense of its position within the system; keep in a principle only the prosaic path to normativity; insist on certain images and metaphors that sustain a particular approach; and, ultimately, following a series of subjective processes, turn an essentially plural and fragmented system into a unitary one, or vice versa.

This multidimensional, ambivalent and constructed nature of unity has been largely ignored in the debate on fragmentation. For the most part, the concept of unity has been used rather intuitively, as referring to the absence of conflict between norms, regimes or decisions. To be sure, this constitutes an important aspect of the question of unity. The fact remains, however, that most discussions about fragmentation take place without the concept of unity being elucidated or even put into question.[33]

[32] Mahmoud Darwish, *La terre nous est étroite* (Paris, Gallimard, 2000) 7 (author's translation).

[33] There are, of course, a few exceptions to this rule. Pierre-Marie Dupuy for instance, in a paper on fragmentation 'and one's perceptions of it', notes that thinking about international law's unity is an essentially 'subjective effort marked by cultures and ideologies' (Pierre-Marie Dupuy, 'Fragmentation du droit international ou des perceptions qu'on en a?' in Rosario Huesa Vinaixa and

The present book takes this ambivalence seriously and seeks to explore the various possible dimensions of unity in an international law context. Rather than listing the different types of unity, in no particular order, I shall proceed by distinguishing between different levels of analysis. Three fundamental perspectives on unity will be considered: the substantial, the cultural and the logical. Rather than speaking of perspectives, it may in fact be useful to think of these as 'families' of unity, for each perspective, as will become clear, contains within itself various possible types of unity: substantial unity can be material or formal; cultural unity can be mental or grammatical; logical unity can be epistemological or axiological, and so on.

Each family or category of unity is premised on a particular vision of international law. Cultural unity, for instance, is premised on a concept of international law as an intellectual project and as a form of argument. Substantial unity refers to the uniformity and formal coherence of 'positive' international law. Logical unity, for its part, considers international law as a rational (epistemological unity) or as a value system (axiological unity). These visions of international law, of course, are fluid and it is not my intention to suggest that they should be strictly separated. The point here is only that it is *theoretically possible* to study law as positive norms, as a language, as an intellectual project or as a value system and that each perspective generates its own notion of unity. These different forms of unity are not mutually exclusive. They *are*, however, different and rest on different sets of objects, dynamics and criteria. They also each have their own range of implications and problems.

Before exploring these different families of unity, however, I shall make a few terminological clarifications and distinguish the question of unity from similar, but nonetheless distinct, *problématiques*.

Karel Wellens (eds), *L'influence des sources sur l'unité et la fragmentation du droit international* (Brussels, Brulyant, 2006) 4. In his Hague lectures on the unity of the international legal order, he then draws a basic distinction between two fundamental types of unity: material and formal (see Pierre-Marie Dupuy, 'L'unité de l'ordre juridique international' (2002) 297 *Collected Courses* 9). Another notable exception is Heko Scheltema who, in a framing paper, considers several possible visions of unity, ranging from totalitarian or absolute unity to interlinked, foundational or opt-in unity (Heko Scheltema, 'The Fragmentation of International Law – Framing the Debate' (2010) Working Paper available at SSRN: ssrn.com/abstract=1581425). His is a work on the various *degrees* of unity, however, rather than a work on the various types of unity in international law. His focus, like that of Dupuy, remains on material norms and their interaction.

3

Unity, Unification, Universality: A Terminological Disambiguation

CERTAIN NOTIONS ARE often used in legal theory alongside the concept of unity. It is not rare, for instance, to see unity discussed in terms of 'unification' or 'universality'. Sometimes, these terms are used interchangeably, as if they were one and the same thing. The present chapter tests this assumption and seeks to bring terminological clarity to the issue. In what follows, I show that the notions of unification and universality – though they bear some relation to it – are semantically distinct from the concept of unity.

I. UNITY AND UNIFICATION

First of all, let us draw an important distinction between unity and unification. Though etymologically very close to unity, the notion of unification is – perhaps paradoxically – semantically quite distant from it. In fact, one could say that the two notions are antithetical, for unification literally signifies the process of uniting *that which is not unitary*. Whilst something cannot be both unitary and fragmented – the two notions being mutually exclusive – a thing can be fragmented and unifying at the same time, since unification necessarily applies to objects which have no unity as of yet. To speak of the unification of an object is thus not the same thing as to say that the object is already one, or indeed to say that it is plural. Instead, unification signifies the movement between one and the other.

Literally, unification is thus not the same thing as unity. But let us now turn to the more specific meaning of unification within the legal discipline. In general, the expression 'unification of law' is taken to mean something different than the establishment of *one* unitary legal system. The great projects for the international unification of private law, for instance, whether that of trade law, family law, or contract law, aim at bringing different national legal systems closer together. Discrepancies between legal systems, it is thought, are bad for the predictability and security of private transactions. Hence the need – for facilitating trade and other exchanges – to create more uniformity in the law.[1]

[1] For an analysis of the values – liberty, wealth, utility and justice – that underpin the discourse on the international unification of law, see Louis Marquis, *International Uniform Commercial Law*

The spirit or philosophy of these projects, however, is never to turn a diversity of legal systems into unity. Rather, it is to create convergence around common standards, to disseminate common principles and to ensure that various legal systems are compatible.[2] Unification is about circulating legal ideas and principles whilst simultaneously preserving the diversity of national systems. In other words, and to borrow from a famous comparative law metaphor, unification happens by way of 'transplants', which are planted into domestic legal orders and which each system then assimilates according to its own techniques, concepts and institutions.[3] Unification is thus first and foremost a matter of interconnectedness of legal cultures.

A variety of examples can be used to illustrate this point. Consider, for instance, the work of the International Institute for the Unification of Private Law (UNIDROIT) and its principles of international commercial contracts.[4] The UNIDROIT principles – first published in 1994 and later extended in 2004 – lay down a series of general rules concerning the formation, validity, interpretation, performance and termination of international commercial contracts. Whilst these principles are intended to serve as a reference point for economic operators and legal actors, and are thought to embody what are perceived as the 'best' solutions to the special problems of international commercial transactions, it is clear that they do not represent the 'one law' for all international commercial contracts. The principles are in essence subsidiary and optional, that is, they only apply where the parties choose them expressly as the rules of law governing their contract.[5] In fact, even where the parties do refer explicitly to the principles, domestic judges are likely to consider that, although this reference amounts to an incorporation of the UNIDROIT principles in the contract, the contract as a whole remains subject to their own national law.[6] In practice, this means that the principles will only govern international contracts inasmuch as they are compatible with – or tolerated by – domestic legal systems.

– *Toward a Progressive Consciousness* (Aldershot, Ashgate, 2005) 35–57. For a sceptical view, see Paul Stephan, 'The Futility of Unification and Harmonization in International Commercial Law' (1999) 39 *Virginia Journal of International Law* 743.

[2] See René David, 'The Methods of Unification' (1968) 16 *American Journal of Comparative Law* 13.

[3] See William Ewald, 'The Logic of Legal Transplants' (1995) 43 *American Journal of Comparative Law* 489.

[4] UNIDROIT, *Principles of International Commercial Contracts* (Rome, Unidroit, 2004) (*PICC*).

[5] Ibid, preamble: 'These principles set forth general rules for international commercial contracts. They shall be applied when the parties have agreed that their contract be governed by them'.

[6] See, eg, *Ostroznik Savo v La Faraona soc. Coop. a.r.l.*, Tribunale di Padova, Sezione di Este, 11 January 2005 (English translation available at: www.cisgw3.law.pace.edu/cases/050111i3.html, in which the court found that a reference by the parties to non-state rules such as the UNIDROIT Principles cannot be considered a veritable choice of law by the parties, with the consequence that these non-state rules will only bind the parties to the extent that they do not conflict with the mandatory rules of the applicable domestic law. See also Michael Joachim Bonell, *An International Restatement of Contract Law – The UNIDROIT Principles of International Commercial Contracts*, 3rd edn (Ardsley, Transnational Publishers, 2005) 180–91.

To be sure, there are situations where the principles may effectively govern the contract to the exclusion of any particular national law, such as when the parties choose the principles and agree to submit their disputes to arbitration.[7] But outside of these situations, the UNIDROIT principles mainly serve as a means for interpreting and supplementing international instruments – such as the UN Convention on Contracts for the International Sale of Goods (CISG) – or the domestic law applicable to commercial contracts. The principles act as a sort of 'intermediate law', that is, as a juridical framework to which contractors, arbitrators, judges and legislators can refer as a useful model or as a restatement of transnational contract law.[8] The point here is not that the UNIDROIT principles play no important role but, simply, that they do not *put an end* to the diversity of legal systems. Their primary functions are to provide, in a clear and simple form, an operational framework for dealing with international commercial contracts, as well as to facilitate the dissemination of recognisable principles based on commercial usage.

Unification therefore differs from unity in two important ways. First, unification is a process, whereas unity is a state or condition. One can sometimes lead to the other. In essence, however, the two are distinct. Second, and perhaps more importantly, in the specific context of transnational law unification is a process whose end-game or horizon is not unity in the strict sense. Legal unification projects do not aim at reducing the multiplicity of legal systems to unity. They maintain the diversity of orders whilst seeking convergence and harmonisation between them. The logic of legal unification is thus one of functional equivalence or compatibility among systems, rather than one of formal integration.[9] Unification seeks to avoid conflicts and to bring order to pluralism. Yet at the same time, unification recognises, manages and, in a way, sustains diversity. In other words, unification *deals* with pluralism but unlike unity, it does not deny or exclude it.

II. UNITY AND UNIVERSALITY

Unification, as has just been shown, does not amount to unity, either in letter or in spirit. The same goes for universality. Whether we understand universality to mean 'omnipresence' or 'generality', to say that law is universal is not the same

[7] Arbitrators, unlike domestic judges, are not bound by a particular domestic legal system. Arbitration also enables the parties to choose rules of law other than national law on which the arbitrators are to base their decision. See *PICC*, above n 4, official commentary 4 to Preamble, 2.

[8] On the notion of 'intermediate law', see Marquis, *International Uniform Commercial Law*, above n 1 at 11.

[9] On the difference between unity and 'functional equivalence' or 'regime compatibility', see Mireille Delmas-Marty, *Les forces imaginantes du droit – Le relatif et l'universel* (Paris, Seuil, 2004) 253–57; as well as Andreas Fischer-Lescano and Gunther Teubner, 'Regime-Collisions: The Vain Search for Legal Unity in the Fragmentation of Global Law' (2004) 25 *Michigan Journal of International Law* 999, 1045–46.

thing as to say that it is 'one' or unitary. Law can be both universal and fragmented. Similarly, a regional or local order can be perfectly unitary. There is no *a priori* or necessary connection between unity and universality. Before considering this notion further, a word must be said about the two basic ways in which one can think of law as universal.

A. Two basic conceptions of universality

At the most fundamental or basic level, the universality of law signifies its omnipresence. Omnipresence here simply means that law can be encountered everywhere at once. It is this notion that we find expressed in the Latin maxim '*ubi societas, ibi jus*': wherever there is society there is law. Any human community, regardless of its size, form or structure, generates its own system of law. To speak of universality in this way is thus merely to mark the pervasive nature of law. It signals law's invariability and ineluctability as a social institution, not its unity.

At a second level, perhaps more familiar to international lawyers, universality means generality – the fact for a legal order to be valid and applicable to all subjects in a given class or category. From this point of view, to say that international law is universal means that it has become accepted by, valid for and binding on all states.[10] International law, the story goes, was once divided into separate spheres: European versus American international law; bourgeois versus socialist international law and so on. But it has since extended to the entire planet and applies equally to all subjects, regardless of their geography, political regime or degree of 'civilisation'. It is, in other words, a 'club' in which all members of the international community are in theory admissible on equal terms.[11]

To say that international law is universal in this second sense is thus to say something about its reach and scope. It signals the all-inclusiveness of the international legal domain but says little about the unity of its forms or substance.

[10] Bruno Simma, 'Universality of International Law From the Perspective of the Practitioner' (2009) 20 *European Journal of International Law* 265, 267. Simma contrasts this vision of universality with what he calls second-level universality, which responds to the question whether international law can be perceived as a coherent whole, and third-level universality, which refers to the establishment of a true 'public order of mankind', ie a value-oriented system promoting collective interests and human rights on a global scale. These alternative visions, however, are not visions of universality properly so called. Simma himself admits that his second-level universality is best understood as referring to the issue of unity, and his third-level universality to universalism as an ethical project.

[11] This does not mean, of course, that there remains no trace of these old principles of division in contemporary international law. As noted by Simma (ibid at 268), the modern rhetoric of 'leagues' or 'alliances' of democracies fighting 'pariah' or 'rogue' states, eg, is reminiscent of the classical splitting of the world into civilised and barbarian nations.

B. Fragmentary universality

Universality, understood as openness and inclusiveness, may be a necessary condition of international law's unity. From a substantive point of view, however, it does not guarantee unity. This is true for a number of reasons. First, it is worth recalling here that universality, by and large, only occurs within small segments of the international juridical spectrum. International law is, for the most part, a special or regional phenomenon, even perhaps a local one.[12] Treaty practice illustrates this point clearly. It is well known that the vast majority of international treaties are bilateral treaties. Multilateral treaties are rare and hardly ever become truly universal.[13] The UN Charter, of course, is an important exception to this rule, having been signed and ratified by nearly all nations. It remains an exception however, and whilst there are other examples of universal or quasi-universal treaties, these are 'islands of universality' in an ocean of more limited or ad hoc treaties, valid for a small number of states only. As a rule, international treaty law develops primarily in regional spaces where geographical, historical, cultural, political or economic proximity creates an environment that is favourable to international agreement.[14]

The point here is not to make a normative judgement about regionalism. Admittedly, regionalism presents both opportunities and challenges for international law. Neither is it to suggest that regionalism necessarily excludes or contradicts universality. In fact, there are situations where the two may be mutually supportive. As law becomes universal, it tends to lose in specificity what it gains in scope. As a result, the development of universal regimes often calls for the parallel development of what could be termed 'secondary regionalism' that is, regional regimes that bring concreteness, thickness and effectiveness to the general/universal law. The best example of this is perhaps Chapter VIII of the UN Charter. This chapter explicitly provides for the possibility of joint actions between the Security Council and 'regional arrangements or agencies' for

[12] See Wladyslaw Czaplinski, 'Universalim, Regionalism and Localism in the Age of Globalization' in Ronald St John Macdonald and Douglas M Johnston (eds), *Towards World Constitutionalism – Issues in the Legal Ordering of the World Community* (Leiden, Martinus Nijhoff, 2005) 255–71.

[13] 70 to 75% of the treaties in the world are bilateral treaties. France, for instance, is a party to 5113 bilateral treaties and only 1965 multilateral treaties (www.doc.diplomatie.fr/pacte/index.html). Figures are similar in the UK (www.fco.gov.uk/en/publications-and-documents/treaties/) and in the US (www.state.gov/s/l/treaty/). It is also estimated that approximately 30% of multilateral treaties are open to universal participation by all states (see Charlotte Ku, 'Global Governance and the Changing Face of International Law' (2001) 2 *ACUN Keynote Papers* 1, 45). From a purely quantitative point of view, it can therefore be said that only 10% of international treaty law has a universal or potentially universal scope.

[14] I use the term regionalism in its widest sense here, as referring not only to geographic regionalism (eg European or African Union), but also to economic (OECD), political (Third World), military (NATO), historical (Commonwealth), religious (Organization of the Islamic Conference) or even linguistic regionalism (Francophonie). For a similar view, see Dietrich Schindler, 'Regional International Law' in *Encyclopedia of Public International Law* (Amsterdam, North-Holland, 1984) 404–05.

dealing with the maintenance of international peace and security. In this particular scenario, there is no opposition between the universal and the regional. The two support each other and coexist in a relation of complementarity, not contradiction.[15]

The fact remains, however, that true normative universality only happens 'fragmentarily', so to speak, in limited areas or branches of the law. Pockets of universality do exist in international law. But these must be contrasted with a large number of special or regional treaty arrangements. There is nothing inevitable about this state of affairs. Things may well change and there are many who consider that the globalisation of the economy and the globalisation of risks (sanitary, environmental or security risks) will inevitably lead to the globalisation of law.[16] The point here is simply that until now, the universality of international law has primarily been a piecemeal affair, in which 'legal universals' coexist with 'legal particulars'.

In fact, this point can be pushed further. It may be the case that universality can only be realised *through* elements of particularism or fragmentation. Universality always requires a good dose of compromise. The establishment of a universal regime requires firm agreement on core purposes and principles as well as some flexibility regarding secondary or peripheral issues. In other words, universality can only be achieved if there is agreement on the essential features of a regime and, at the same time, some room for marginal variance and deviation.

The institution of reservations in the law of treaties is perhaps the best illustration, in positive law, of this general principle. In the interest of encouraging state participation in treaties and thereby maximising their impact, the law of treaties has long accepted that parties should be able to compromise the integrity or completeness of a treaty by excluding or modifying the legal effect of certain provisions.[17] Provided that such reservations are compatible with the treaty's aim and purpose, a treaty may enter into force even though the agreement between the parties – the cornerstone of the treaty – is incomplete or imperfect. We are thus in a situation where greater universality is achieved by compromising the treaty's unity.[18] Universality, in this case, does not simply coexist with fragmentation. It rests on it.

[15] See, on this point, Haro van Panhuys, 'Regional or General International Law? A Misleading Dilemma' (1961) 8 *Netherlands Journal of International Law* 146.

[16] On the globalisation of risks as an 'involontary', but nonetheless very real, vector of legal universalisation, see Jürgen Habermas, *La paix perpétuelle: le bicentenaire d'une idée Kantienne* (Paris, Editions du Cerf, 1996) 74.

[17] *Vienna Convention on the Law of Treaties*, 23 May 1969, art 19.

[18] On this theme, see especially Catherine Redgwell, 'Universality or Integrity? Some Reflections on Reservations to General Multilateral Treaties' (1993) 64 *British Yearbook of International Law* 245.

C. Conflicts of universals

Let us note, for the sake of completeness, that even in the hypothesis of a truly universal legal order – a system without regional, local or bilateral variations – universality would still not be synonymous with unity. This is because of the possibility of conflicts between legal universals, that is, incompatibilities or even antinomies between the rationality, teleology, rights and obligations of universal regimes.[19] This possibility is far from theoretical in modern international law. In fact, some very real conflicts have already occurred, such as that between WTO law and other branches of international law. The conflict between the GATT and certain multilateral environmental agreements (MEAs) is perhaps the best-known example of tension between universal regimes. This conflict is perhaps inevitable, since the GATT aims at de-regulating the market whilst MEAs are intended to re-regulate the economy in areas where the free market fails to account for environmental 'externalities'.[20]

Legally speaking, this tension between WTO law and MEAs can create some very real normative conundrums, including cases where it is impossible for the parties to comply with their obligations under the different treaties. One well-known example of such conflict involves the *Convention on International Trade in Endangered Species* (CITES), a treaty that prohibits or tightly regulates the trade of certain animal and vegetal species.[21] Another famous example is the *Montreal Protocol* on the ozone layer, which bans parties from importing certain ozone-depleting chemicals.[22] In both instances, the MEA provisions are genuinely incompatible with the GATT, since the latter prohibits all forms of trade restrictions other than customs duties and genuine taxes.[23] We are thus in a situation where the law is universal or quasi universal – for the three regimes count 153 (GATT), 175 (CITES) and 193 (Montreal Protocol) parties respectively – but where the law is contradictory and does not form a coherent or unitary whole.

III. INTERMEDIATE CONCLUSIONS – COMPLEXITY ON THE GLOBAL MARKETPLACE OF LAW: THE MOX PLANT DISPUTE

The juridical field is becoming increasingly open-ended and law is arguably undergoing a process of internationalisation and globalisation. This process, however, is happening rather randomly or accidentally. Law is developing at

[19] On the concept of normative conflict, see below ch 4.

[20] On this inherent tension, see Mario Prost, *D'abord les moyens, les besoins viendront après – Commerce et environnement dans la jurisprudence du GATT et de l'OMC* (Brussels, Bruylant, 2006) 191–97.

[21] *Convention on International Trade in Endangered Species*, 3 March 1973, art III–V.

[22] *Montreal Protocol on Substances that Deplete the Ozone Layer*, 16 September 1987, arts 2–4.

[23] *General Agreement on Tariffs and Trade*, 30 October 1947, art XI.

different levels and on different 'scales' (local, national, regional, global, etc), but with no blueprint or overall plan.[24] The globalisation of law is also marked by phenomena of 'asynchrony', that is, speed variations between legal developments in different social spheres. The slow pace of universalism in human rights law, for instance, is contrasted with the fast pace of globalisation in economic law.[25] From one 'scale', field or rationality to the other, the law is characterised by important deviations, in both time and space. As it is becoming more universal, the juridical landscape is thus becoming ever more complex, slowly turning into what some may call a 'global marketplace' of law.[26]

The notion that law can experience universalisation *and* complexification – perhaps even fragmentation – may be best illustrated by reference to a recent example. The MOX dispute between Ireland and the United Kingdom demonstrates the problems of coexistence and competition that can occur when different spheres of law – at the national, regional and universal levels – are all applicable to the same situation. This dispute concerned access to information in a case involving the construction of a nuclear fuel reprocessing plant in Sellafield, on the British coast, some 100 miles away from Ireland. Anxious about the environmental and sanitary impact of the project, most notably about the risk of radioactive discharges into the Irish Sea, Ireland sought to block the construction and operation of the reprocessing plant. Following failed attempts by environmental groups to obtain the suspension of administrative authorisations in the English courts, Ireland requested access to all relevant information regarding the MOX plant. Although two reports were made available to Ireland, the British authorities retained sections on grounds of commercial confidentiality, without which, Ireland argued, the economic justification and environmental impact of the MOX plant could not be fully reviewed. Dissatisfied with the lack of cooperation from the British authorities, and having exhausted all diplomatic channels, in 2001 Ireland initiated a full-scale judicial offensive against the United Kingdom. In addition to the domestic proceedings before the English courts, Ireland fought a battle on no less than four different fronts, involving four international tribunals.

1) Proceedings were first initiated under the *Convention for the Protection of the Marine Environment of the North-East Atlantic* [OSPAR Convention], which establishes a right of access to all information 'on the state of the maritime area [and] on activities or measures adversely affecting or likely to affect it'.[27] An ad hoc arbitral tribunal was set up in accordance with the

[24] I borrow this notion of juridical 'scale' from Boaventura de Sousa Santos, 'Law: A Map of Misreading. Toward a Postmodern Conception of Law' (1987) 14 *Journal of Law and Society* 279, 287–91.

[25] Mireille Delmas-Marty, *Ordering Pluralism: A Conceptual Framework for Understanding the Transnational Legal World* (Oxford, Hart Publishing, 2009) 119–33.

[26] Yves Dezalay, *Vers une sociologie de l'internationalisation du champ de l'expertise: du marché du droit à la politique du droit* (Paris, Centre de Recherche Interdisciplinaire, 1994).

[27] *Convention for the Protection of the Marine Environment of the North-East Atlantic*, 22 September 1992, (1992) 32 *ILM* 1069, art 9.

Convention's arbitration clause and under the auspices of the Permanent Court of Arbitration.[28]

2) A second arbitral tribunal was established under Annex VII of the *United Nations Convention on the Law of the Sea* [UNCLOS] in order to deal, this time, with the alleged breach by the United Kingdom of the Convention's provisions on the protection and preservation of the marine environment.[29]
3) Additionally, and considering that the proceedings before the UNCLOS tribunal would be in vain if the United Kingdom were to start operating the MOX plant before the tribunal could deliver its judgment on the merits, Ireland filed a request for the indication of provisional measures with the International Tribunal on the Law of the Sea [ITLOS] asking the tribunal to order the United Kingdom to suspend the authorisation of the MOX plant.
4) Lastly, the European Commission, being of the opinion that this dispute fell within the ambit of Community law, initiated proceedings against Ireland in the European Court of Justice (ECJ) for failing to submit the dispute to the exclusive jurisdiction of the Court.

The same set of facts is therefore covered simultaneously by three treaty regimes, operating at the micro-regional (OSPAR), the macro-regional (EU) and the universal levels (UN). And to add complexity to an already complex situation, the various tribunals involved in this dispute took very different views on this issue of regime overlap and on the principles guiding the relation between different rule-complexes:

1) The OSPAR tribunal acknowledged that the dispute may not fall exclusively within the ambit of the OSPAR Convention. It took the view that at least some elements of the dispute may fall within the jurisdiction of the ECJ, in particular those involving access to environmental information, an issue also governed by Community law.[30] At the same time, the tribunal held that the OSPAR Convention was a 'self-contained' system of dispute settlement and that the jurisdiction of the ECJ was no bar to its own.[31] The tribunal did not rule out the possibility of taking into account, if only for the purpose of interpretation, other international treaties or rules of customary inter-

[28] *Dispute Concerning Access to Information Under Article 9 of the OSPAR Convention (Ireland v United Kingdom of Great Britain and Northern Ireland)*, 2 July 2003, (2003) 42 *ILM* 1118 [hereinafter OSPAR award].

[29] *United Nations Convention on the Law of the Sea*, 10 December 1982, (1982) 21 *ILM* 1261.

[30] See Council Directive 90/313/EEC of 7 June 1990 on the Freedom of Access to Information on the Environment [1990] OJ L158/56, later repealed by Directive 2003/4/EC on Public Access to Environmental Information [2003] OJ L41/26.

[31] OSPAR award, above n 28 at para 143: 'the OSPAR Convention contains a particular and self-contained dispute resolution mechanism . . . The similar language of the two legal instruments . . . does not limit a Contracting Party's choice of a legal forum to only one of the two available, i.e. either the ECJ or an OSPAR tribunal. [It does not] create precedence of one set of legal remedies over the other'.

national law.[32] In the tribunal's view, however, the OSPAR Convention and Community law are two distinct and separate regimes, each with its own sources and remedies, and each equally capable of governing the dispute. As a result, the OSPAR tribunal found it possible to fully exercise its jurisdiction and to rule on the merits of the case based exclusively on the provisions of the OSPAR Convention.

2) The ITLOS tribunal, in its order for provisional measures, adopted a slightly more ambiguous attitude towards the issue of regime overlap. The tribunal took note of the proceedings instigated by Ireland under the OSPAR Convention, as well as of the possibly exclusive jurisdiction of the ECJ to hear some aspects of the dispute.[33] However, and despite finding that the OSPAR Convention and the EC Treaty contain rights and obligations similar to those set out in the UNCLOS Convention, the tribunal held that these different regimes 'have a separate existence from [the UNCLOS] Convention'.[34] Though not speaking of 'self-contained regimes', the tribunal maintained that each regime had its specificity and that differences existed in their 'respective contexts, objects and purposes'.[35] Since the dispute was concerned exclusively with the application and interpretation of the UNCLOS Convention the ITLOS tribunal concluded that 'only the dispute settlement procedures under the [UNCLOS] Convention [were] relevant to that dispute'.[36] Based on this, the tribunal declared itself competent to order provisional measures, pending the decision on the merits by the Annex VII tribunal.

3) The position adopted by the Annex VII tribunal was radically different. Although the tribunal saw no reason to disagree with the ITLOS' finding that it had *prima facie* jurisdiction, it nonetheless had to satisfy itself that it had jurisdiction in a definitive sense to decide the merits, especially in view of the competing proceedings initiated under the OSPAR Convention and of a possible conflict of jurisdiction with the ECJ.[37] The tribunal ruled that the OSPAR proceedings were not an obstacle to its own jurisdiction, since these proceedings did not directly involve the interpretation and application of the UNCLOS Convention.[38] The tribunal did find, however, the 'interrelation' between the

[32] Ibid at para 175: 'It should go without saying that the first duty of the Tribunal is to apply the OSPAR Convention. An international tribunal, such as this Tribunal, will also apply customary international law and general principles, unless and to the extent that the Parties have created a *lex specialis*'.

[33] *The Mox Plant Case – Request for Provisional Measures (Ireland v United Kingdom)*, 3 December 2001, (2002) 41 *ILM* 405, paras 40–42.

[34] Ibid at para 50.

[35] Ibid at para 51.

[36] Ibid at para 52.

[37] *The MOX Plant Case (Ireland v United Kingdom) – Suspension of Proceedings on Jurisdiction and Merits, and Request for Further Provisional Measures*, Order no 3, 24 June 2003, (2003) 42 *ILM* 1187, para 14.

[38] Ibid at para 18. The tribunal did recognise, however, that some aspects of the dispute may be governed by the OSPAR Convention and that Irish claims arising under other treaties or instruments may be inadmissible (para 19).

law of the sea and Community law to be a much more problematic question.[39] The Community and its members all being parties to the UNCLOS Convention, the tribunal observed that there was a 'real possibility' that jurisdiction regarding the law of the sea had been transferred to the European Community in a way that may preclude its jurisdiction.[40] The tribunal recognised that the dispute touched upon matters 'which essentially concerne[d] the internal operation of a separate legal order (namely the legal order of the European Community)' and, as a result, that the dispute may be better settled 'within the institutional framework of the European Communities'.[41] In order to avoid a conflict of jurisprudence that would be detrimental to the peaceful settlement of the dispute, and bearing in mind considerations of mutual respect and comity, the tribunal therefore decided to suspend further proceedings pending clarification on the ECJ's jurisdiction.[42]

4) The ECJ, for its part, adopted what could be termed a 'hegemonic' posture on the issue of regime overlap. The Court began its 2006 judgment by observing that, under a well-established jurisprudence, international treaties adopted by the Community (now the Union) form an integral part of the Community legal order.[43] The UNCLOS Convention, however, is a mixed agreement, that is, a treaty adopted jointly by the Community and its member states on the basis of shared competences.[44] The mixed nature of the UNCLOS Convention means that only parts of the treaty fall within Community competences (and thus within ECJ jurisdiction),[45] whilst others remain within the competence of the member states (and may thus be submitted to a forum other than the ECJ). The real question, for the ECJ, was therefore to establish whether the provisions in dispute between Ireland and the United Kingdom (protection of the marine environment) fell within the former or the latter category. In answering this question, the Court based itself on a very liberal interpretation of the 'declaration of competence' of the Community. This document, attached to the EC ratification of the UNCLOS Convention, details the nature and extent of the competences

[39] Ibid at para 20.

[40] Ibid at para 21.

[41] Ibid at paras 24–26.

[42] Ibid at paras 28–29. The suspension was initially pronounced for a period of five months. It was subsequently extended *sine die*, after the European Commission decided to authorise the institution of proceedings against Ireland in respect of Community law issues. Proceedings were eventually terminated after Ireland withdrew its claim against the United Kingdom. See ibid, orders 4 and 6 (www.pca-cpa.org/showpage.asp?pag_id=1148).

[43] Case C-459/03 *Commission v Ireland* [2006] ECR I-04635, para 82.

[44] On the status of mixed agreements in European Union law, see Joni Heliskoski, *Mixed Agreements as a Technique for Organizing the International Relations of the European Community and its Member States* (The Hague, Kluwer Law International, 2001).

[45] Under European Union law, the ECJ has exclusive jurisdiction to settle disputes concerning the interpretation or application of the constitutive treaties. See *Treaty on the Functioning of the European Union*, art 344: 'Member States undertake not to submit a dispute concerning the interpretation or application of the Treaties to any method of settlement other than those provided for therein'.

> transferred by the member states to the Community in matters governed by the Convention. This declaration clearly stipulates that the Community shall have exclusive competence in areas where Community rules are already in operation *and* where these rules are affected by the provisions of the UN Convention.[46] Otherwise, competence rests with the member states. In other words, the only areas of the UNCLOS Convention that fall within the exclusive jurisdiction of the Community are areas in which the Community has, in practice, already become the primary actor/legislator.[47] Despite these rather clear provisions, the ECJ decided that a transfer of competence had taken place regarding the protection of the marine environment even 'without any of the Community rules concerned being affected'.[48] For the Court, it was sufficient to find that *some* rules had been enacted by the Community, 'irrespective of what may otherwise be the scope and nature of those rules'.[49] As a result, the Court found that the UNCLOS provisions that Ireland relied on were in effect Community rules, which could only be subject to Community dispute resolution processes. This decision can be regarded as hegemonic in the sense that it affirms that certain provisions of the UNCLOS Convention can only be adjudicated by the ECJ, irrespective of the scope and extent of the Community's 'legislative investment' in these matters.[50] In other words, this decision artificially 'Communitarises' whole portions of the law of the sea and asserts, in absolute terms, the autonomy and superiority of the Community system over the universal regime of the UN.[51]

What does the MOX Plant dispute tell us about international law's unity? The first lesson is that, in spite of law's gradual universalisation in areas such as the law of the sea or environmental protection, the same dispute can give rise to no less than five parallel proceedings, at four different regulatory levels, and can be

[46] Council Decision 98/392/EC of 23 March 1998 Concerning the Conclusion by the European Community of the United Nations Convention of 10 December 1982 on the Law of the Sea and the Agreement of 28 July 1994 Relating to the Implementation of Part XI Thereof [1998] OJ L179/1, annex II: 'The Community has exclusive competence for certain matters and shares competence with its Member States for certain other matters . . . with regard to the provisions on maritime transport, safety of shipping and the prevention of marine pollution . . . the Community has exclusive competence only to the extent that such provisions of the Convention or legal instruments adopted in implementation thereof affect common rules established by the Community'.

[47] See Robin Churchill and Joanne Scoot, 'The MOX Plant Litigation: the First Half-Life' (2004) 53 *International and Comparative Law Quarterly* 643, 664–66.

[48] *Commission v Ireland*, above n 43 at para 105.

[49] Ibid at para 108.

[50] For a similar analysis, see Freya Baetens, 'Muddling the Waters of Treaty Interpretation? Relevant Rules of International Law in the MOX Plant OSPAR Arbitration and EC-Biotech Case' (2008) 77 *Nordic Journal of International Law* 197, 202.

[51] The prevalence of this 'Community-focused reasoning' is apparent in several other sections of the Court's decision. See *Commission v* Ireland, above n 43 at para 123: 'an international agreement cannot affect the allocation of responsibilities defined in the Treaties and, consequently, the autonomy of the Community legal system'; and para 154: 'the institution and pursuit of proceedings before the [Annex VII] Arbitral Tribunal . . . involve a manifest risk that the jurisdictional order laid down in the Treaties and, consequently, the autonomy of the Community legal system may be adversely affected'.

governed simultaneously by four regimes, with no *a priori* law of organisation or fixed hierarchy to resolve problems of jurisdictional overlap.

The second lesson is that, when confronted with problems of regime overlap, international judges and arbitrators tend to adopt very different attitudes. Some assert the autonomy and self-containedness of their regime – in relative or in absolute terms – and read their law in 'clinical isolation' from its broader normative environment. Others, prompted by considerations of mutual respect and comity, insist on the inter-connectedness of their regimes and look for ways to achieve 'systemic integration' between different spheres of legality.

Lastly, the MOX Plant dispute illustrates how, in a given policy area (law of the sea), even a universal regime (UNCLOS) can be affected by the existence of regional regimes or systems (EU law). The 'communitarisation' of the law of the sea, that is, its integration into the European Union legal order, affects the nature, substance and justiciability of the rights and obligations contained in the UN Convention. It affects their nature, first of all, for the rules of the UNCLOS Convention effectively become Community rules and, as such, are directly applicable and enforceable in the territory of the member states, without the need for incorporation of the treaty provisions into domestic law.[52] It also affects their substance, since as Community rules, the UNCLOS provisions become subject to the general principles and methods of interpretation of EU law.[53] Lastly, the communitarisation of the law of the sea affects its justiciability, for the EU legal order, unlike the UN regime, features a system of general and compulsory jurisdiction open to member states, Union institutions and, to some extent, to natural and legal persons.[54]

As a final but no less important point, and this constitutes an ultimate element of complexification, it must be recalled that the law of the sea is internalised in the Union legal order if and only to the extent that Union institutions have already legislated on matters governed by the UN Convention. As a result, the regime is far from homogenous *even among member states of the Union*, with portions of the law of the sea being governed by EU law and other matters remaining within the ambit of the UN Convention.

What the above demonstrates is that the universalisation of law is in large part coextensive with its complexification. Universalisation results in irregular and unstable mixtures between scattered juridical objects, rather than in the unity, or even the unification, of international law. This trend or movement is

[52] Case 12/86 *Meryem Demirel v Stadt Schwäbisch Gmünd* [1987] ECR I-03719, para 14: 'a provision in an agreement concluded by the Community with non-member countries must be regarded as being directly applicable when . . . the provision contains a clear and precise obligation which is not subject, in its implementation or effects, to the adoption of any subsequent measure'.

[53] On EU law's specific methods of interpretation, see eg, Ian McLeod, 'Literal and Purposive Techniques of Legislative Interpretation: Some European Community and English Common Law Perspectives' (2003) 29 *Brooklyn Journal of International Law* 1109.

[54] Treaty on the Functioning of the European Union, art 263: 'any natural or legal person may, under the conditions laid down in the first and second paragraphs, institute proceedings against an act addressed to that person or which is of direct and individual concern to them, and against a regulatory act which is of direct concern to them and does not entail implementing measures'.

not irreversible. As international law is becoming more universal and has to deal with problems of regime overlap, it is starting to develop rules of interpretation and principles of organisation which, imperfect though they may be, enable law-appliers to build systemic relationships between rule-complexes, to resolve conflicts of norms, or at the very least to justify their preferences in a legal, rational manner.[55] The fact remains, however, that universality can entail competition between different spheres of law, which all have their own coherence and rationality, and whose interaction is not unlike that of separate systems of municipal law.[56] Whether faced with regional deviations or with conflict of universals, it becomes clear that universality is simply not the same thing as unity.

[55] See the approach taken by the International Law Commission in *Fragmentation of International Law: Difficulties Arising from the Diversification and Expansion of International Law – Report of the Study Group of the International Law Commission* (finalised by Martti Koskenniemi), UN Doc A/CN.4/L.682 (2006), para 20: 'This report is about legal reasoning. Although it does not purport to give ready-made solutions to problems [of fragmentation] it does provide a toolbox with the help of which lawyers dealing with [such] problems may be able to proceed to a reasoned decision'.

[56] For an early account, see Wilfried Jenks, 'The Conflict of Law-Making Treaties' (1953) 30 *British Yearbook of International Law* 400, 403.

4

Material Unity

THE STAGE IS set. In the last two chapters, I have discussed two themes that are essential to our understanding of international law's unity. I have shown, first of all, that the concept of unity is fundamentally ambivalent and contested. One can apprehend unity at different semantic levels and from different perspectives, none of which is self-evident or objectively truer than the others. In international law, there is more than one way of being 'one'. Lawyers can express preference for one or the other perspective. But the conceptual pluralism of unity can hardly be ignored. To speak of unity from a substantive point of view is not the same thing as to speak of it from generic, teleological or axiological points of view. International law, as shall become clear in the rest of this book, can be at once unitary and fragmented, depending on the perspective from which the analysis is conducted.

The second important theme considered thus far has been to exclude certain notions from the ambit of this book, which bear some relation to the concept of unity but are nonetheless distinct from it. I have attempted to show, in particular, that important differences exist between the concept of unity and those of unification and universality. The notion of unification refers, in legal scholarship, to processes of harmonisation between separate legal systems. The notion of universality, for its part, points to the degree of openness and inclusiveness of the juridical field. Unification and universality, though important and worthy of analytical consideration, must therefore be distinguished from the concept of unity.

Having set forth the general approach and ambit of this book, I now turn to its main argument. In the following chapters, I take the conceptual complexity or 'thickness' of unity seriously and explore what I consider the six principal ways in which one can think of law in general, and international law in particular, as 'one'. I begin in the present chapter with a consideration of 'substantive' unity, the type of unity that is used, explicitly or implicitly, in most of the fragmentation literature. My choice to speak of 'substantive' unity is justified by the fact that unity is understood in relation to law's normative content, that is, to its juridical substance. Unity, from this perspective, springs not from legal science, juridical thought, doctrine or any other cognitive activity, but rather from the compatibility or orderly arrangement of legal norms themselves. What matters, in other words, is not the 'spirit' but the 'body' of positive law.

That said, the substantive unity of international law can be understood in at least two ways, depending on whether unity is assessed in relation to primary or secondary norms.[1] In the first instance, unity is measured by considering the extent to which consistency and coherence exist among individual norms of conduct. In the second instance, unity refers not to the compatibility or identity of individual norms, but rather to the processes by which these are combined and assembled together. I shall speak of 'material' unity in the first case and of 'formal' unity in the second.[2] The current chapter explores the former type of unity whilst I consider the latter form of unity in chapter five.

I. THE 'NO CONFLICT' THEORY OF UNITY

Most lawyers intuitively think of the unity of law as something that concerns the uniformity of the substantive rules of a legal system. The emphasis is generally placed upon *primary* rules, that is (to borrow from Hart's *Concept of Law*) rules that directly govern the conduct of legal subjects and by which these subjects are required to do or abstain from certain actions.[3] To think of substantive unity from this point of view is to consider the degree of harmony that exists among the constituent 'parts' of the system – the primary rules – which form the raw material, the elementary normative fabric of the legal order. Here, unity is measured by reference to law's normative *content* and is achieved when different rules applicable to the same problem prescribe similar or compatible solutions.[4]

In general, lawyers espouse this form of unity somewhat spontaneously and instinctively. As a result, material unity is rarely theorised or clearly articulated in the literature. More often than not, recourse is had to rather indistinguishable formulations that are mere variations on the general themes of uniformity and coherence. Some say, for instance, that there is legal unity 'where a uniform legislation has been put in place'.[5] Others consider that material unity rests on the existence of 'a certain homogeneity of interpretation and application of legal norms'.[6] Others see unity where the law 'treats all legal subjects in the same way'.[7]

[1] For a similar analysis, see Pierre-Marie Dupuy, 'L'unité de l'ordre juridique international' (2002) 297 *Collected Courses of the Academy of International Law* 9.

[2] I borrow this basic distinction from Joseph Raz, 'The Identity of the Legal System' (1971) 59 *California Law Review* 795, 796.

[3] HLA Hart, *The Concept of Law* (Oxford, Clarendon Press, 1961) 78–80.

[4] For a similar analysis, see Henri Battifol, *Aspects philosophiques du droit international privé* (Paris, Dalloz, 1956) 49. Battifol speaks of rules as forming legal 'wholes' (*ensembles*) 'by reason of their content' (*à raison de leur contenu*).

[5] Blaise Knapp, 'Fédéralisme et unité du droit' (1986) 46 *Annales de Droit de Louvain* 309, 315.

[6] Denise Bindschelder, 'Le règlement des différends relatif au statut d'un organisme international' (1969) 128 *Collected Courses of the Hague Academy of International Law* 453, 507.

[7] Jean-Michel Lemoyne de Forges, 'Le juriste arrive toujours plus tard' in Jean-Bernard Auby et al (eds), *L'unité du droit – Mélanges en hommage à Roland Drago* (Paris, Economica, 1996) 485.

International lawyers, who often speak of unity and fragmentation, are rarely more specific in their definition of material unity. Here again, unity is usually understood to denote 'coherence among rules of international law'.[8] And by coherence, international lawyers generally mean the existence of 'identical or comparable rules',[9] the 'uniform development of jurisprudence'[10] or 'judicial harmony'.[11]

Judges, finally, who are often regarded as the 'guardians of unity',[12] are no less elusive in their approach to unity: an American tribunal mentions the 'harmony' and 'symmetry' of laws;[13] the High Court of Australia speaks of the 'identity of applicable substantive rules';[14] Justice Cançado Trindade, in an individual opinion appended to a decision of the Inter-American Court of Human Rights, measures the unity of public international law in terms of its 'aptitude to regulate legal relations in distinct contexts with equal adequacy and effectiveness'.[15]

'Uniformity', 'homogeneity', 'harmony', 'symmetry' or 'continuity': the analysis of unity remains mired in theoretical vagueness, in which one fuzzy concept is replaced by another. In order to understand more fully what material unity is, it may thus be useful to turn to negative definitions of the concept, that is, to what unity is *not*. As often with fuzzy concepts, negative definitions are useful to the extent that they narrow one's general area of investigation and allow one to get closer to one's object of inquiry. In this regard, lawyers generally think of the unity of law as the absence of deviating norms, of inconsistent decisions, or of any other element of heterogeneity that may lead to uncertainty as to which norm should apply to a given situation.[16] Unity, in other words, is understood as the *absence of conflict* in the law. This way of thinking about the

[8] Stephan Wittich, 'Domestic Implementation and the Unity of International Law' in Andreas Zimmermann and Rainer Hofmann (eds), *Unity and Diversity in International Law* (Berlin, Duncker & Humbolt, 2006) 345.

[9] Beate Rudolf, 'Unity and Diversity of International Law in the Settlement of International Disputes' in Andreas Zimmermann and Rainer Hofmann (eds), *Unity and Diversity in International Law* (Berlin, Duncker & Humbolt, 2006) 398.

[10] Shigeru Oda, 'Dispute Settlement Prospects in the Law of the Sea' (1995) 44 *International and Comparative Law Quarterly* 863, 864.

[11] Pemmaraju Sreenivasa Rao, 'Multiple International Judicial Forums: a Reflection of the Growing Strength of International Law or its Fragmentation?' (2004) 25 *Michigan Journal of International Law* 929, 961.

[12] See, eg, Pierre-Marie Dupuy, 'The Unity of Application of International Law at the Global Level and the Responsibility of Judges' (2007) 2 *European Journal of Legal Studies* 1.

[13] *Ex parte Mode* (1915) 77 Tex Crim 432, 462: 'where two enactments separately made are read *in pari materia*, they are treated as having formed in the minds of the enacting body parts of a connected whole . . . Such a principle is in harmony with the actual practice of legislative bodies and is essential to give unity to laws, and connect them in a symmetrical system'.

[14] *McKain v RW Miller & Co (South Australia) Pty Ltd* [1991] HCA 56, in which the High Court of Australia insists upon 'the unity of the law of this country and the consistency and predictability of the identity of applicable substantive rules under that national legal system'.

[15] *Caesar v Trinidad and Tobago (Petition no 12.147)* [2005] 21 BHRC 305, para 46.

[16] For this way of thinking about unity, see eg, Joost Pauwelyn, *Conflict of Norms in Public International Law: How WTO Rules Relate to Other Rules of International Law* (Cambridge, Cambridge University Press, 2003).

unity of international law can be found, for instance, in the International Law Commission's report on fragmentation. There, the Commission conceptualises fragmentation in terms of 'conflicting and incompatible rules, principles, rule-systems and institutional practices', adding that when such deviations become general and frequent, they create 'problems of coherence in international law' and 'the unity of the law suffers'.[17]

In the field of legal theory, Kelsen articulated this notion of unity in the most explicit and systematic manner. Kelsen's theory of the unity of law, as we shall see below, is not free from ambiguities. At times, Kelsen advocated a strict theory of unity, claiming that valid norms *necessarily* form a unitary system. At other times, he presented a softer theory of unity, merely observing that valid laws, as a matter of fact, do generally form coherent wholes. Located somewhere between an epistemological postulate and an empirically verifiable fact, unity is for Kelsen as central as it is ambivalent.[18] The fact remains, however, that the notion of normative conflict is critical to Kelsen's understanding of the unity of law.

In the first edition of his *Reine Rechtslehre*, for instance, Kelsen writes that 'the negative criterion of unity is noncontradiction . . . One cannot claim that two norms whose content is . . . mutually exclusive are valid at the same time, that is, one cannot claim that *A* ought to be and, at the same time, not-*A* ought to be, just as one cannot claim that *A* is and, at the same time, not-*A* is'.[19] In the second edition of the *Pure Theory of Law*, Kelsen reiterates that the unity of law 'is expressed by the fact that a legal order may be described in rules of law that do not contradict each other', adding that a conflict of norms exists 'if one norm prescribes a certain behaviour, and another norm prescribes another behaviour incompatible with the first. For example, if one norm prescribes that adultery ought to be punished, and another norm that it ought not to be punished; or if one norm prescribes that theft ought to be punished by death, and another by imprisonment'.[20]

To define material unity as the absence of normative conflict, as the previous quotations illustrate, only gets us halfway to fully understanding it. For the question then becomes what, juridically, constitutes a conflict. This question may appear rather uncontroversial when a contradiction exists between, say, one traffic norm prescribing 'priority on the right' and another prescribing 'priority on the left', or between one norm making religious teaching at school compulsory and another banning it. But can one say with the same degree of

[17] *Fragmentation of International Law: Difficulties Arising from the Diversification and Expansion of International Law – Report of the Study Group of the International Law Commission* (finalised by Martti Koskenniemi), UN Doc A/CN.4/L.682 (2006) [ILC Fragmentation Report] paras 14–15.

[18] See on this point HLA Hart, 'Kelsen's Doctrine of the Unity of Law' in Howard Kiefer and Milton Munitz (eds), *Ethics and Social Justice* (Albany, SUNY Press, 1968) 171–72.

[19] Hans Kelsen, *Introduction to the Problems of Legal Theory* (Oxford, Clarendon Press, 1992) 112.

[20] Hans Kelsen, *Pure Theory of Law* (Berkeley, University of California Press, 1967) 205.

certainty that a conflict exists between one norm *authorising* overtaking on the left and another *authorising* overtaking on the right? Likewise, is there a normative conflict if two norms simply diverge, for instance if one norm provides protection of intellectual property rights for a period of 50 years and another for a period of 70 years? There is no simple or evident answer to these important questions and definitions of norm conflicts vary widely, both in theory and in practice.

II. THE DEFINITION OF 'NORM CONFLICT' IN THEORY AND PRACTICE

The purpose of the present section is to highlight the diversity of theoretical perspectives on the issue of norm conflicts. I identify and analyse three fundamental perspectives, each with its own ramifications and sub-categories. *Stricto sensu* conflicts, otherwise known as deontic antinomies, refer to situations where two or more norms are intrinsically, mechanically and mutually exclusive. *Medio sensu* conflicts are premised on the same notion of normative incompatibility but encompass what are known as potential conflicts, that is, contradictions between obligations and permissions. *Lato sensu* conflicts, for their part, refer not so much to strict normative incompatibilities as to divergences or dissonances between norms that have different purposes and 'get in each other's way'.

Before examining these different forms of conflict further, I must make two preliminary points. The first point is that, if lawyers disagree on the definition, nature and logic of normative conflicts, so too do they disagree, and perhaps at a more fundamental level, on the *object* of conflicts, that is, on the elements that are susceptible of conflicting in the first place. If most lawyers, for instance, believe that conflicts of jurisprudence are normative conflicts properly-so-called, which undermine the coherence and the unity of international law,[21] some consider that conflicts of norms and conflicts of jurisprudence are two different things.

Joost Pauwelyn, who has written extensively on norm conflicts in international law, considers for instance that judicial decisions cannot be at issue in

[21] See, eg, Gilbert Guillaume, 'L'unité du droit international public est-elle aujourd'hui en danger?' (2003) 55 *Revue Internationale de Droit Comparé* 23; Pierre-Marie Dupuy, 'The Danger of Fragmentation or Unification of the International Legal System and the International Court of Justice' (1998) 31 *New York University Journal of International Law & Politics* 791; Nele Matz-Lück, 'Promoting the Unity of International Law: Standard-Setting by International Tribunals' in Doris König et al (eds), *International Law Today: New Challenges and the Need for Reform?* (Berlin, Springer, 2008). Even authors who consider that the risk of fragmentation is exaggerated or merely virtual often view contradicting judicial decisions as forms of normative conflict which pose problems of coherence and unity. See, eg, Jonathan Charney, 'Is International Law Threatened by Multiple International Law Tribunals?' (1998) 271 *Collected Courses of the Hague Academy of International Law* 101, 104: 'decisions reaching different conclusions on the same international law subject by a variety of tribunals may undermine the appearance, if not the fact, of a unitary international legal system'.

norm conflicts.[22] In his view, judicial decisions are not, in and of themselves, norms of international law. They are particular instances of application of legal norms, in the limited context of a given dispute. Judicial decisions are 'accurate statements' of what the law is, as between two parties and as applied to a particular set of circumstances, but they are not the law itself.[23] Moreover, for a conflict to arise, says Pauwelyn, there must be an overlap *ratione personae*, *personae* and *temporis* between norms or norm-complexes. In other words, the norms or norm-complexes must apply to the same subject matter, to the same parties, and at the same time.[24] Because judicial decisions never truly overlap – the facts, parties and issues being different from one dispute to the other – conflicts of jurisprudence, in Pauwelyn's opinion, are not really conflicts of norms.

The second point is that, conversely, where there is overlap, there is not necessarily conflict. Norms can interact and overlap in a number of ways, many of which do not constitute conflict. One norm, for example, can confirm or consolidate another. Article 5 of the Treaty on European Union, for instance, merely confirms a key principle of the law of international organisations – the principle of 'speciality' – when providing that the Union shall act only 'within the limits of the competences conferred upon it by the Member States in the Treaties to attain the objectives set out therein'.[25] A norm can also add rights and obligations to existing ones. A norm regulating trade in services can for instance complement a norm regulating trade in goods. In this case, the two norms overlap, for they both apply to trade, but they do not contradict each other. There is, between them, a relation of accumulation, not conflict.[26] There is, finally, the possibility for a norm to provide for an exception to another rule. Article 51 of the UN Charter (inherent right of self-defence), for instance, does not 'conflict' with article 2(4) (prohibition of the use of force) for it explicitly holds that 'nothing in the Charter' shall impair the right of legitimate self-defence. The two norms have different scopes or functions: one is the rule, the other the exception. They themselves organise their mutual interaction by holding that, in certain circumstances, one norm will displace the other. In all these situations where one norm serves to apply, interpret, clarify, update or modify

[22] Pauwelyn, *Conflicts of Norms in Public International Law*, above n 16 at 109.

[23] Ibid at 110.

[24] Ibid at 165. See also Francesco Capotorti, 'Interférences dans l'ordre juridique interne entre la Convention et d'autres accords internationaux' in Walter Van der Meersch (ed), *Les droits de l'homme en droit interne et en droit international* (Brussels, Presses Universitaires de Bruxelles, 1968) 123: 'pour qu'il y ait interférence entre deux accords, il faut qu'ils aient au moins un point de contact subjectif et un point de contact objectif; subjectif en ce sens qu'un ou plusieurs Etats sont parties à ces deux accords; objectif en ce sens qu'une même matière ou des matières connexes sont réglées, dans les deux accords, par une ou plusieurs dispositions'.

[25] For a classical formulation of the principle of speciality, see *Jurisdiction of the European Commission of the Danube*, 8 December 1927, PCIJ Reports (1927), Ser B, No 14, 64: 'the European Commission is not a State, but an international institution with a special purpose, it only has the functions bestowed upon it by the Definitive Statute with a view to the fulfilment of that purpose'.

[26] See Pauwelyn, *Conflicts of Norms in Public International Law*, above n 16 at 161–64.

another, there is no normative conflict. The various norms are applied in conjunction with one another.[27]

There are cases, however, where norms do not merely 'accumulate' and where a genuine conflict may arise. It is then necessary to choose between the various applicable norms. This much is rather uncontroversial. Problems arise, however, when trying to find a commonly accepted definition of conflicts. Most authors who deal with the interaction or hierarchy of norms provide no definition and adopt an 'I know it when I see it' attitude. In such situations, one is often forced to deduce how the authors define conflict from the examples used to support their argument. In doing so, one generally finds rather broad definitions of conflict at work in the literature. Where definitions are explicitly provided, however, authors generally favour a more restrictive approach to norm conflicts. This section begins with this narrow or strict definition of conflicts and then progresses to wider definitions.

A. *Stricto sensu* conflicts

The strict or narrow definition of conflicts refers to the logical impossibility of applying two particular norms simultaneously. From this point of view, there is a conflict where two norms can *in no way* be applied at the same time. In practice, this type of complete and irresolvable conflict, which Alf Ross calls 'deontic antinomies',[28] will occur in three situations:

- When one norm prescribes the very opposite of another. This constitutes the most obvious case of conflict. It will occur, for instance, if one traffic norm provides 'priority on the right' and another provides 'priority on the left'; or if one norm, after a divorce, entrusts child custody to the mother whilst another awards it to the father.
- When one norm prescribes a conduct which, although not diametrically opposite, is nonetheless incompatible with that prescribed by another norm. This would happen, for instance, if one norm was to require Mr Smith to attend a court hearing at Oxford Magistrates' Court at 9am on Monday morning and another asked him to present himself, on the same day and at the same time, at his local police station; or if one and the same debt claim was subject to different orders of priority for repayment of the creditors.
- The third hypothesis concerns situations where one norm prescribes that which another explicitly forbids. It would be the case, for instance, if one norm made compulsory the sanitary inspection of all goods crossing the

[27] On the distinction between relations of 'interpretation' and relations of 'conflict', see *Conclusions of the Work of the Study Group on the Fragmentation of International Law: Difficulties Arising from the Diversification and Expansion of International Law*, UN Doc A/61/10 (2006) (ILC Fragmentation Conclusions) para 2.

[28] Alf Ross, *Directives and Antinomies* (New York, Humanities Press, 1968) 168–74.

border whilst another prohibited all non-tariff barriers to trade; or if one norm made religious teaching at school compulsory and another banned it.

Here we have situations where the law, according to Ross, is 'directively nonsensical'.[29] Legal directives (that is, norms of conduct) are incompatible, either because they impose obligations that point in opposite directions, or because one directive prohibits that which another requires.[30] This approach to conflicts is narrow in the sense that it only covers situations where norms are *genuinely*, *necessarily* and *mutually* exclusive. As a result, conflicts known as 'potential' and 'apparent' conflicts are excluded from this strict definition.

- The strict definition excludes, first of all, potential conflicts, that is, conflicts between an obligation (to do or *not* to do something) and a mere permission (to do or *not* to do something). Such would be the case, for instance, between norm A prohibiting quantitative restrictions to trade (obligation not to restrict trade) and norm B allowing certain restrictive measures regarding dangerous products or endangered species (permission to restrict trade). In such a situation, the conflict will only materialise if the permission is *effectively acted upon*. Although the two norms are potentially incompatible, they do not *necessarily* or *automatically* exclude each other.
- The narrow definition of conflicts also excludes apparent conflicts, that is, situations where two norms are different but are not mutually exclusive. Such is the case, first of all, in situations where two norms govern the same subject matter and one is stricter than the other. One can imagine, for instance, a situation where norm A prescribes a speed limit of 80 mph and norm B prescribes a limit of 70 mph. There is, of course, a difference between A and B. And this difference will create problems of predictability and certainty for legal subjects. A driver will need to know, in our scenario, which speed limit to obey. Yet, the conflict can be regarded as apparent in the sense that the divergence between A and B can be resolved by complying with the strictest norm (that is, by driving below 70 mph). A conflict will also be apparent where the contradiction between two norms can be resolved by way of interpretation. If norm A, for instance, prohibits the use of vehicles in the park and norm B provides for the organisation of cycling competitions in the park on Sundays, there is a contradiction between A and B. But this contradiction can be avoided or overcome if the term 'vehicles' is construed as applying to motor vehicles only. In all these situations, one will say that the conflict is only apparent, not genuine, since there is a 'window of compatibility' between the diverging norms.

This narrow understanding of norm conflicts, which only includes *genuine* and *necessary* conflicts, generally prevails in the literature and jurisprudence, both

[29] Ibid at 174.

[30] For a similar approach, see Chaïm Perelman, *Logique juridique: nouvelle rhétorique* (Paris, Dalloz, 1979) 39.

domestically and internationally. At the domestic level, this narrow definition is often used in federal systems, where judges are regularly called upon to rule on the interaction between federal and national/provincial legislation. In Canadian constitutional law, for instance, the federal/provincial distribution of legislative powers is governed by the doctrine of 'paramountcy'. This doctrine provides that, where a conflict exists between federal and provincial laws, federal laws prevail and provincial laws are rendered inoperative to the extent of the inconsistency.[31] By definition, however, the doctrine of paramountcy only applies where (1) the federal and the provincial laws are both valid; and (2) they conflict with one another.[32] The notion of conflict is therefore of the utmost importance to the operation of this doctrine. Canadian tribunals have adopted a rather restrictive interpretation of conflicts, holding that paramountcy only applies in cases of explicit and genuine contradiction. The Supreme Court of Canada, in particular, has considered that a conflict only arises if 'compliance with one law involves breach of the other'.[33] There must be an 'operational incompatibility' between the federal and the provincial laws, or else these laws continue to operate concurrently and must be reconciled by way of interpretation.[34] Although, as we shall see below, the Supreme Court has somewhat revisited this approach in its recent case law, the traditional criterion of conflict in Canadian constitutional law is thus one of impossibility of simultaneously complying with two norms. As summarised by Supreme Court Chief Justice Dickson, there is an actual conflict in operation 'where one enactment says "yes" and the other says "no"'.[35]

This restrictive approach also prevails in the field of international law. Wilfried Jenks, in a classic piece on the conflict between law-making treaties, insisted that a conflict 'arises only where a party to two treaties cannot simultaneously comply with its obligations under both treaties'.[36] In his view, other types of divergence between treaties do not constitute conflicts in the strict sense, even when they defeat the object of one of the treaties. Although Jenks recognised that these divergences could have serious practical implications, he maintained that a genuine conflict only exists when two instruments cannot be reconciled and the obligations they contain cannot be performed at the same time.[37] Since Jenks, most international lawyers have adopted similar views. Wolfram Karl, in an encyclopaedia entry on conflicts between treaties, adopted the view that 'technically speaking, there is a conflict between treaties when two (or more) treaty instruments contain obligations which cannot be complied

[31] On the doctrine of paramountcy, see eg, WR Lederman, 'The Concurrent Operation of Federal and Provincial Laws in Canada' (1963) 9 *McGill Law Journal* 185; Luanne Walton, 'Paramountcy: a Distinctly Canadian Solution?' (2004) 15 *National Journal of Constitutional Law* 335.

[32] See Peter W Hogg, *Constitutional Law of Canada*, 3rd edn (Toronto, Carswell, 1992) 419.

[33] *Smith v The Queen* [1960] SCR 776, 800.

[34] Ibid.

[35] *Multiple Access v McCutcheon* [1982] 2 SCR 161, 191.

[36] Wilfried Jenks, 'The Conflict of Law-Making Treaties' (1953) 30 *British Yearbook of International Law* 400, 426.

[37] Ibid at 427.

with simultaneously'.[38] In line with Jenks, he added that mere divergences only represent 'prima facie conflicts' and that a true incompatibility between treaty instruments remains a *sine qua non* condition of conflicts.[39] Czaplinski and Danilenko, in an article on conflicts of norms in international law, also found that 'one can speak of the conflict of treaties when one of the treaties binding on the parties obliges party A to take action X, while another stipulates that A should take action Y, and X is incompatible with Y'.[40] Similarly, Gabrielle Marceau, whilst recognising that conflicts can be defined strictly or widely, depending on one's conception of the international legal order, nonetheless adopted a rather narrow definition of conflict as the situation where two treaties impose 'mutually exclusive obligations'.[41]

The prevalence of this restrictive view on conflicts arises from a number of factors. The primary reason is certainly that conflicts are widely regarded as juridical anomalies. To most lawyers, conflicts have a negative connotation and must therefore be avoided as far as possible. From this point of view, giving conflicts a narrow definition is a convenient way to resolve a number of contradictions by simply positing, at the outset, that they fall outside the scope of norm conflicts. In other words, the proponents of the narrow definition seek to solve part of the problem of norm conflicts by avoiding interpretations that may lead to the conclusion that a conflict exists in the first place.[42]

The narrow definition of conflicts may also be explained by the influence of domestic law thinking. In domestic law, most problems of contradiction are resolved, in advance, by strict hierarchies. It is well established that a prescription or prohibition imposed by legislation always prevails over an individual right (save of course for fundamental rights). For instance, a contract whose object is unlawful, in that it is contrary to an express provision of law, will always be regarded as void. As a result, most domestic legal systems do not regard contradictions between commands and permissions as genuine conflicts but rather as mere contradictions, which the legal system itself is able to resolve.

Although no such hierarchy exists in international law, the narrow vision of conflicts continues to prevail, not only in doctrine, but also in the practice of courts and tribunals. The case law of the WTO offers some salient examples. In the *Indonesia – Automobiles* case, the European Community, Japan and

[38] Wolfram Karl, 'Conflicts Between Treaties' in Rudolf Bernhardt (ed), *Encyclopedia of Public International Law – Vol IV* (Amsterdam, Elsevier, 1992) 936.

[39] Ibid.

[40] W Czaplinski and G Danilenko, 'Conflicts of Norms in International Law' (1990) 21 *Netherlands Yearbook of International Law* 3, 12.

[41] Gabrielle Marceau, 'Conflicts of Norms and Conflicts of Jurisdiction – The Relationship Between the WTO Agreement and MEAs and Other Treaties' (2001) 6 *Journal of World Trade* 1081, 1083–86.

[42] See, on this point, Pauwelyn, *Conflicts of Norms in Public International Law*, above n 16 at 171: 'Carving out certain situations as not being conflicts "in the strict sense" or "technically speaking" (as Jenks and other authors do) is focusing on one type of conflict only, thereby ignoring the complexity of the potential forms of interplay between norms. Doing so, one essentially solves part of the problem by ignoring it'.

the United States lodged a complaint against Indonesia, alleging that certain tax and duties exemptions granted to 'national vehicles' were in violation of Indonesia's obligations under, *inter alia*, Article III of the GATT (non-discrimination between imported and domestic products). Indonesia, for its part, argued that as a developing country it was entitled to special derogations under the Agreement on Subsidies and Countervailing Measures (SCM Agreement). The SCM Agreement, in its view, constituted a *lex specialis* and, as such, prevailed over GATT provisions. Before considering the application of the *lex specialis* doctrine, the panel had to be satisfied that a conflict existed between the GATT and the SCM Agreement. When examining this matter, the panel resorted to a strict definition of conflict:

> In international law for a conflict to exist between two treaties, three conditions have to be satisfied. First, the treaties concerned must have the same parties. Second, the treaties must cover the same substantive subject matter . . . Third, the provisions must conflict, in the sense that the provisions must impose mutually exclusive obligations[43]

Based on this narrow definition, the panel concluded that there was no conflict between the GATT and the SCM Agreement. In its views, the two treaties did not have the same coverage and did not impose the same types of obligations. Article III of the GATT was concerned with discrimination between domestic and imported products whilst the SCM Agreement dealt with the provision of subsidies. More importantly perhaps, the GATT explicitly *prohibited* discrimination whilst the SCM Agreement merely *authorised* the provision of certain subsidies contingent on the use of domestic goods.[44] Consequently, the panel found that the two treaties were not mutually exclusive. A window of compatibility existed between them: all Indonesia had to do to avoid a contradiction was to comply with the strictest norm of non-discrimination.[45]

The following year, another WTO panel confirmed this narrow interpretation – which excludes 'potential' conflicts – in the *Turkey – Textile* dispute. This case concerned the relationship between two provisions of the GATT, one prohibiting quantitative restrictions (article XI) and the other providing for the possibility that regional trade agreements may depart from certain provisions of the GATT (article XXIV). When examining the tension between the two provisions, the panel recalled that the *lex specialis* principle, invoked by Turkey, could only apply if a 'formal conflict' existed between them. On this point, the panel referred expressly to Jenks' classical definition and found that 'there is no conflict if the obligations of one instrument are stricter than, but not incompatible with those of another, or if it is possible to comply with the obligations of one instrument by refraining from exercising a privilege or discretion accorded by

[43] *Indonesia – Certain Measures Affecting the Automobile Industry*, Panel Report (adopted 2 July 1998) WT/DS54/R, WT/DS55/R, WT/DS59/R, WT/DS64/R, para 14.28.

[44] Ibid at paras 14.33–14.36.

[45] Ibid at para 14.99.

another'.[46] As in the *Indonesia – Automobile* case, the panel concluded that no conflict existed between the two GATT provisions (a prohibition and a permission) and that Turkey should have complied with the strictest obligation contained in article XI, when exercising its rights under article XXIV.[47]

B. *Medio sensu* conflicts

Although the strict definition of conflict generally prevails in doctrine and in practice, other less narrow definitions exist that recognise different forms of incompatibilities as constituting a conflict. One such definition, in particular, regards so-called 'potential conflicts' as conflicts properly-so-called. In legal theory, Kelsen has been a notable proponent of this position. Initially, he adopted a rather narrow and conventional approach to conflicts, similar to that described in the previous section. In the first edition of the *Pure Theory of Law*, for example, Kelsen held the classic view that a conflict exists when two norms, whose content is mutually exclusive, cannot be obeyed at the same time.[48] Kelsen, however, has developed his theory of law over a period of more than 60 years. Inevitably, and despite being committed to preserving the 'purity' and coherence of his jurisprudence, Kelsen did change his mind about certain issues. Kelsen's theory of unity evolved, in parallel with many of his other ideas, across the different 'periods' of his general theory of law.[49] Kelsen, to begin with, changed his mind on the very *possibility* of a conflict arising between two norms belonging to the same system. In his early work, Kelsen took the view that a conflict of norms is *logically impossible*. In his view, all the norms in a given system are bound by a single and continuous chain of validity or creation. Consequently, if two norms are in contradiction, this can only mean one thing: that one of them is invalid.[50] The idea that two norms may be valid and directively incompatible is, in Kelsen's earlier work, unconceivable, even meaningless from a normative point of view.[51] Later, however, Kelsen came to recognise that conflicts between valid norms are conceivable. Despite seeing conflicts as anomalies, Kelsen eventually took the view that such conflicts are logically possible,

[46] *Turkey – Restrictions on Imports of Textile and Clothing Products*, Panel Report (adopted 31 May 1999) WT/DS34/R, para 9.92.

[47] Ibid at para 10.1.

[48] Kelsen, *Introduction to the Problems of Legal Theory*, above n 19 at 112.

[49] On the different 'periods' of Kelsen's theory of law, see Stanley Paulson, 'Four Phases in Hans Kelsen's Legal Theory? Reflections on a Periodization' (1998) 18 *Oxford Journal of Legal Studies* 153. See also Jörg Kammerhofer, 'Kelsen – Which Kelsen? A Reapplication of the Pure Theory to International Law' (2009) 22 *Leiden Journal of International Law* 225.

[50] Kelsen, *Pure Theory of Law*, above n 20 at 205–06.

[51] Ibid. See also Hans Kelsen, *General Theory of Law and State* (Harvard, Harvard University Press, 1949) 375: 'two norms which by their significance contradict and hence logically exclude one another cannot be simultaneously assumed to be valid'.

and in fact rather common in practice: 'a conflict of norms is an undesirable state of affairs, but it is possible and not all that infrequent'.[52]

As well as changing his mind on the possibility of norm conflicts, Kelsen changed views on the definition of conflict. Despite initially regarding conflicts as the strict impossibility of simultaneously applying two norms (a prescription and a prohibition), Kelsen later widened the scope of his definition to include potential conflicts, that is, conflicts between an obligation (to do or not to do something) and permission. In his *General Theory of Norms*, in particular, Kelsen wrote that a conflict can very well occur between a command and permission: 'if we must consider "commanding" and "permitting" as two different normative functions, then it is undeniable that being-permitted and being-commanded are mutually exclusive'.[53] In Kelsen's later view, conflicts of norms are thus not limited to strict and automatic conflicts: a conflict occurs whenever obedience with one norm 'necessarily *or possibly* involves the violation of the other'.[54]

Others have adopted this more expansive definition of conflict, which involves the whole spectrum of normative functions, including permissions. Karl Engisch, for instance, has taken the view that a conflict exists 'if conduct of a given type is at the same time prohibited and permitted, or prohibited and prescribed, or prescribed and not prescribed in a given legal order'.[55] Similarly, Hart has held that conflicts include contradictions between commands and permissions: 'if one rule prohibits and another permits the same action by the same person at the same time, joint conformity will be logically impossible and the two rules will conflict'.[56]

In international law doctrine, a few authors have adopted this approach to norm conflicts. This is the case of Joost Pauwelyn, who has taken the view that two norms are in a relationship of conflict 'if one constitutes, has led to, or may lead to, a breach of the other'.[57] A conflict, in Pauwelyn's view, does not only arise when two obligations (be they a command or a prohibition) are mutually exclusive. Permissions too can be at play in conflicts of norms: 'an obligation to do X under one norm (say, to liberalize trade) and an explicit right to do –X under another (say, a permission to ban a particular import under an environmental treaty), can constitute conflict'.[58] For Pauwelyn, all normative functions – commands, prohibitions and permissions – are susceptible to conflict. Only 'apparent conflicts', that is, contradictions that are explicitly regulated by the

[52] Hans Kelsen, *General Theory of Norms* (Oxford, Clarendon Press, 1991) 125.

[53] Ibid at 99.

[54] Ibid at 123.

[55] Karl Engisch, *Die Einheit der Rechtsordnung* (Heidelberg, C Winter, 1935) 46; as translated by Erich Vranes, 'The Definition of "Norm Conflict" in International Law and Legal Theory' (2006) 17 *European Journal of International Law* 395, 406.

[56] Hart, 'Kelsen's Doctrine of the Unity of Law', above n 18 at 185.

[57] Pauwelyn, *Conflicts of Norms in Public International Law*, above n 16 at 175–76.

[58] Joost Pauwelyn, 'Unity and Fragmentation of International Law – Introductory Report on the World Trade Organization' in Rosario Vinaixa and Karel Wellens (eds), *L'influence des sources sur l'unité et la fragmentation du droit international* (Brussels, Bruylant, 2006) 117.

law itself in the form, for instance, of a rule-exception relationship, are not to be regarded as conflicts properly-so-called.[59] Similarly, Erich Vranes has recently argued that the 'adequate' definition of conflict is that which covers incompatibilities between permissive norms and obligations. In his view, 'there is a conflict between norms, one of which may be permissive, if in obeying or applying one norm, the other norm is necessarily or potentially violated'.[60]

This wider definition of norm conflict has occasionally been adopted in international case law, albeit sporadically and often implicitly. In the *Lockerbie* case, for instance, the International Court of Justice inferred that the contradiction between a positive obligation and a right may constitute a conflict. In this case, the United Kingdom and the United States relied upon two UN Security Council resolutions to argue that Libya was under an obligation to surrender two of its nationals suspected of participation in the Lockerbie bombing.[61] Libya, for its part, objected that, under the Montreal Convention on air safety, it had the right to maintain the suspects on its territory for the purpose of prosecution.[62] Although the Court did not provide a definition of conflict, it found that, pursuant to article 103 of the UN Charter, 'the obligations of the Parties [contained in the Security Council resolution] prevail over their obligations under any other international agreement, including the Montreal Convention'.[63] Since article 103 only comes into play 'in the event of a conflict' between Charter obligations and other international agreements, the Court, in reaching its conclusion, must have regarded the contradiction between a command (to surrender the suspects) and a right (to refuse extradition and submit the case to one's own authorities) as constituting a conflict.

[59] Pauwelyn, *Conflicts of Norms in Public International Law*, above n 16 at 176.

[60] Vranes, 'The Definition of "Norm Conflict" in International Law and Legal Theory', above n 55 at 418. See also Seyed Ali Sadat-Akhavi, *Methods of Resolving Conflicts Between Treaties* (Leiden, Martinus Nijhoff, 2003) 5–6 who defines conflict as the situation where it is impossible to comply with all requirements of two norms and who uses the term 'comply' in a broad sense 'so as to include not only compliance with an obligation but also making use of a permission'.

[61] Security Council Resolution 731, UN Doc S/RES/731 (21 January 1992): 'The Security Council, . . . deeply concerned over the results of investigations, which implicate officials of the Libyan Government . . . in relation to the attacks carried out against Pan Am flight 103 . . . 3. Urges the Libyan Government immediately to provide a full and effective response to the requests [addressed by France, the UK and the US] so as to contribute to the elimination of international terrorism'. Security Council Resolution 748, UN Doc S/RES/748 (31 March 1992): 'The Security Council . . . deeply concerned that the Libyan Government has still not provided a full and effective response to the requests in its resolution 731 . . . 1. Decides that the Libyan Government must now comply without any further delay with resolution 731 regarding the requests addressed to the Libyan authorities by France, the UK and the USA'.

[62] *Convention for the suppression of unlawful acts against the safety of civil aviation*, 23 September 1971, art 7: 'The Contracting State in the territory of which the alleged offender is found shall, if it does not extradite him, be obliged, without exception whatsoever and whether or not the offence was committed in its territory, to submit the case to its competent authorities for the purpose of prosecution'.

[63] *Case Concerning Questions of Interpretation and Application of the 1971 Montreal Convention Arising From the Aerial Incident at Lockerbie (Libyan Arab Jamahiriya v United States of America)*, request for the indication of provisional measures, 14 April 1992, ICJ Reports (1992) 114, para 42.

In the WTO context, this wider definition of conflicts was used in at least one case, although the prevailing view of WTO panels is that genuine conflicts only arise between mutually exclusive *obligations*. In the *Banana III* dispute, Ecuador, Guatemala, Honduras, Mexico and the United States lodged a complaint against the European Communities. The complainants alleged that the Community regime for the importation, sale and distribution of bananas – which granted preferential treatment to bananas originating in ACP (Africa, Caribbean, Pacific) countries – was inconsistent with the Community's obligations under, *inter alia*, the GATT, the Import Licensing Agreement and the Agreement on Trade Related Investment Measures (TRIMs Agreement). In order to settle the dispute, the panel had to examine the relationship between the GATT and the other two agreements, a relationship governed by an interpretative note appended to the Marrakesh Agreement Establishing the WTO. The interpretative note provides that, in the event of conflict, special agreements shall prevail over the GATT.[64] As a preliminary issue, the panel therefore found it necessary to define the notion of conflict. On this occasion, it held that conflict covers two situations: '(i) clashes between obligations contained in the GATT and obligations contained in [another WTO] agreement, where those obligations are mutually exclusive in the sense that a Member cannot comply with both obligations at the same time, and (ii) the situation where a rule in one agreement prohibits what a rule in another agreement explicitly permits'.[65] The second part of the definition makes it clear that the panel views potential conflicts between obligations and permissions as genuine conflicts for the purpose of WTO law. Although the panel noted that Members could theoretically avoid such conflicts by simply refraining from invoking the rights or the permissions contained in the other WTO agreements, it found potential conflicts to be just as disruptive as automatic or inherent conflicts between commands and/or prohibitions, and concluded that the former should therefore be resolved in the same way as the latter.[66]

C. *Lato sensu* conflicts

The definition of conflict described in section B, whilst wider than the strict definition examined in section A, continues to limit the notion of conflict to situations where the implementation of one norm involves, necessarily or potentially, the breach of another. In both definitions, a conflict arises when norms

[64] *Agreement Establishing the World Trade Organization*, 15 April 1994, general interpretative note to Annex 1A: 'in the event of conflict between a provision of the General Agreement on Tariffs and Trade 1994 and a provision of another [WTO] agreement, the provision of the other agreement shall prevail to the extent of the conflict'.

[65] *European Communities – Regime for the Importation, Sale and Distribution of Bananas*, Panel Report (adopted 22 May 1997) WT/DS27/R, para 7.159.

[66] Ibid at para 7.159 and fn 401.

are directively incompatible. What differs between the two sets of definitions is the object, not the criterion, of conflict. However, there is a third way in which conflicts of norms can be defined and understood. Rather than limiting the notion of conflict to true normative antinomies, this 'third way' recognises as conflicts mere normative divergences, that is, situations where two norms, without being necessarily and strictly incompatible, work at cross-purposes. I shall label these situations *lato sensu* conflicts.

Elements of this third definition can be found in both domestic and international law. At the domestic level, this extensive definition of conflict has been used, for instance, in the recent case law of the Supreme Court of Canada. Traditionally, and as noted above, the Supreme Court has limited the notion of conflict to situations of explicit contradiction – situations where obedience to one norm automatically involves disobedience to another. In two important decisions issued in 1990 and 2001, however, the Supreme Court revisited its traditional approach and substantially modified the criterion of conflict so as to include situations where application of one norm simply frustrates the object and purpose of another.

The first case, *Bank of Montreal v Hall*, concerns a Saskatchewan farmer who contracted loans from the Bank of Montreal and, as collateral, granted two mortgages on his real property in favour of the Bank, as well as a security interest in a piece of farm machinery.[67] When Hall defaulted on his loan, the Bank seized the machinery and commenced action to enforce its real property mortgage loan agreement. Hall objected to the proceedings, arguing that the Bank had not served the Notice of Intention to Seize, as required under the Saskatchewan Limitation of Civil Rights Act. The Bank, for its part, alleged that its actions were not subject to provincial law and were consistent with the Federal Bank Act, which did not require prior notification. The task of the Court in this case was therefore to decide which of the provincial or the federal law should govern the loan agreement. In answering this question, the Court had to establish, as a preliminary issue, whether a conflict existed between the two laws, which would justify applying the doctrine of federal paramountcy.

On this point, the Court departed from the traditional approach taken in the *Multiple Access* case. Rather than asking if compliance with one law would automatically involve a breach of the other, the Court found it necessary to consider the extent to which 'operation of the provincial act is compatible with the federal legislative *purpose*'.[68] The key criterion in defining conflict is no longer the existence of a literal contradiction between the two laws. Instead, it becomes the extent to which the two acts differ 'in the approach taken to the problem'.[69]

Applying this criterion to the facts at hand, the Court took the view that the essence of the federal legislation was to facilitate producers' access to capital by providing, on a nationwide basis, for a uniform security mechanism allowing

[67] *Bank of Montreal v Hall* [1990] 1 SCR 121.
[68] Ibid at para 64.
[69] Ibid.

banks to realise their collateral more easily, so as to make lending less complicated and therefore more affordable. To require banks to defer to the provincial legislation and procedures would, from this point of view, 'set at naught the very purpose' behind the federal security mechanism.[70] It would, in the Court's opinion, 'frustrate Parliament's legislative purpose'.[71] As a result, the Court found the two statutes to be 'in conflict' and, applying the doctrine of paramountcy, declared the Saskatchewan Act inoperative.[72]

The Supreme Court confirmed its approach to conflicts of norms in several subsequent cases, most notably in *Law Society of British Columbia v Mangat*.[73] In this case, the Law Society of British Columbia (BC) contested the right of an immigration consultant, who was not a qualified lawyer, to appear as counsel on behalf of foreign nationals before the Immigration and Refugee Board (IRB). The difficulty in this case was that this practice, although prohibited under BC law, was allowed under federal immigration law. As in *Bank of Montreal*, the Supreme Court had to decide whether a conflict existed between federal and provincial law for the purpose of applying the doctrine of paramountcy.

Despite the window of compatibility between the two laws (compliance with both laws was possible by obeying the stricter one) the Supreme Court again relied on a teleological test when examining the issue of conflict. Justice Gonthier, writing for the majority, took the view that 'there will be a conflict in operation where the application of the provincial law will displace the legislative purpose of Parliament'.[74] Whether dual compliance is possible 'at a superficial level' is irrelevant. What matters, says the Court, is whether the purpose of the provincial law is compatible with the 'legitimate objective' of the federal law.[75]

In that particular instance, the Court took the view that the objective of the federal law, in line with Canada's 'humanitarian tradition', was to facilitate the representation of immigrants before the IRB.[76] The Court noted that non-lawyers may provide a useful service to people who are subject to IRB proceedings, since it may be difficult to find lawyers who are fluent in other languages and who are familiar with different cultures. The objective of the federal legislation was, in other words, to establish an informal, accessible and expeditious process before immigration tribunals.[77] To require counsels to be members in good standing of the bar or to refuse the payment of a fee to non-lawyers would, from this point of view, 'frustrate' Parliament's purpose.[78] The Court therefore concluded that, although not automatic or express, the conflict between provin-

[70] Ibid at para 63.
[71] Ibid at para 62.
[72] Ibid at para 66.
[73] *Law Society of British Columbia v Mangat* [2001] 3 SCR 113.
[74] Ibid at para 69.
[75] Ibid at para 72.
[76] Ibid at para 60.
[77] Ibid at para 72.
[78] Ibid at para 23.

cial and federal law was real: it was impossible to comply with the provincial statute without thwarting the legitimate purpose of the federal law.

These two cases illustrate the contrast between the restrictive and the extensive criterion of conflict. The traditional approach to conflicts places the emphasis on firm and direct contradictions, that is, on the material impossibility of complying with two norms at once. The wider approach adopted by the Supreme Court in its recent case law, on the other hand, defines conflict not so much in terms of logical antinomies or contradictions but rather in terms of purposive tensions. The focus has shifted from the letter to the *telos* of the law. What matters is no longer the literal margin of compatibility between contradictory norms but the extent to which these norms differ in their approach to legal problems.

This understanding of normative conflicts can be qualified as *non-deontic* and *functional*. The problem of conflict is no longer tied to the concepts of breach and obedience but instead to the notion of interference in the operation of concurrent norms. In this perspective, conflicts do not only arise when joint compliance is impossible. They also take place when two norms 'get in each other's way', that is, when one norm interferes with the intended functioning of another or pursues an objective which is hostile to that of another.[79] Such a conflict would arise, for instance, if one law provided tax credits for energy saving improvements in existing homes and another deregulated the energy industry. In this scenario, no deontic antinomy exists between the two laws: compliance with the former does not involve a breach of the latter. In fact, the two laws do not really overlap. However, a functional conflict can be said to exist between them. Whilst the first law is designed to encourage energy savings, the second law, by creating the conditions for cheaper energy, may have the very opposite effect of maintaining, or even increasing, energy consumption. There is a clash of purposes: one norm reinforces the behaviour that another seeks to discourage.

This definition of conflict applies to a much wider range of phenomena than traditional analyses and covers situations in which two norms, without being mutually exclusive, do not 'get along' and thus hinder each other's operation. Kelsen, who originally advocated a rather narrow approach to conflicts, began to suggest a similar analysis in some of his later writings. Without completely abandoning the analysis of conflicts as deontic incompatibilities, Kelsen observed in his *General Theory of Norms* that a conflict of norms may in fact be something entirely different from a pure logical contradiction: 'a conflict of norms can be compared – if at all – not with a logical contradiction, but with two forces acting in different directions on the same point'.[80] Although the metaphor is somewhat elusive, it does suggest an analytical move from the strict logic of deontic antinomy to a logic of tension or friction between opposing forces.

[79] See Hamner Hill, 'A Functional Taxonomy of Normative Conflict' (1987) 6 *Law and Philosophy* 227.

[80] Kelsen, *General Theory of Norms*, above n 52 at 125.

In international law doctrine, where lawyers have traditionally adopted narrow definitions of conflicts, it is possible to detect a similar movement from *stricto sensu* to *lato sensu* conflicts. Typically, the functional approach to conflicts is used more implicitly than explicitly. Some authors, for instance, have spoken of a 'conflict of norms' between international humanitarian law and human rights law simply because these two regimes, whose scope of application increasingly overlap, are based on different histories, philosophies and teleologies.[81] The conflict is not the result of direct normative incompatibilities between humanitarian law and human rights law. It merely reflects the fact that these two branches of the law have different ways of dealing with similar problems and are rooted in different projects. Similarly, it has been argued that a conflict exists between the Stockholm Convention on Persistent Organic Pollutants and WTO Law, due to the tension between the 'requirements' of international trade law and the 'needs and goals' of international environmental law.[82] Here again, the notion of conflict seems to be understood, albeit implicitly, in terms of functional interference between norm-complexes.

Some international law scholars, however, have articulated a more explicit theory of functional conflicts. Christopher Borgen, for instance, argues for the widening of the definition of norm conflicts in international law. In an important study on the resolution of treaty conflicts, he takes the view that traditional definitions are too restrictive and overlook important causes of fragmentation, most notably situations where joint compliance is possible but where one treaty thwarts the goals of another. In response to this problem, Borgen defines treaty conflicts more broadly 'as when a state is party to two or more treaty regimes and either the mere existence of, or the actual performance under, one treaty will frustrate the purpose of another treaty'.[83] In Borgen's view, a typical example of this type of 'structural conflict' arises between trade and environmental treaties or between trade and human rights treaties, which reflects deeper and inherent tensions between instruments that seek to liberalise the economy and instruments that seek to regulate it.[84]

Rüdiger Wolfrum and Nele Matz have also taken the view that conflicts and contradictions between international treaties can take a variety of forms, some of which have not traditionally been considered conflicts in a legal sense.[85] The two authors consider, in particular, that mere 'collisions' and 'divergences'

[81] See, eg, Heike Krieger, 'A Conflict of Norms: The Relationship Between Humanitarian Law and Human Rights Law in the ICRC Customary Law Study' (2006) 11 *Journal of Conflict and Security Law* 265, 266–68; Anthony Cassimatis, 'International Humanitarian Law, International Human Rights Law, and Fragmentation of International Law' (2007) 56 *International and Comparative Law Quarterly* 623.

[82] See, eg, Dean Batchelder, 'An Analysis of Potential Conflicts Between the Stockholm Convention and Its Parties' WTO Obligations' (2006) 28 *Michigan Journal of International Law* 157, 173.

[83] Christopher Borgen, 'Resolving Treaty Conflicts' (2005) 37 *George Washington International Law Review* 573, 575.

[84] Ibid at 580.

[85] Rüdiger Wolfrum and Nele Matz, *Conflicts in International Environmental Law* (Berlin, Springer-Verlag, 2003) 6.

between treaties, even when they do not establish strictly contradictory norms, can have just as negative an effect as *stricto sensu* conflicts. For this reason, Wolfrum and Matz take the view that the notion of conflict should be taken to include what they term 'conceptual conflicts' as well as 'political conflicts'. The first category refers to divergences in the conceptual or philosophical approaches underlying different norms or norm-complexes.[86] The authors consider, for instance, that a conflict of this type exists between the Convention on the Conservation of Antarctic Marine Living Resources and the UN Convention on the Law of the Sea. The conflict is said to arise from the fact that the first instrument takes an 'eco-systemic' approach to the marine environment, in which the environment is apprehended as an ecological whole, whilst the second takes a more economic or utilitarian approach, in which emphasis is placed on the sustainable exploitation of natural resources.[87] The second type of conflict refers to the fact that different treaty instruments pursue divergent goals or policy objectives.[88] The more salient example of this type of conflict is, once again, that which exists between environmental treaties, which aim at re-regulating the economy, and trade agreements, whose primary policy objective is the eradication of trade barriers. Here again, the term conflict does not refer to strict normative antinomies but rather to the tension between opposing policy forces.

It is noteworthy that this very broad approach to conflicts has largely been sanctioned by the International Law Commission in its work on fragmentation. Martti Koskenniemi devotes an entire section of his final report to the definition of normative conflicts. There, he suggests a definition that is reminiscent of Kelsen's metaphor of the 'forces in tension'. There is a conflict, he writes, 'if two different rules or sets of rules are invoked in regard to the same matter' and if 'the relevant treaties seem to point to different directions in their application'.[89] Further, however, Koskenniemi asks: 'what does "pointing in different directions" mean'?[90] Whilst noting that a rather literal interpretation of this criterion generally prevails in theory and in practice (the impossibility-of-joint-compliance test), the rapporteur takes the view that focusing entirely on logical incompatibilities 'mischaracterises legal reasoning as logical subsumption'. He thus advocates a much wider approach. The definition suggested in the report and endorsed by the Commission deserves to be quoted in full, for it summarises perfectly the essence of the functional approach to normative conflicts:

> A treaty may sometimes frustrate the goals of another treaty without there being any strict incompatibility between their provisions. Two treaties or sets of rules may possess different background justifications or emerge from different legislative policies or aim at different ends. The law of State immunity and the law of human rights, for example, illustrate two sets of rules that have very different objectives. Trade law and

[86] Ibid at 7–8.
[87] Ibid.
[88] Ibid at 8–9.
[89] *ILC Fragmentation Report*, above n 17 at para 23.
[90] Ibid at para 24.

environmental law, too, emerge from different types of policy and that fact may have an effect on how the relevant rules are interpreted or applied. While such 'policy-conflicts' do not lead into logical incompatibilities between obligations upon a single party, they may nevertheless also be relevant for fragmentation. This Report adopts a wide notion of conflict as a situation where two rules or principles suggest different ways of dealing with a problem.[91]

III. INTERMEDIATE CONCLUSIONS

At this point in our study, one thing is already apparent. Even if limited to its material dimension, the concept of unity presents itself as a complex analytical object that is not easily grasped and cannot be reduced to one single formula or criterion. If there is near-consensus in the literature on the fact that material unity refers to the absence of conflict in the law (the 'no-conflict' thesis), there are, however, a great many ways in which the nature, the object and the criterion of a conflict can be interpreted. The pathways and the levels of analysis are manifold. I have suggested three fundamental perspectives, three general ways of understanding the concept of 'norm conflict', which are accepted to varying degrees in theory and practice:

- *Stricto sensu conflict*: in its strictest version, which I have equated with the notion of deontic antinomy, the term conflict refers to the situation in which it is materially impossible to comply with two norms simultaneously. One norm says 'yes' whilst the other says 'no' and obedience to the former necessarily involves a breach of the latter. This definition is doubly restrictive. For one thing, it only concerns genuine and automatic conflicts, that is, conflicts between norms which, in and of themselves, are mutually exclusive. For another, it only covers conflicts between obligations (commands or prohibitions) which overlap *ratione materiae*, *personae* and *temporis*.
- *Medio sensu conflict*: in its intermediate version, the term conflict rests on the same criterion (the 'impossibility-of-joint-compliance' test) but applies to a wider range of norms. Whilst following the deontic logic of mutual exclusiveness, its scope includes permissions as well as commands and prohibitions.
- *Lato sensu conflict*: in its most expansive version, the notion of conflict refers to a different logic altogether. Rather than designating express and literal antinomies, it covers situations where norms diverge in their way of dealing with a problem and get in each other's way. The criterion of conflict is no longer mutual exclusiveness but functional interference between norms or norm-complexes with clashing policy objectives or teleologies.

The multi-layeredness of the notion of conflict raises a number of questions, both practical and theoretical. From a practical point of view, the choice of a

[91] Ibid at paras 24–25.

particular perspective on conflicts may have direct consequences in terms of applicable law and may even command the outcome of a dispute. The *Indonesia–Automobiles* case discussed above illustrates this point.[92] In that case, Indonesia argued that one set of rules (the SCM Agreement) should prevail over another (the GATT) under the *lex specialis* doctrine. The panel, however, took the view that no genuine conflict existed between the two instruments. The conflict was only apparent: Indonesia could have avoided contradiction simply by complying with the strictest norms contained in the GATT. A window of compatibility existed between the two treaties and, absent any real conflict, there was no reason to set the GATT rules aside in favour of the SMC Agreement. Had the panel adopted a different approach to conflicts, however, the outcome may have been very different. In all likelihood, the use of a wider definition of conflict would have resulted in a finding that a conflict did exist between the two treaties. In that case, the *lex specialis* doctrine would have operated and would have justified Indonesia's measures under the SCM Agreement. In other words, Indonesia might have won its case, or at least part of it.[93]

From a theoretical point of view, the multi-dimensional nature of conflict has far-reaching consequences, most notably on one's reading of international law's unity. Consider, for instance, the following scenario: two regional courts – say the European and the Inter-American Courts of Human Rights – deliver contradictory judgments on the extradition of suspected terrorists to countries where they may be at risk of torture or inhuman/degrading treatment. The facts in the two cases are identical but the two courts reach opposite conclusions. The former takes the view that the risks to public security outweigh the risks of torture and thus permits extradition. The latter considers that the prohibition of torture is absolute and can never be compromised, even in the name of public security. It therefore rules against extradition. Does the divergence between the two courts threaten the unity of international law? If unity is understood as the absence of conflicts in the law, then the response to this question will largely depend on one's understanding of conflict. At least five intellectual positions can be envisaged:

- Position No 1: Norms, not judicial decisions, come into play in normative conflicts. Differences of view between international tribunals are not directly relevant to the issue of fragmentation. Such divergences may of course create problems of 'readability' and 'predictability' for legal subjects. They may also preclude the formation or consolidation of customary rules at the global level. Strictly speaking, however, conflicts of jurisprudence do not, in and of themselves, affect the material unity of international law.
- Position No 2: Judicial decisions can in principle be at issue in normative conflicts. For this to happen, however, these decisions must overlap *rationae*

[92] See above n 43 and corresponding text.

[93] For a similar view, see Pauwelyn, *Conflicts of Norms in Public International Law*, above n 16 at 193–94.

materiae, *personae* and *temporis*. Although the decisions issued by the two courts deal with the same subject matter, there is between them no subjective overlap: the parties in each dispute are different and the decisions are not addressed to the same subjects. The divergence between the two courts is therefore not a normative conflict *per se*, but merely the expression of regional variations in the field of international human rights law.

- Position No 3: The fact that the two decisions and the two regional human rights regimes only partially overlap does not, in and of itself, exclude the possibility of a normative conflict. There must nonetheless be a genuine conflict between them. In our case, the divergence between the two courts involves an obligation (not to extradite to countries in which torture is practised) and permission (to extradite suspected terrorists in order to safeguard public security). Conflicts between obligations and permissions are not genuine conflicts, but merely potential conflicts that can be avoided simply by not acting upon the permission. There is no true antinomy in this case and the material unity of international law is therefore not directly compromised.
- Position No 4: Conflicts of norms are not limited to strict and automatic conflicts between obligations. A conflict occurs whenever obeying one norm necessarily or possibly involves violating the other. Permissions are just as capable of conflicting as commands and prohibitions. The conflict between the two courts is thus a true normative conflict, which creates problems for the material unity of international human rights law.
- Position No 5: The fact that the conflict involves a prohibition and permission is irrelevant. The truth of the matter is that on an issue as important as extradition in the face of torture, two courts disagree and have issued rulings that 'point in different directions'. Two opposing forces are at play on the same question and they clearly 'get in each other's way'. This, in itself, compromises the coherence and the material unity of international law.

The same demonstration and the same type of reasoning could be carried out in relation to trade and environmental law, sovereign immunities and human rights, *Nicaragua* and *Tadic*.[94] The main point, however, has already been established. Even when unity is understood in its most elementary form, as the absence of conflicts among primary norms, theoretical perspectives abound and no perspective is self-evident. Material unity can be understood in a great many ways, depending on one's perception of the nature, object and criterion of conflicts. What some see as a mere accumulation of norms, others may see as a genuine conflict. I take this point further in the next chapter and show that what is true of material unity is equally true, and perhaps to an even greater degree, of formal unity.

[94] On the various possible readings of the *Tadic* case, see the general conclusion.

5

Formal Unity

MATERIAL UNITY, AS noted above, represents the most immediate and elementary form of legal unity. Legal unity exists, in this perspective, where there is a unity of meaning and direction. Law is apprehended as a set of directives, and unity stems from the fact that these directives point the same way. However, the substantial unity of law in general, and international law in particular, can be thought of as something different from mere 'directive consistency' (that is, the absence of normative conflicts). Rather than pointing to notions of consistency and compatibility among individual norms, another way to look at unity is to consider the processes by which these norms are combined and arranged together. The emphasis is placed, in this perspective, on the 'whole' and its internal structure, not on the 'parts'. Here, law is unitary by reason of the formal relations that unite its norms. I shall therefore speak of formal unity to designate this way of thinking about unity.

I will now move from the analysis of law as individual norms to the analysis of law as a dynamic system or order.[1] The question then becomes: what gives a legal system its structure, identity and integrity as a complex whole? Needless to say, this is an eminently difficult question and I shall not attempt to develop my own theory of the legal system. Others, in jurisprudence and in international law doctrine, have discussed the systemic paradigm at length and the purpose of this chapter is not to add to the already long list of doctrinal contributions on the subject.[2] The spirit of this book, as previously discussed, is to shed light on

[1] I use the terms 'order' and 'system' interchangeably in this chapter as referring to the existence of specific relations of interdependence and of a certain structure among the constituting elements of a complex whole. In other words, the terms 'order' and 'system' in law both signal the existence of something more than a mere body or collection of norms. See, on this point, Michel Van de Kerchove and François Ost, *The Legal System between Order and Disorder* (Oxford, Oxford University Press, 1993) 3–6.

[2] In international law doctrine, see eg, Serge Sur, 'Système juridique international et utopie' (1987) 32 *Archives de Philosophie du Droit* 35; Joe Verhoeven, 'L'Etat et l'ordre juridique international' (1978) 82 *Revue Générale de Droit International Public* 751; Jean Combacau, 'Le droit international: bric-à-brac ou système?' (1986) 31 *Archives de Philosophie du Droit* 85; Yoram Dinstein, 'International Law as a Primitive Legal System' (1986) 19 *New York University Journal of International Law and Politics* 1; Anthony D'Amato, 'International Law as an Autopoietic System' in Rüdiger Wolfrum and Volker Röben (eds), *Developments of International Law in Treaty Making* (Berlin, Springer, 2005); Eyal Benvenisti, 'The Conception of International Law as a Legal System' (2008) 50 *German Yearbook of International Law* 393.

the conditions of possibility of discourse regarding international law's unity and to complicate the rather static and one-dimensional picture of unity that prevails in the literature. The main purpose of the present chapter is not therefore to offer a coherent and all-encompassing vision of formal unity but instead to examine the conventional approaches to formal unity and, where necessary, to show their limits, contradictions and shortfalls. My argument will be twofold.

First, I shall attempt to show that a plurality of theoretical perspectives exists on the issue of formal unity and that there are more ways than one for a legal order to be formally 'one'. The form of the legal order can be imagined and apprehended at different levels, all premised on different 'laws of unity' or 'categorial predicates', to use Husserl's terminology. Each type of formal unity, as I will discuss, rests on a particular causal relation between the constituent parts of the system. This can be a relation of authority between norms and social institutions (institutionalist theories), a relation of validity between different types of rules (normativist theories), or a hermeneutic relation between norms and law-appliers (post-normativist theories). The principal goal of this first section is to explore the various 'candidate conceptions' of formal unity and to insist on their specificity.

My second argument will centre more explicitly on Hart's conception of the legal order. I do so not because I regard Hart's theory as correct or as the best theory for debating the formal unity of international law, but rather because nearly all discussions on formal unity in the fragmentation literature take his theory as a starting point. I shall try to show that the use of Hart's theory is often oversimplified – if not simplistic – and that two primordial aspects of his theory of the unity of law – which pertain to the 'determinacy' and the 'acceptance' of secondary norms – are too seldom recognised in the fragmentation literature. After a brief consideration of the function of determinacy and acceptance in Hart's theory, I use a series of concrete examples to shed light on the sorts of problems that these notions raise in the field of international law. My intention in doing so is not to suggest that international law lacks formal unity but rather to take Hart seriously and to consider the conditions under which his theory can be used as a meaningful paradigm of unity in international law.

I. THREE CONCEPTIONS OF THE LEGAL ORDER

One of the major lessons learned from legal positivism is that law cannot be satisfactorily defined and analysed from the standpoint of norms considered in isolation. Law is not a miscellaneous collection of norms, a grab-bag of disconnected rules. Legal norms do not exist in a vacuum. Their validity, meaning and efficacy depend upon the relation they maintain with other norms and institutions. To grasp the specific nature of law, something must therefore be learnt about its systematicity, that is, about the ways in which its rules are arranged, assembled and organised.

The fact that law exists in a systematic form is hardly contested today, at least in modern Western legal contexts. More disputed, however, are the questions of what makes law a system, and what sort of system law is. Models and paradigms abound on the systematicity of law, from theories of 'living' or 'organic systems'[3] to conceptions of law as an 'open',[4] 'autonomous' or 'autopoietic' system.[5] In these various models, the systematicity of law is at times 'static' and at other times 'dynamic'.[6] At other times still, it is 'dual' or even 'melodic'.[7] The approaches and conceptions vary almost infinitely. Among these, however, three fundamental categories emerge: the 'institutionalist', the 'normativist' and the 'post-normativist' perspectives. In the following paragraphs, I briefly describe these perspectives and their approach to formal unity. In doing so, I seek to show that the concept of formal unity, like that of material unity, is multi-faceted and multi-layered. The formal unity of a system such as international law can be apprehended in a great many ways, which involve different 'laws of organisation', different 'logics' and criteria. Limiting formal unity to the mere existence of secondary norms, as is often the case in the fragmentation discourse, is thus unsatisfactory. This type of approach makes the error of overlooking law's organisational complexity, that is, the fact that formal unity is rarely ever monocausational and often rests on a complex web of forces and dynamics.

A. The institutionalist approach

Santi Romano was one of the first legal theorists to defend the idea that the essence of law cannot be reduced to the sum of its parts (that is, to its norms) and that the nature of law must instead be grasped from the standpoint of the legal order (*ordinamento giuridico*). For Romano, traditional definitions of law, which regard norms as the central element in the phenomenon of law, are not false or untrue. They are, however, 'inadequate and insufficient'.[8] Law, in Romano's view, exists beyond its norms. To understand law, one must understand something about the nature and structure of the system as a whole.

[3] See, eg, Christophe Grzegorczyk, 'Evaluation critique du paradigm systémique dans la science du droit' (1986) 31 *Archives de Philosophie du Droit* 286, 284–85; François Ost and Michel van de Kerchove, 'L'idée de jeu peut-elle pretender au titre de paradigm de la science juridique?' (1993) 30 *Revue Interdisciplinaire d'Etudes Juridiques* 191.

[4] Joseph Raz, *Practical Reason and Norms* (Oxford, Oxford University Press, 1999) 152–54.

[5] Gunther Teubner, *Law as an Autopoietic System* (Oxford, Blackwell, 1993).

[6] On the difference between static and dynamic systematicity, see Van de Kerchove and Ost, *The Legal System between Order and Disorder*, above n 1 at 28–35.

[7] Paul Amselek, 'Réflexions critiques sur la conception kelsénienne de l'ordre juridique' (1978) *Revue du Droit Public* 5.

[8] Santi Romano, *L'ordre Juridique* (Paris, Dalloz, 1975) 2; first published in 1918 as *L'ordinamento Giuridico* (Pisa, Nuova Edizione).

Defining law, in other words, involves defining the legal order in its totality and its unity.[9]

Recognising that norms are simply the constituent parts of a broader whole, however, is only the starting point, and Romano himself concedes that this is a commonplace of legal theory, though one that deserves reiterating. For Romano, in order to comprehend the special nature of the legal order, one must therefore consider a number of elements which are not norms: 'the multiple mechanisms and gear wheels, the relations of authority and of force which create, modify, apply, and impose respect for legal norms but are not legal norms themselves'.[10]

According to Romano, the key distinction between legal norms and other types of norms, most notably moral norms, lies in the fact that legal norms possess certain formal attributes which make law a truly 'obligatory' system. One such attribute is objectivity – the fact that law 'transcends and rises over' the subjectivity and individuality of its subjects.[11] If law loses its critical distance vis-a-vis individual interests, says Romano, it can no longer fulfil its role as 'superior social consciousness', as a mediator of justice and power among social subjects. As a result, law must be, and continue to be, a 'kingdom of objectivity'.[12]

Law's other formal attribute, which characterises the difference between the legal and the non-legal, is that of 'sanction'. For Romano, this may in fact be the 'only truly distinctive formal characteristic of law'.[13] Romano, it must be noted, takes a broad view of sanction and does not equate it, as did his predecessors, with force or coercion. For him, the idea of sanction covers a wide range of consequences attached to non-compliance, 'whether direct or indirect, mediate or immediate, preventative or repressive, actual or potential'.[14] That said, Romano's argument regarding sanction is twofold. First, there must be mechanisms for ensuring that legal norms are obeyed by their legal subjects, or else law ceases to be law. Second, the enforcement of one norm cannot depend upon another norm. If this were the case, one would never see the end of law: the enforcement of the second norm would imply the existence of a third norm, whose enforcement would in turn require the existence of a fourth norm of control, and so on.

From these two formal elements – objectivity and sanction – Romano reaches a fundamental conclusion regarding the nature of the legal order: legal norms are never self-sufficient (although legal orders can be). Their existence and efficacy as legal norms depends entirely upon the existence of a structured and structuring power capable of expressing the objective 'social consciousness' and of controlling the production, development and operation of norms. It is this structuring power which Romano labels 'institution'. Romano does not limit

[9] Ibid at 7. Despite defining each legal order as a unity, Romano was an early legal pluralist, taking the view that legal orders exist both beyond and within the state.

[10] Ibid at 10.

[11] Ibid at 12.

[12] Ibid.

[13] Ibid at 15.

[14] Ibid.

institutions to organic and hierarchical structures. To him, an institution can be any social agency or social body which has a stable and concrete existence and which forms an independent entity with a life of its own (the family, the church, the state, etc). The point remains, however, that in Romano's institutionalist theory, the unity of the legal order has little to do with the material consistency among individual norms. Unity lies in the social substructure, which gives law its shape and identity as an independent order. Where there is an institution, there is an autonomous and unitary legal order. Legal order, institution and unity are, in Romano's theory, interchangeable. The equivalency between these concepts, he wrote, 'is necessary and absolute'.[15]

B. The normativist approach

(i) Kelsen

More than Romano perhaps, Kelsen has helped to consolidate the vision of law as a system. Like Romano, Kelsen believed that a theory of law is only meaningful if it explains the nature and working of law as legal order. Legal norms, in Kelsen's opinion, are not autonomous entities 'standing coordinatedly side by side'.[16] A legal norm exists 'only as part of a system'.[17] As a result, says Kelsen, all law must be understood 'in one system – that is, from one and the same standpoint – as one closed whole'.[18]

By speaking of law as a 'closed whole', Kelsen marks his difference with Santi Romano, who thought of legal orders as 'open' systems. In Romano's theory of the legal order, law is not self-sufficient and can only be explained in relation to an organised social order (that is, an institution). Kelsen, for his part, sees norms as the only constituent parts of the legal order. Everything, in Kelsen's theory, has to do with norms and their mutual relations. Kelsen does not deny the importance of institutions, particularly that of the state. In his view, however, one of the most significant peculiarities of the law is that 'it regulates its own creation and application'.[19] Law's systematicity, in other words, lies in its capacity for self-organisation.

That said, what, according to Kelsen, are the principles of formal unity in normative orders? Kelsen, in answering this question, identifies two principles: a static and a dynamic principle.[20] According to the first, norms are deduced from each other and are united through their content. One norm is valid because its content can be traced back to another norm under whose content the content of the norm in question can be subsumed. For example, says Kelsen, the norms 'do

[15] Ibid at 19.
[16] Hans Kelsen, *Pure Theory of Law* (Berkeley, University of California Press, 1967) 202.
[17] Ibid at 47.
[18] Ibid at 328.
[19] Ibid at 71.
[20] Ibid at 195–98.

not lie', 'do not give false testimony' or 'do fulfil a promise' can all be derived from a general norm that prescribes truthfulness. Similarly, the norms 'do not harm one's fellow man', 'do not damage him physically or morally' and 'do help him in need' can all be derived from the general norm to 'love one's neighbour'. And these two general norms, in turn, could be reduced to a higher norm still (for example, 'live in harmony with the universe') on which a whole order may be founded. According to Kelsen, this type of unity, in which norms are linked by their content, is characteristic of moral orders.[21]

Legal orders, however, rest upon a different – dynamic – principle of unity. Under this second principle, norms are united through ascending chains of validity: each norm finds its reason for validity in a superior norm, which in turn is founded on another norm and so on. Eventually, all norms can be traced back to one single over-arching norm – the *Grundnorm* – which confers unity and validity upon the entire legal order. Under this second principle of unity, relations between norms are purely formal, for the superior norm supplies only the reason for validity, not the content of the norms based on it.[22] Superior norms merely 'habilitate' inferior norms – that is, they stipulate how these norms ought to be created, and under what conditions they are to become part of the system. The formal unity of law, in this perspective, is therefore a 'unity of foundation', to use Husserl's terminology.[23] It is premised on two key ideas: 1) all the norms in a legal system are mutually dependent and are linked by chains of validity; and 2) these chains of validity all lead to a single *Grundnorm*, which acts as a crystallising agent, or an Archimedean point for the system as a whole.

(ii) Hart

Hart and Kelsen's theories have much in common, most notably the fact that they both conceptualise the legal order as a system in which the lifecycle of certain norms is governed by other norms. The comparison, however, has its limits and these similarities must not be allowed to obscure the very real differences that exist between the two authors. Contrary to what some have argued, Hart's theory is far from being a mere 'derivative' of Kelsen's work, written in a clearer and less ambiguous language.[24] In fact, Hart's analytical positivism differs from the pure theory of law in several ways.

The first point of divergence concerns Hart's rejection of the claim, central in Kelsen's work, that law is a coercive order.[25] The notion that law is 'command

[21] Ibid at 196.

[22] Ibid at 197.

[23] See above ch 2, n 28 and corresponding text.

[24] On this point, see Jeffrie G Murphy and Jules L Coleman, *Philosophy of Law – An Introduction to Jurisprudence* (San Francisco, Westview Press, 1990) 27.

[25] Kelsen, *Pure Theory of Law*, above n 16 at 54: 'a definition of law which does not determine law as a coercive order must be rejected (1) because only by including the element of coercion into the definition of law is the law clearly distinguished from any other social order; (2) because coercion is a factor of great importance for the cognition of social relationship and highly characteristic of the social orders called "law"'.

backed by threat' is in Hart's opinion unsustainable. It misrepresents the standard way in which law functions in everyday life, as well as the way in which legal officials and citizens relate to legal norms 'from their internal point of view'.[26] Rather than tying law to the notions of command and force, Hart's concept of law revolves around the combined existence of two types of rules: primary and secondary rules. Primary rules are duty-imposing rules of conduct. They are concerned with the actions that individuals must or must not do. Criminal rules that provide that one shall not kill or steal are typical examples of such rules. Secondary rules are of a different nature. They do not impose duties but instead confer powers on legal agents (officials or citizens), such as the power to 'make' law by way, for instance, of legislation or contract.[27] Characteristically, the object of secondary rules is not individual behaviour but rather the primary rules themselves, whose 'lifecycle' they govern. Secondary rules, which in a way are the basic 'rules of the game' – some would say the 'rules about rules'[28] – have three essential functions in Hart's theory: they set out the criteria for the recognition, change and adjudication of primary norms. Rules of recognition, as is well known, provide explicit standards for determining the content or scope of a given rule. In other words, they enable legal agents or organs to identify the norms that belong to – or form part of – the system. Rules of change, for their part, set out the conditions under which new rules of conduct are introduced and old ones are repealed or amended. Finally, rules of adjudication both define the procedures to be followed when a primary rule has been broken and identify which authority will determine the consequences for such a breach.[29]

The principle of unity in Hart's theory lies in the union of primary and secondary rules. Hart does not reject the possibility of legal orders consisting exclusively of primary rules (international law, in his view, being a prime example).[30] But he does not see these orders as legal systems properly-so-called. Instead, they are viewed as primitive orders that suffer from a number of flaws (they are uncertain, static and inefficient).[31] In Hart's theory, law as a unitary system exists if three conditions are met: 1) the valid rules of conduct are generally obeyed; 2) their existence and operation is governed by a set of secondary rules; and 3) this union of primary and secondary rules is ultimately founded upon a single, ultimate rule of recognition, which constitutes the supreme criterion of validity for the system as a whole and is accepted as such by the system's officials.[32]

Here the links between Hart and Kelsen's theories become apparent. The ultimate rule of recognition, like the *Grundnorm*, rests on the notion that rules are

[26] HLA Hart, *The Concept of Law* (Oxford, Clarendon Press, 1961) 20–25.
[27] Ibid at 78–79.
[28] Prosper Weil, 'Le droit international en quête de son identité' (1992) 237 *Collected Courses of the Hague Academy of International Law* 9, 131.
[29] Hart, *The Concept of Law*, above n 26 at 92–96.
[30] Ibid at 213–37.
[31] Ibid at 89–91.
[32] Ibid at 102–04.

bound in chains of validity. One norm is valid insofar as it has been authorised or recognised as such by another, more general norm. And in both theories, this ascending chain of validity must necessarily come to a stop somewhere, with a founding and all-encompassing norm that cannot be justified by another norm. But here again these similarities must not be exaggerated. Real differences exist between the two authors. Hart, for instance, does not see this fundamental norm as a necessary condition for the existence of a legal system. The ultimate rule of recognition, he writes, 'is not a necessity, but a luxury', found mostly in advanced and sophisticated social systems.[33] More importantly perhaps, Hart disagrees with Kelsen on the very nature of the fundamental norm. In Kelsen's theory, the *Grundnorm* is a logical-transcendental postulate that cannot be verified. The existence and validity of this superior norm cannot be questioned and must not be sought. The *Grundnorm* has to be presupposed.[34] In Hart's concept of law, on the other hand, the ultimate rule of recognition is a *socially constructed* principle of unity. It is an observable *fact* that can be verified by ascertaining whether or not, as a matter of practice, it is accepted by system officials.[35] Hart's notion of acceptance, as we shall see below, is somewhat ambiguous and it is not always clear what Hart meant by it. It remains, however, a central tenet of his concept of law that demonstrates, to a large extent, the originality of his work, not only in relation to classical Austinian positivism but also in relation to Kelsen's normativism.

C. The post-normativist approach

While differences exist between Hart and Kelsen's theories of the legal system, both are premised on the notion that legal systems are made up exclusively of norms. It is precisely this notion that post-normativist approaches – such as those of Raz and Dworkin – partially or wholly reject.

(i) Raz

Raz's theory of the legal system is in large part affiliated with that of Kelsen – which he seeks to improve by ridding it of unsatisfactory or unnecessary elements[36] – and with that of Hart, his teacher at Oxford, who he considered did not go far enough in the critique of classical positivism.[37] In his *Concept of a Legal System*, Raz posits as a fundamental hypothesis that the nature of law cannot be reduced to norms considered in isolation. A normative system, he writes, is a legal system only if it has a minimum degree of complexity. In order

[33] Ibid at 235.
[34] Kelsen, *Pure Theory of Law*, above n 16 at 197.
[35] Hart, *The Concept of Law*, above n 26 at 102–07.
[36] Joseph Raz, *The Concept of a Legal System* (Oxford, Clarendon Press, 1970) 121.
[37] Ibid at 183.

to grasp the nature of law as a complex system, one must understand something about the variety of legal norms that populate the system and about their mutual relations.[38] Legal systems, in other words, are more than haphazard assemblages of norms. They are intricate webs of interconnected laws.

That said, Raz's approach to the legal system, and to its unity, differs from that of Kelsen and Hart in two respects. First, Raz argues that legal systems are not made up exclusively of norms. As a starting point, Raz borrows from Hart's distinction between primary and secondary norms. Without completely adhering to Hart's terminology, he argues that two fundamental types of laws operate in every legal system. These are what he calls 'duty-imposing laws' – or D-laws – and 'power-conferring laws' – or P-laws.[39] In his view, the nature and structure of the legal system entirely depends upon the 'genetic' and 'operative' bonds that tie these different types of law together. Like Hart, Raz believes that the legal system's defining feature is that one group of norms governs the existence and operation of the other (that is, its validity, change and sanction).[40] Unlike Hart, however, Raz argues that a legal system contains other types of laws that are not norms. In this he differs from his predecessors. Bentham, Austin and Hart all agreed on one thing: every law is a norm. Raz, on the other hand, takes the view that, although normativity is an important aspect of the law, some laws simply do not qualify as norms, for they do not attempt to guide human behaviour – that is, they do not prescribe a particular course of conduct.[41] This is true, for instance, of 'laws instituting rights'. A law that stipulates that a wife has a right to maintenance or that an individual has the right of ownership in immovable property does not impose a conduct. It merely states the existence of a legal relation between legal subjects or between a subject and an object of right.[42] The same goes for 'categorizing rules', which explain how to translate actions, events, and other facts into appropriate legal categories, or so-called 'rules of scope', which merely fix the scope of other rules.[43] These laws, for Raz, are important components of the legal system. They are not, however, legal norms in the proper sense of the term.

Another important aspect of Raz's post-normativism is the fact that, in his vision of the legal system, formal unity rests not on a superior principle of validity but instead on an *institutional fact of recognition*. In a way, Raz rejects the idea of an 'ultimate' rule of recognition. He does not regard it as a necessary component of legal systems.[44] The identity and the self-containedness of the system lie, in his view, in the empirically verifiable fact that the laws of the system are effectively accepted by the system's primary organs, that is, the organs that possess the authority to make binding and applicative decisions (for

[38] Ibid at 121–22 and 140–41.
[39] Ibid at 147–66.
[40] Ibid at 183–86.
[41] Ibid at 168.
[42] Ibid at 180–83.
[43] Ibid at 224–25.
[44] Ibid at 100–05.

example, courts and tribunals). Formal unity, from this point of view, consists in law-applying organs being able to draw the boundaries of the system on the basis of commonly accepted 'criteria of membership' – that is, criteria that determine which laws are part of the system and which are not.[45]

(ii) Dworkin

More than Raz perhaps, Dworkin is at variance with classical positivism, and Hart's in particular.[46] Dworkin, however, shares Raz's conviction that the identity of legal systems does not reside in a 'master-norm' or a superior rule of recognition that trickles down to the whole system and ensures its consistency and unity.[47] For Dworkin, the identity and the self-contained nature of legal systems does not depend upon 'a test of pedigree' but rather on a key concept (the principle) and its use by a key figure (the judge).

Behind rules, says Dworkin, are a number of standards that are not rules but 'principles' and 'policies'. By 'policy', Dworkin means a standard that sets out a goal to be reached and that generally represents some sort of progress for the community.[48] This progress can either be economic (for example, full employment) or socio-political (for example, access to housing, gender equality and so on). In any case, a policy points towards a socially desirable goal. A 'principle', on the other hand, is a standard that is to be observed, not because it advances or secures a desirable goal, but because it is required by justice or fairness or some other dimension of morality.[49] Thus, says Dworkin, 'the standard that automobile accidents are to be decreased is a policy, and the standard that no man may profit by his own wrong a principle'.[50]

The key distinction employed by Dworkin, however, is that between legal rules and principles. Although both types of standards point to particular decisions in particular circumstances, Dworkin considers that rules and principles work differently and play different roles in a legal system. Rules, he writes, are applicable in an 'all-or-nothing' fashion: if the facts that a rule stipulates are given (for example, a theft or housebreaking), then the answer it supplies (for example, the penalty) must be accepted. If the facts, on the other hand, are not given, then the rule does not apply and it contributes nothing to the decision.[51] This is not, however, the way principles operate. Principles, unlike rules, do not set out legal consequences that follow automatically from the occurrence of

[45] Ibid at 189–97.

[46] On the famous 'Hart/Dworkin debate', see eg, Michael Mandel, 'Dworkin, Hart, and the Problem of Theoretical Perspective' (1979) 14 *Law and Society Review* 57; Scott Shapiro, 'The "Hart-Dworkin" Debate: A Short Guide for the Perplexed' (2007) 77 *University of Michigan Public Law Working Paper* 1.

[47] Ronald Dworkin, 'The Model of Rules' (1967) 35 *University of Chicago Law Review* 14, 45.

[48] Ronald Dworkin, *Taking Rights Seriously* (Cambridge, Harvard University Press, 1977) 22.

[49] Ibid at 90.

[50] Ibid.

[51] Ibid at 24.

certain facts. In fact, principles rarely – if ever – stipulate the circumstances in which they ought to operate. They are simply propositions that provide underlying justificatory values or reasons: 'they state a reason that argues in one direction, but do not necessitate a particular decision'.[52] The principle according to which, for instance, car manufacturers have special responsibilities in connection with the construction, promotion and sale of their cars is not a rule in the traditional sense of the term. It does not prescribe a particular conduct or course of action. It does, however, suggest that automobile manufacturers – who produce potentially dangerous machines – may be held to higher standards than other manufacturers and may consequently be less entitled to rely on a freedom of contract argument to escape these special obligations.[53]

For Dworkin, the unity of a legal system does not reside in the absence of conflicts between valid rules – he sees such conflict as logically impossible[54] – or in the existence of 'secondary' rules that govern the existence and operation of primary rules of conduct. Instead, formal unity stems from the interpretative activity of the judge informed by legal principles. This point is made by Dworkin in relation, in particular, to 'hard cases' – that is, cases in which the result is not clearly dictated by statute or precedent. The traditional positivist theory of adjudication posits that judges should use their discretion to resolve hard cases. Dworkin rejects this argument, or rather qualifies it. Judges' discretion, he writes, is like the hole in a doughnut: 'it does not exist except as an area left open by a surrounding belt of restriction'.[55] It is wrong, in other words, to assume that the judge, when exercising discretion, is not bound by any standards. The judge is always constrained, at minimum, by legal principles. This is not to say that principles command a particular outcome. If this were the case, they would be rules, not principles. They do, however, 'generate' particular decisions – that is, they provide grounds of justification on which to found a proper decision.[56]

Dworkin's principle of unity is thus a *principle of decision* according to which judges must read and interpret rules as if they were the product of a single author, the community personified, expressing a particular conception of justice and equity. And if rules themselves do not provide explicit guidance, the judge must look for justifications in the underlying principles of the legal order. Dworkin illustrates this point by his famous metaphor of the 'chain novel'. Judges, he writes, are like a group of authors writing a chain story. The novel is passed along from author to author, each adding a new chapter based on the plotline of preceding chapters. In this story, the role of each novelist/judge is twofold: 'every novelist but the first has the dual responsibilities of interpreting

[52] Ibid at 26.
[53] Ibid.
[54] Dworkin, 'The Model of Rules', above n 47 at 40: 'if two rules conflict, one of them cannot be a valid rule'.
[55] Dworkin, *Taking Rights Seriously*, above n 48 at 31.
[56] Ibid at 83–84.

and creating because each must read all that has gone before in order to establish, in the interpretivist sense, what the novel so far created is. He or she must decide what the characters are "really" like; what motives guide them; what the point or theme of the developing novel is; how far some literary device or figure, consciously or unconsciously used, contributes to these, and whether it should be extended or refined or trimmed or dropped in order to send the novel further in one direction or the other'.[57]

Everything thus happens as if the judge had to write the best possible novel based on the material passed on to him (that is, statutes, precedents and so on) and on what he has to add to it (that is, his interpretation). To achieve this, the judge must uncover the principles (the plotlines, stories, characters) that are already in place, which give the system (the story) its identity and integrity. This hermeneutic uncovering, for Dworkin, has nothing to do with arbitrariness or pure discretion, for it is controlled by legal principles, if only, at minimum, the principle according to which each judge has to take previous decisions, stories and interpretations into account.

Here, formal unity is conceptualised not as a chain of validity but as a chain of interpretation. In this perspective, whether judges reach similar decisions or resort to similar interpretations is almost irrelevant. The integrity and unity of the system is maintained as long as judges play by the book, locate their interpretative activity (that is, their part of the story) within the 'unfolding narrative' of the legal order, and adopt the decision that best 'fits' the law as a whole (that is, the story to date).[58] Dworkin's theory of unity is thus rooted in the *practice of adjudication* and lies in the hermeneutical act of tying explicit rules to underlying principles in search of the 'right answer' to moral/legal dilemmas.

D. Conventional discourses on formal unity: two forms of reductionism

Perspectives on law's systematicity and formal unity, as the above demonstrates, are plentiful. Principles and criteria of unity vary, depending on the standpoint from which the unity of the system is examined. In institutionalist approaches, the degree of unity of a legal system largely depends on the degree of coherence of the social order that lies behind or underneath the law (that is, the institution). In normativist approaches, formal unity rests upon the dynamic relationships that unite different classes of norms, in which one type of norm governs the 'lifecycle' of the other. Post-normativist approaches, for their part, place the emphasis on the mutually constitutive relations between certain types of norms, rules or principles and the law-applying organs of the system.

The conventional discourse on formal unity in international law tends to regard these various perspectives in isolation from each other, as if they were

[57] Ronald Dworkin, *A Matter of Principle* (Cambridge, Harvard University Press, 1985) 158–59.

[58] Ronald Dworkin, *Law's Empire* (Cambridge, Belknap Press, 1986) 247ff.

mutually exclusive. Yet there is no reason to believe that law forms a unitary whole by virtue of only one of these dynamics. Institutions, ascending chains of validity and collective chains of interpretation are elements of any legal system. Surely, assessing the degree of formal unity of a system like international law requires looking at the intersection between these different forces or criteria of unity. Formal unity is not mono-causational. Law, understood as a complex system of norms, always involves a number of rules and principles that are socially constituted, and whose meaning and operation depends at least in part on what interpretative communities think and make of them. Law's complexity means precisely this: that the identity of legal orders can never be reduced to either one of these three dimensions alone. Law is not rules *or* institutions *or* the practice of adjudication. It is all of them at once.

To focus on one dynamic at the expense of the others would be a simplification. Any system of law is characterised by powerful cross-currents, with uniting and pluralising forces running in opposite directions. The degree of unity of a system will always depend on the tension and balance between these forces. On this point, it must be noted that conventional approaches to formal unity in international law often offer one-dimensional explanations of – and, as a result, suggest one-dimensional solutions to – problems of unity/fragmentation. In fact, and as already discussed, international law's systematicity, and its formal unity, are often more assumed than explained. But where formal unity is theorised or rationalised, it tends to be reduced to one dynamic, dimension or explanation, generally involving the interaction between different classes of norms.[59] Whether they are debating the multiplication of international organisations, the proliferation of tribunals or the autonomisation of special regimes, international lawyers almost always conceptualise formal unity in terms of secondary norms. The line of reasoning is nearly always the same: in a world in which international law is becoming ever more complex and dense, the unity of international law as a system is measured by looking at the existence, beyond the diversity of rules and institutions, of a stable core of general and structuring rules (that is, of secondary rules).[60]

This argumentative structure is analysed in greater detail in the rest of this chapter. The point, for now, is to identify a first form of reductionism. International lawyers tend to use Hart's theory of secondary rules, often explicitly, as the sole and exclusive paradigm of formal unity. The problem, of course,

[59] Two notable exceptions are William Burke-White, 'International Legal Pluralism' (2004) 25 *Michigan Journal of International Law* 963 (one of the few authors to consider that the study of unity/fragmentation requires an exploration of a number of 'trends' (he counts seven of them) and the ways in which they interact); and Tomer Broude, 'Fragmentation(s) of International Law: On Normative Integration as Authority Allocation' in Tomer Broude and Yuval Shany (eds), *The Shifting Allocation of Authority in International Law: Considering Sovereignty, Supremacy and Subsidiarity* (Oxford, Hart Publishing, 2008) (who takes the view that two forms of unity exist – the unity of norms and the unity of authority – which cannot be studied in isolation from one another).

[60] See eg, Andreas Zimmermann and Rainer Hofmann (eds), *Unity and Diversity in International Law* (Berlin, Duncker & Humblot, 2006); and LANM Barnhoom and Karel Wellens (eds), *Diversity in Secondary Rules and the Unity of International Law* (The Hague, Martinus Nijhoff, 1995).

is not the use of Hart's theory *per se*, although it is ironic that international lawyers, in debating the integrity and unity of their law, are resorting to an author who was notoriously sceptical about the international law being a system of law properly-so-called.[61] The use of Hart's theory becomes problematic, however, when it excludes other possible explanations, forms or logics of unity. Often, the question asked is whether international law is equipped with a system of secondary rules as if this question alone exhausted the debate about formal unity.

By doing so, one risks overlooking a score of questions regarding the intersection between normative, institutional and hermeneutical dynamics. How, for instance, does the inter-normative dynamic of unity relate to the institutional dynamic in international law? Assuming that a system of secondary norms exists in international law, do these norms rest upon a coherent social structure (that is, an institution) capable of providing institutionally secured normative consistency? Can one speak, for instance, of an 'international society' generating law in an integrated fashion so as to bring global answers to global problems? Or does international law today spring from autonomous 'villages' or functionally distinct fragments of society (the merchant society, the humanitarian society, the environmentalist society, etc), each generating its own normative and institutional apparatus on the basis of distinct goals and preferences?[62]

Similarly, how does the interaction between primary and secondary rules relate to interpretative or hermeneutic dynamics? Can one speak, for instance, of a community of judges in international law, all bound in continuous chains of interpretation? Despite the lack of a formal judicial system, are international judges part of a common hermeneutic venture or 'story'? Are they committed to common standards or principles? Do they talk to each other? Does 'cross-fertilisation' take place among international courts and tribunals?[63]

Though some recent contributions have started addressing these important questions,[64] these have largely been ignored in the literature. By focusing almost exclusively on the issue of secondary norms, one tells only part of the story, leaving entire aspects of the concept of formal unity in the dark. This represents an important limit in the conventional discourse on unity/fragmentation. It is

[61] Hart, *The Concept of Law*, above n 26 at 208–31.

[62] On this theme, see especially, Andreas Fischer-Lescano and Gunther Teubner, 'Regime-Collisions: The Vain Search for Legal Unity in the Fragmentation of Global Law' (2004) 25 *Michigan Journal of International Law* 999.

[63] On these issues, see the debate within the field of human rights law: Antonio Augusto Cançado Trindade, 'The Merits of Coordination of International Courts on Human Rights' (2004) 2 *Journal of International Criminal Justice* 309; Thomas Buergenthal, 'The European and Inter-American Courts of Human Rights: Beneficial Interaction' in Paul Mahoney (ed), *Studies in Memory of Rolv Ryssdal* (Köln, Heymanns, 2000); Hector Gros Espiell, 'La Cour Interaméricaine et la Cour européenne des droits de l'homme' in *Liber Amicorum Marc-André Eissen* (Paris, LGDJ, 1995).

[64] See, eg, Ruti Teitel and Robert Howse, 'Cross-Judging: Tribunalization in a Fragmented but Interconnected Global Order' (2009) 41 *New York University Journal of International Law and Politics* 959; and Harlan Cohen, 'Finding International Law, Part II: Our Fragmenting Legal Community' (2011) 44 *New York University Journal of International Law and Politics* 1.

not the only one, however. Another form of reductionism can be observed in the literature. Conventional approaches to formal unity in international law are not only one-dimensional, focusing almost exclusively on the structuring role of secondary norms. They also tend to adopt over-simplifying – not to say simplistic – views of Hart's theory of the legal system. Often, the category of secondary norms is used as a free-standing and all-explaining category, without ever being located in Hart's broader and more complex concept of the legal system. As a consequence, important elements of Hart's systems theory are overlooked, in particular those that pertain to the 'determinacy' and the 'acceptance' of secondary rules. This would not be a problem if these elements, as is the case in domestic systems, were somehow obvious or self-evident. In what follows, however, I show through concrete examples that they are not, and that both determinacy and uniform acceptance of secondary norms cannot be assumed to exist in international law. These examples are not meant to suggest that international law today fails as a unitary system. Instead, they are used to examine the conditions under which Hart's theory of secondary norms can serve as the basis for debating the formal unity of international law. In other words, and as in the previous sections, my aim here is not only to pluralise but also to complicate the doctrinal picture of formal unity that prevails in the international law literature.

II. TAKING HART SERIOUSLY: SECONDARY RULES, DETERMINACY AND ACCEPTANCE

What, then, is this doctrinal picture? What views do most international lawyers hold about Hart, secondary rules and the formal unity of international law? In the vast majority of cases, this vision of unity rests on a narrow interpretation of Hart's theory of the legal system and takes the following syllogistic form:

1) A legal system enjoys formal unity if it is based on a set of secondary rules that control the recognition, change and adjudication of primary rules;
2) There are secondary rules in international law;
3) Therefore international law possesses formal unity.

This way of thinking about unity is articulated in its most explicit form in the work of Pierre-Marie Dupuy, one of the rare authors to have developed a complete theory of unity in international law. At a symposium organised at the New York University Law School on the multiplication of international tribunals, Dupuy was the first to distinguish between material and formal unity in international law, a key distinction that would later form the basis of his general Hague Lectures.[65] In his symposium contribution, Dupuy argues that formal unity 'is basically composed of what Hart calls "secondary rules" in his book *The Concept*

[65] Pierre-Marie Dupuy, 'The Danger of Fragmentation or Unification of the International Legal System and the International Court of Justice' (1998) 31 *New York University Journal of International Law & Politics* 791.

of Law'.[66] Contrary to what Hart contended, however, Dupuy takes the view that international law is endowed with 'a full set of secondary rules', in particular rules of change and rules of adjudication, which are 'fundamentally the same whatever the object of the international primary rules'.[67] In Dupuy's view, this fact alone is sufficient to conclude that international law possesses formal unity.

In his Hague Lectures, Dupuy largely confirms his vision of formal unity. He writes that formal unity is 'for the most part related to the use of the same secondary rules' in all branches of public international law, most notably rules that concern the 'production of norms' and the 'conditions of their implementation'.[68] Despite a lengthy treatment of formal unity, Dupuy's vision remains, at its core, a simple one: international law 'can be said to constitute a legal order in the formal sense of the term because it is endowed with a system of secondary norms, in particular secondary norms of production'.[69]

This conception of formal unity has two central characteristics. First, it uses Hart's theory without comparing it to other theories of the legal order or considering the way in which it may interact with other forms or dynamics of unity.[70] Second, it reduces Hart's theory to its simplest form, which can be summarised in a single a succinct proposition: formal unity, in Dupuy's own words, follows from the fact that international law possesses '*a certain number of formal rules*, all secondary norms pursuant to Hart's theory'.[71]

The problem is not that this proposition borrows from Hart's theory of the legal system. Hart is amongst the most influential legal philosophers of the twentieth century and his concept of secondary norms has long permeated the analysis of international law, as shown for instance in the International Law Commission's work on state responsibility.[72] The problem, however, comes from the fact that Dupuy's proposition ignores large portions of Hart's systems theory and treats the existence of secondary norms as an end in itself, whereas Hart himself concedes they are but starting points. In the *Concept of Law*, Hart clearly states that, once the union of primary and secondary rules has

[66] Ibid at 793.

[67] Ibid at 793–94.

[68] Pierre-Marie Dupuy, 'L'unité de l'ordre juridique international' (2002) 297 *Collected Courses of the Hague Academy of International Law* 9, 39 and 94.

[69] Ibid at 119.

[70] It must be noted that Dupuy, in his Hague Lectures, does begin his analysis of formal unity by reviewing three general conceptions of the legal order. After having briefly examined the theories of Romano, Kelsen and Hart, however, he goes on to develop his vision of formal unity based solely on Hartian premises, without providing a justification for this choice.

[71] Pierre-Marie Dupuy, 'A Doctrinal Debate in the Globalisation Era: On the "Fragmentation" of International Law' (2007) 1 *European Journal of Legal Studies* 1, 19 (emphasis added). For a similar analysis, see also Oriol Casanovas, *Unity and Pluralism in Public International Law* (The Hague, Martinus Nijhoff, 2001) 249: 'Public international law is a legal system the unity of which derives, in the first place, from the structure maintained between the rules which make it up: primary rules and secondary rules'.

[72] See James Crawford, *The International Law Commission's Articles on State Responsibility – Introduction, Text and Commentaries* (Cambridge, Cambridge University Press, 2002) 14–16 (endorsing Hart's distinction between primary and secondary norms).

been established as the basis upon which the legal system is founded, 'a range of fascinating and important questions confronts us'.[73] In what follows, I shall only address two of these questions: that of the determinacy and that of the uniform acceptance of secondary rules. This choice was not made randomly. It results from the fact that these two questions, although central to Hart's theory of the unity of legal systems, have received virtually no attention in today's fragmentation debate.[74]

A. The determinacy of secondary rules

Hart's theory of the legal system is rooted in a simple but fundamental premise: law's function is to guide and control the behaviour of its subjects (citizens and officials) by setting out certain standards and rules of conducts. Hart, it must be noted, does not dwell long on this question. The aim of his *Concept of Law* is essentially descriptive. Hart seeks to provide a theory of what law *is*, and how different types of norms interact in practice. His is not a justificatory enterprise but rather an analytical depiction of how law works.[75] That said, Hart's fundamental premise regarding the function of law remains relatively clear: law's principal purpose is to designate – through rules – certain types of behaviour as standards for the guidance of individuals or groups of individuals, as well as to identify other kinds of conduct that are socially undesirable.[76]

Law, then, is a guide. It limits and constrains its subjects' freedom of action. Certain behaviours are made non-optional, that is, in some sense obligatory.[77] In Hart's theory, one important consequence flows from this fundamental premise: in order to fulfil their role as 'controllers' of social behaviour, rules must be determinate, or at least determinable by the lay person, without further direction or intervention from system officials. If rules fail to provide clear guidance as to the conduct to be followed, they risk losing their very *raison d'être* and, according to Hart, 'nothing that we now recognize as law could exist'.[78] In other words, law's successful operation depends in large part on its ability to communicate general standards of conduct with a minimum degree of certainty and predictability.

To be sure, Hart does recognise the existence in any legal system of an element of doubt and uncertainty. In response to arguments formulated by realists and other 'rule sceptics', Hart concedes that law, to some extent, possesses an

[73] Hart, *The Concept of Law*, above n 26 at 107.

[74] The situation is not without irony, for international lawyers themselves have long criticised Hart for his simplistic views on international law. See, eg, Ian Brownlie, 'The Reality and Efficacy of International Law' (1981) 52 *British Yearbook of International Law* 1, 5–8.

[75] This point is made clear in the 'postface' to the second edition of the *Concept of Law* (Oxford, Clarendon Press, 1994) 239–40.

[76] Hart, *The Concept of Law*, above n 26 at 27 and 38.

[77] Ibid at 6 and 80.

[78] Ibid at 121.

'open texture' and that uncertainties as to the form of behaviour required by rules may emerge in particular cases.[79] This, Hart explains, is an unavoidable consequence of the fact that law is a product of human societies and of the open texture of language itself. Human beings are not gods. They are neither prophets nor omnipotent. Human legislators cannot possibly foresee all the combinations of circumstances that the future may bring. For law to function properly, legislators are forced to communicate rules in general terms and there will always be hard, complex or borderline cases in which it is unclear that particular circumstances fall within the scope of a general rule. Law's 'open texture' is thus the price to be paid for the use of general classifying terms. Human beings' inability to predict future brings with it the inescapable possibility of cases not anticipated by the legislator that do not neatly fit the operational parameters of the existing law.[80]

The 'open texture' thesis, however, has its limits. For one thing, Hart considers that normative uncertainty can only be tolerated if it remains marginal, that is, at the borderline. Whilst admitting that a 'fringe of vagueness' is inevitable – perhaps even desirable – in any system of law, Hart insists that law can only fulfil its function of social guidance if rules, on the whole, possess an established 'core of certainty'.[81] For another, Hart takes the view that uncertainties in primary rules of conduct – and the judicial discretion that may follow from it – are only acceptable if they are governed by a stable and coherent set of secondary rules. Law's indeterminacy, in other words, must not only remain relative. It must be *controlled by law itself*.[82]

To better understand this second point, it may be useful to reiterate that secondary rules, in Hart's theory of the legal system, play a distinct and defined role: they are *remedies* for the flaws and defects of primitive orders, that is, normative orders composed exclusively of primary rules. Primitive orders, according to Hart, suffer from three fundamental imperfections: they are uncertain, static and inefficient.[83] Secondary rules are required precisely because they fix these problems. They bring a solution to the issue of inefficiency by endowing certain individuals or groups of individuals with the power to decide if wrongful acts have been committed and what the consequences of these wrongful acts should be (rules of adjudication).[84] They bring a solution to the static character of primitive regimes by setting out procedures by which primary rules can be amended, repelled or replaced by new ones, so as to meet the changing needs of society (rules of change).[85] Last but not least, secondary rules solve the issue of

[79] Hart's *Concept of Law* can be read in large part as a response to American realism and rule scepticism, as stated by Hart himself at the outset of his book, which he presents as a response to the 'perplexities' of authors like Llewellyn and Holmes.

[80] Ibid at 121–26.

[81] Ibid at 119–20.

[82] Hart, *The Concept of Law*, 2nd edn, above n 75 at 272–76.

[83] Ibid at 89–91.

[84] Ibid at 94–95.

[85] Ibid at 93–94.

uncertainty by setting out the conditions of validity of primary rules, that is, the conditions under which they can be regarded, with some degree of confidence, as part of the system (rules of recognition).[86]

Secondary rules are thus the means by which to *dispel doubts* about the existence, scope and operation of primary rules. They specify the way in which the primary rules may be conclusively and decisively ascertained and instances of their violation conclusively identified. If a certain degree of uncertainty or indeterminacy is bound to exist in any legal system, this element of uncertainty must thus stop with secondary rules. These rules are, in a sense, 'ultimate rules' or rules of 'last resort'.[87] They constitute the systemic response to law's open texture and, if they are to fulfil their function, they must therefore be determinate. This, for Hart, is a 'necessary' and 'crucial' condition of law's unity and integrity as a system.[88]

B. The unified and general acceptance of secondary rules

If the determinacy of secondary rules matters, so too does their general and uniform acceptance by the system's 'officials'. What, exactly, does Hart mean by this? Hart, it will be recalled, insists that the mere existence of secondary rules is not sufficient to prove the existence of a unitary and autonomous system of law. The effective existence and integrity of a system of law, Hart claims, rests on a certain relation or *rapport* to law. Hart insists, in particular, on the fact that secondary rules must be effectively 'internalised' by the system's officials.[89] What is crucial, says Hart, 'is that there should be a unified or shared official acceptance of the rule of recognition containing the system's criteria of validity'.[90]

The concept of acceptance is key to Hart's theory of the legal system and this, perhaps more than anything else, distinguishes it from that of his predecessors (Bentham and Austin in particular). This concept, however, is rather ambiguous and Hart's explanations in this regard are not always helpful. In fact, Hart never really provides a positive definition of acceptance. He does, however, provide elements of a negative definition and insists in particular on the fact that acceptance covers a wide range of 'attitudes', which: (1) are not to be confused with the notion of general obedience; and (2) do not necessarily involve total moral adherence or loyalty to the law.

The first element in this negative definition concerns the distinction between acceptance and mere habits of obedience. Hart does not discount the importance of habitual obedience for legal systems. In fact, he firmly believes that

[86] Ibid at 89–90.
[87] Ibid at 102 and 107.
[88] Ibid at 92 and 147–48.
[89] Ibid at 111.
[90] Ibid.

there can be no legal system if rules are not generally obeyed. At the same time, Hart insists that the relation of 'ordinary citizens' to primary rules of conduct must not be confused with that of the system's officials to secondary rules. Mere citizens stand in what Hart calls an 'external' relation with (primary) rules. By this, Hart means that ordinary citizens normally obey legal rules not because they feel it is the 'right' or 'correct' thing to do, but rather in fear of the negative social consequences (that is, sanctions) attached to rule violations. Obedience to primary rules of conduct need not involve a value judgement regarding the legitimacy or fairness of rules, or their importance as standards of behaviour for the social group. The obedient citizen, to be sure, *may* hold the view that what she does is the right thing for her or for others to do. But according to Hart, regular obedience *need not* involve such thought or judgement on the part of the person obeying the rule.[91]

This 'external' relation to primary rules is, in Hart's view, fundamentally different from that which the officials of the system *must* entertain with secondary rules. If officials, and in particular judges, were to apply rules in this passive and uncritical manner, simply for fear of sanctions or because this is what they are paid for, then 'the characteristic unity and continuity of a legal system would disappear'.[92] For Hart, the existence of a single and unitary legal system demands a 'critical reflective attitude' from the system's officials, that is, a degree of adherence, rather than mere submission, to secondary rules.[93] This is what Hart calls the 'internal point of view', that is, the belief that a rule must be obeyed not simply because it is valid and obligatory, but more fundamentally because it constitutes a public standard of validity, decision or behaviour. Acceptance, from this perspective, means holding the view that there are good reasons for abiding by the system's secondary rules and that deviations from these rules are therefore of critical concern. Hart, it is worth stressing, claims that acceptance can be motivated by a variety of reasons (tradition, collective interest, conformity with usage, etc), none of which is intrinsically superior to the others.[94] In fact, the specific reasons for accepting the authority of law are almost irrelevant to Hart. What really matters is the notion that officials should somehow pledge allegiance to the system's structuring (that is, secondary) norms.

Whilst speaking of 'allegiance', 'legitimacy' and 'good reasons' for abiding by the system's secondary rules, Hart insists at the same time that this 'internal point of view' must not be understood as a moral point of view. Those who accept the authority of law from the internal point of view need not believe that it is *morally* right to do so. A judge, for instance, may very well consider that it is morally wrong to apply a secondary rule and yet, for a variety of other rea-

[91] Ibid at 111–12.
[92] Ibid at 113.
[93] Ibid at 56.
[94] Hart, *The Concept of Law*, 2nd edn, above n 75 at 198.

sons, continue to accept it.[95] This undoubtedly represents one of the most ambiguous, not to say paradoxical, aspects of Hart's theory of the legal system. Indeed, if accepting the law entails believing that its demands are justified, how can a judge regard a rule as morally unjustified and yet, at the same time, accept it?[96] Paradoxical though it may be, Hart's notion of acceptance remains central to his conception of the legal system and covers a set of attitudes that are *more* than mere habits of obedience but *less* than a true moral ratification. It would be wrong to regard uniform and general acceptance as a secondary or peripheral requirement. To Hart, acceptance is not merely a matter of the efficiency or well-being of the legal system. It is, much more fundamentally, 'a necessary condition of our ability to speak of the existence of a single legal system'.[97]

C. Two unexplored conditions

Despite the importance of determinacy and acceptance to Hart's theory of the legal system, the fragmentation literature has paid little or no attention to these two important themes. More often than not, international lawyers take the rather 'short' view that there is formal unity in the law if it can be established that the system possesses 'a certain number' of secondary rules. As such, the argument is insufficient as it remains purely quantitative. It largely ignores the fact that it is by reason of their particular quality as norms of last resort that secondary rules are able to turn a primitive and disorganised set of norms into a coherent and autonomous system.

The conventional discourse on formal unity also ignores the notion of acceptance, that is, the internalisation of secondary rules by the system's officials, lawmakers and law-appliers. Often, formal unity is found to exist simply because different branches have a 'common denominator' or 'common structures'. Formal unity, in other words, is equated with the fact that different regimes or norm-complexes resort to similar techniques of law-making and implementation.[98]

The problem with this argument is not that it is empirically false. The problem lies in the fact that it says nothing about the attitude of international 'officials' – states and judges in particular – vis-a-vis the secondary rules of public international law. Is there such a thing, in international law, as a general and uniform acceptance of a stable set of secondary rules? Or are we simply dealing with converging 'habits of obedience'? These are important questions,

[95] Ibid at 199.

[96] On this contradiction, see Richard Holton, 'Positivism and the Internal Point of View' (1998) 17 *Law and Philosophy* 597, 600–06.

[97] Hart, *The Concept of Law*, above n 26 at 112–13.

[98] See, eg, James Crawford, *International Law as an Open System: Selected Essays* (London, Cameron May, 2002) 5–37 (who claims that international law, despite deep transformations and rapid change, remains a relatively stable and unitary system, due to the fact that some elements are invariable across regimes and institutions, including the 'same old concepts' of consent, treaty and authority, and the 'same old techniques' of ascertainment and interpretation).

for whoever adopts a sufficiently high level of abstraction may find common 'trends' or 'traits' in virtually all things. Merely finding that different regimes resemble each other in their functioning does not prove the existence of a single and coherent system. It merely suggests a form of generic unity, that is, a unity based on the fact that different regimes belong to the same normative genus (international law, as opposed to domestic law).

A *reductio ad absurdum* may help clarify this point. If one were to judge from the highest possible level of abstraction, one would find that all domestic legal systems exhibit the same structure or features: all domestic systems rests on a division of juridical labour between the government, the legislator and the judge; all use the same normative technology, comprising of statutes, decrees, regulations, customs and precedents; and all attach similar consequences to unlawful conducts (restitution, remedies and a blend of symbolic, pecuniary and physical sanctions). Is this to say, then, that only one law exists on the planet of which national legal orders are but mere parts or variations? The argument seems strange, to say the least. It shows, however, that identifying 'common trends' or 'identical structures' is not the same as proving the existence of a single, formal system of law.

What the above demonstrates is that formal conceptions of unity in international law doctrine often stop short of asking the real or 'hard' questions. They debate the doctrine of sources or rules on state responsibility, but fail to consider whether these rules are determinate, that is, whether they possess the intrinsic quality of certainty that is necessary to maintain unity in the system.[99] They identify general trends and tendencies among different regimes, but leave open the question of whether these commonalities are produced by mere habits of obedience or whether they reflect a uniform and general acceptance by international law officials, that is, the common conviction that they are part of the same system of law, whose secondary rules they regard as authoritative and justified.

All of this would not matter too much if these questions were somewhat straightforward or evident in international law, as they often are in domestic legal systems. But international law, as is well known, is largely devoid of the hierarchical and integrating structures (written constitution, government, legislator, Supreme Court, etc) that give domestic systems a sense of immediate and palpable unity. International law is a 'disincarnate' or 'disembodied' legal order, in which the allocation of juridical authority – that is, the authority to make, interpret and implement the law – is uncertain, shifting and contested.[100] This does not mean that international law cannot possess unity. It means, however,

[99] The most prominent exception to this rule is Martti Koskenniemi's *From Apology to Utopia: The Structure of International Legal Argument* (Cambridge, Cambridge University Press, 2005) which is almost entirely dedicated to demonstrating international law's indeterminacy. I discuss this work further in ch 6.

[100] See Tomer Broude and Yuval Shany (eds), *The Shifting Allocation of Authority in International Law: Considering Sovereignty, Supremacy and Subsidiarity* (Oxford, Hart Publishing, 2008).

that the determinacy and the general acceptance of secondary norms cannot simply be assumed. In the absence of 'external signs of unity', determinacy and acceptance must be engaged with as complex questions, the answers to which are neither certain nor self-evident. The following paragraphs seek to do just that. Through two concrete examples, I show that, if there is little doubt today that international law does possess a number of secondary rules, in the Hartian sense of the term, whether these rules are determinate and uniformly accepted is a fundamentally open and contested question. My purpose here is not to answer or to settle this question once and for all. It is, rather more simply, to point out the *sort of issues* that Hart's theory of formal unity, if taken seriously, raises in the field of international law.

III. ISSUES OF DETERMINACY: QUESTIONING THE SOURCES OF INTERNATIONAL LAW

Let us first consider the question of sources, which many regard as the primary foundation of formal unity in international law.[101] The question of sources is of course not a new issue. It may in fact be one of the most recurring – some would say obsessive or constitutive – questions in the discipline of international law.[102] But the fact that the doctrine of sources is an old and persistent question should not prevent us from discussing it. On the contrary, the question's enduring presence is an indication of its uncertain, contested and indeterminate nature.

In what follows, I do not intend to discuss the notion of sources *per se*. Neither will I address in details specific aspects of the law of treaties or customary law processes. Instead, I shall ask a series of simple questions about the sources of international law: does international law possess, as is often claimed, a stable and coherent infrastructure of secondary rules of recognition? Is the question of sources sufficiently settled to constitute the 'core of certainty' that Hart sees as necessary to a single, unified legal system? How much is really known about law-making processes, criteria of validity and methods of ascertainment in international law? To these simple but important questions, I shall offer an ambivalent answer: we know a lot and a little at the same time.

When asked 'where does international law come from', international lawyers are able to provide certain elements of a response. We know, for instance, that most international law comes from two fundamental sources: treaties, that is,

[101] See, eg, Christian Tomuschat, General Course, Coll Courses, at 307: 'any legal system needs as its foundation uncontested – or largely uncontested – rules of recognition . . . In the absence of such agreement, the unity of the system could not be maintained'.

[102] See Prosper Weil, 'Le droit international en quête de son identité' (1992) 237 *Collected Courses of the Hague Academy of International Law* 9, 133: 'the debate over the sources of international law . . . continues, generation after generation, to fascinate lawyers . . . The problem of sources is at the crossroad of all the great controversies in international law, it reveals and magnifies lawyers' thoughts and agendas. All roads in international law come from sources, and all lead to them' (author's translation).

written agreements creating rights and duties for their parties; and custom, that is, an unwritten and 'spontaneous' process that reflects a general practice accepted as law.[103] This much is uncontroversial. Save for one historical exception,[104] the general consensus is that treaties and customs are the basic and elementary sources of international law.[105]

We know more about treaties. The Vienna Convention on the Law of Treaties, which represents the end-product of two long decades of codification, provides clear, specific, and determinate answers to a wide range of questions concerning, *inter alia*, the capacity to conclude treaties, their adoption and entry into force, conditions of validity, interpretation, and procedures of suspension/termination/invalidation.[106] Of course, a number of questions remain open, such as the effect of hostilities on treaties or the admissibility of certain types of reservations. Save for these few questions, however, the Vienna Convention constitutes a rather stable, specific and coherent set of rules that governs the most important aspects – whether formal, substantial or procedural – of treaties' existence.[107] Treaties, it seems, are thus a clear and consistent source of international law, a universally accepted category, the contours of which are uncontroversial and fairly determinate.[108]

Beyond this point, however, the question of sources enters a much more open, shifting and uncertain terrain. This is true, first of all, of the catalogue of formal sources. Tradition has it, of course, that article 38 of the ICJ Statute provides an 'authoritative' list or description of international law sources.[109] The systematic reference to article 38, however, is made principally by default and

[103] On the 'spontaneous' nature of custom, see Roberto Ago, 'Science juridique et droit international' (1956) 90 *Collected Course of the Hague Academy of International Law* 851, 929.

[104] The socialist doctrine of international law has, for a time, rejected the notion that custom is an autonomous source of international law arguing, instead, that it represents a form of tacit agreement among states. On this point, see eg, Grigorii Tunkin, *Theory of International Law* (Cambridge, Harvard University Press, 1974) 133.

[105] Vaughan Lowe, *International Law* (Oxford, Oxford University Press, 2007) 34; Ian Brownlie, *Principles of Public International Law*, 6th edn (Oxford, Oxford University Press, 2003) 5; Robert Jennings and Arthur Watts (eds), *Oppenheim's International Law*, vol 1 (London, Longman, 1996) 24; Hersch Lauterpacht, 'International Law – The General Part' in Elihu Lauterpacht (ed), *International Law – Being the Collected Papers of Hersch Lauterpacht, Vol 1* (Cambridge, Cambridge University Press, 1970) 53.

[106] *Vienna Convention on the Law of Treaties*, 23 May 1969.

[107] Ian Sinclair, *The Vienna Convention on the Law of Treaties* (Manchester, Manchester University Press, 1984) 5; Anthony Aust, *Modern Treaty Law and Practice* (Cambridge, Cambridge University Press, 2000) 6; Paul Reuter, *Introduction au droit des gens* (Paris, Armand Colin, 1972) 25.

[108] The only controversy seems to be that which concerns the question of whether treaties are a source of law (ie general rules applicable to all states) or merely a source of obligations (ie contractual obligations binding on their parties only). On this point, see Gerald Fitzmaurice, 'Some Problems Regarding the Formal Sources of International Law' in *Symbolae Verzijl* (The Hague, Martinus Nijhoff, 1958) (treaties as mere sources of obligations) and, *contra*, Maurice Mendelson, 'Are Treaties Merely a Source of Obligation?' in William Butler (ed), *Perestroika and International Law* (Dordrecht, Martinus Nijhoff, 1990).

[109] Lauterpacht, 'General Rules of the Law of Peace' in *Collected Papers*, above n 105 at 231: 'Article 38 of the Statute of the Court, containing as it does an authoritative definition of the sources of international law, has done much to deprive [previous controversies on the subject]'.

for lack of a better option. Its authority as a list of sources springs principally from the absence of competing texts. This is not to say that article 38 does not play an important role. It filled a gap in 1945 and, since then, has enjoyed a very high 'pragmatic' status as a starting point for any discussion of sources.[110] The fact remains, however, that article 38 is first and foremost a clause of 'applicable law' that provides direction to the court and defines the various materials that it ought to take into account when deciding disputes submitted to it.[111] Nothing indicates that the drafters intended to give article 38 constitutional status or to provide an authoritative list of international law sources.[112]

The absence of a constitutional text defining in advance the sources of law is not necessarily a bar to the existence of a single legal system. Hart himself concedes that constitutions are a luxury found only in the most advanced and developed systems.[113] An autonomous and coherent system can therefore exist without a constitution, as long as a minimal consensus exists among legal actors as to the system's secondary rules, and in particular its formal sources.[114]

Yet no such consensus seems to exist in the field of international law. Beyond the ritual reference to article 38 of the ICJ Statute, all agreement among scholars and practitioners seems to vanish. The only point on which there is relative consensus is the fact that 'other sources' do exist beyond treaties and custom. That agreement ends, however, as soon as the identity and the nature of these sources are debated.[115]

This is true, first of all, of the other sources listed in article 38. Consider, for instance, the status of general principles of law. To some commentators, general principles are a source of law proper, with their own, autonomous criteria of validity: if a rule is recognised by all states *in foro domestico*, as part of their legal system, and if this rule is applicable in the realm of international relations, then it must be regarded as a valid rule of international law. It can thus be invoked directly by the parties to a dispute, independently of treaty and customary law.[116]

[110] On the 'pragmatic' value of art 38 as a rallying point for debates on the topic of sources (rather than as a meta-law on sources-creation) see Jorg Kammerhofer, *Uncertainty in International Law: A Kelsenian Perspective* (London, Routledge, 2011) 208–10.

[111] Alain Pellet, 'Article 38' in Andreas Zimmermann et al (eds), *The Statute of the International Court of Justice – A Commentary* (Oxford, Oxford University Press, 2006).

[112] Robert Jennings, 'General Course on Principles of International Law' (1967) 121 *Collected Courses of the Hague Academy of International Law* 9, 323–30. Fitzmaurice, 'Some Problems Regarding the Formal Sources of International Law', above n 108 at 160.

[113] See above n 33 and corresponding text.

[114] For an argument in this direction, see Michel Virally, 'The Sources of International Law' in Max Sorensen (ed), *Manual of Public International Law* (New York, St Martin Press, 1968) 119–20 (who claims that a stable system of secondary rules can emerge 'spontaneously' from the communal practice and relations of legal actors).

[115] Myres McDougal and Michael Reisman, 'The Prescribing Function in World Constitutive Process: How International Law is Made' (1980) 6 *Yale Studies in World Public Order* 249, 259–61.

[116] See, eg, Paul Guggenheim, 'Contribution à l'histoire des sources du droit des gens' (1958) 94 *Collected Courses of the Hague Academy of International Law* 1, 78; Jenning and Watts, *Oppenheim's International Law*, above n 105 at 29; Nguyen Quoc Dinh, Patrick Daillier and Alain Pellet, *Droit International Public*, 6th edn (Paris, LGDJ, 1999) 112–13; Dominique Carreau, *Droit international*, 5th edn (Paris, Pedone, 1997) 284–90.

Others, however, take the view that general principles are not an autonomous source of international law. It has been argued, for instance, that general principles are simply the expression of universal customary principles that are so widely accepted by the interpretative community (governments, judges, doctrine) that they become in some way evident and inherent to the international legal order. General principles, in this perspective, are not formally a law-making process but rather a set of undeniable or cardinal customs.[117] Equally, it has been argued that the reference to general principles in article 38 is best understood as a mandate given to the court to fill the lacunae in the body of treaty and customary rules. Here again, general principles are not construed as a source of law *per se*, but rather as a pool of implicit principles from which the judge can draw inspiration in areas where treaties and custom provide no guidance.[118]

The same type of controversy is found with regard to case law. Conventional wisdom has it that judicial decisions do not, in and of themselves, create new rules of international law. Instead, they constitute a method of ascertaining treaty and customary law.[119] Jurisprudence, in other words, is merely a source of identification or interpretation, rather than a formal source of norm-creation. Proponents of this position often acknowledge that judges are not simply phonographs that mechanically recite positive law and assert that decisions play an important role in the 'progressive development' of international law. Judges, it is argued, are like juridical 'midwives' helping to reveal or deliver norms-in-the-making.[120] The traditional position remains, however, that judicial decisions, authoritative though they may be, are merely 'statements' of the law or, as provided by article 38, 'subsidiary means for the determination of rules of law'.[121]

Others have argued, however, that in practice judicial decisions operate like sources of law proper and not merely as methods for ascertaining existing treaty or customary rules. International judges, they claim, are engaged in a creative activity and their function is not simply to apply existing rules to facts. More

[117] See, eg, Thomas Franck, 'Non-Treaty Law-Making: When, Where and How?' in Rüdiger Wolfrum and Volker Röben (eds), *Developments of International Law in Treaty Making* (Berlin, Springer, 2005) 423; Virally, 'The Sources of International Law', above n 114 at 144–46; Georges Scelle, *Manuel élémentaire de droit international public* (Paris, Montchrestien, 1944) 400.

[118] See, eg, Antonio Cassese, *International Law*, 2nd edn (Oxford, Oxford University Press, 2005) 188–89; Robert Kolb, 'Principles as Sources of International Law (With Special Reference to Good Faith)' (2006) 53 *Netherlands International Law Review* 1; Peter Malanczuk, *Akehurst's Modern Introduction to International Law*, 7th edn (London, Routledge, 1997) 48–49.

[119] See, eg, Jenning and Watts, *Oppenheim's International Law*, above n 105 at 25; Georg Scharzenberger, *International Law – Vol I: International Law as Applied by International Courts and Tribunals*, 3rd edn (London, Stevens, 1957) 26–28; Vladimir Degan, *Sources of International Law* (The Hague, Kluwer Law International, 1997) 14–17; Godefridus van Hoof, *Rethinking the Sources of International Law* (Deventer, Kluwer Law, 1983) 169–72; Joe Verhoeven, *Droit international public* (Brussels, Larcier, 2000) 314–15.

[120] Georges Abi-Saab, 'Cours général de droit international public' (1987) 207 *Collected Courses of the Hague Academy of International Law* 9, 133–34.

[121] See, eg, Louis Henkin, *International Law: Politics and Values* (Dordrecht, Martinus Nijhoff, 1995) 123; Daillier and Pellet, *Droit international public*, above n 116 at 394–95; Carreau, *Droit international*, above n 116 at 305–07.

importantly perhaps, their decisions are almost always regarded as binding 'precedents', whether it be upon other judges or upon states themselves, who generally refer to judicial decisions as elements of positive law.[122] Judicial decisions, in other words, do not simply exert authority over a given dispute. In a system lacking a single legislator with the power to make law for the community as a whole, judicial decisions are a primary form of law-making and their influence is far deeper than what article 38 suggests. For proponents of this position, the doctrinal orthodoxy is therefore misleading, for it ignores the fact that judicial decisions, in practice, do not merely state the law but create it, most notably in areas where treaties and customs are silent.[123]

The same could be said about doctrine as a source of international law, with some authors claiming that doctrine merely serves to 'reveal', 'disseminate' or 'digest' positive law,[124] whilst others argue that, in areas in which law is silent or uncertain, a 'good book' will often be regarded in Foreign Offices as an acceptable source of law (or legal justification).[125] The main point, however, has already been made: even within the limited confines of article 38, the question of sources is far from settled. Whilst relative consensus exists on the fact that treaties and custom are the two principal sources of international law, a question as fundamental as the status of judicial decisions remains unsettled, with persistent disagreement occurring among legal commentators, states and other actors.

Things become even more complicated at the level of the so-called 'other sources' of international law. From a fairly indeterminate terrain, the question of sources moves into radically open and uncertain territory. Consider, for instance, two of the classical 'candidate sources' of international law: unilateral acts of states and resolutions of international organisations. In both cases, international lawyers are in fundamental disagreement. To some, unilateral acts and resolutions possess normative value only if and to the extent that they fit traditional forms of treaty and customary law-making. Unilateral acts of states, for instance, are taken to 'make' law insofar as they express their author's

[122] See, eg, Mohamed Shahabuddeen, *Precedent in the World Court* (Cambridge, Cambridge University Press, 1996) 2–3; Brownlie, *Principles of Public International Law*, above at 105 at 19–23; Hersch Lauterpacht, *The Development of International Law by the International Court* (London, Stevens & Sons, 1958) 5; Rosalyn Higgins, *Problems and Process: International Law and How We Use It* (Oxford, Oxford University Press, 1993) 202.

[123] See, eg, Alan Boyle and Christine Chinkin, *The Making of International Law* (Oxford, Oxford University Press, 2007) 266–69; Malanczuk, *Akehurst's Modern Introduction to International Law*, above n 118 at 51; Lauterpacht, 'International Law – The General Part' in *Collected Papers*, above n 105 at 78–80.

[124] On the 'revealing' function of doctrine, see René-Jean Dupuy, 'La contribution de l'Académie au développement du droit international' (1973) 138 *Collected Courses of the Hague Academy of International Law* 45. On the 'digestive' function of doctrine, in the fragmentation context in particular, see Mario Prost and Julien Fouret, 'La multiplication des juridictions internationales: de la nécessité de remettre quelques pendules à l'heure' (2002) 15 *Revue Québécoise de Droit International* 117, 136–38.

[125] See Louis Sohn, 'Sources of International Law' (1996) 25 *Georgia Journal of International and Comparative Law* 399, 400–02.

consent to be bound by a rule and if tacit acceptance of that rule can also be inferred from the behaviour of other nations (in which case law is created by 'implicit contract').[126] Resolutions of international organisations, for their part, are regarded as manifestations of state practice that merely give shape to pre-existing or emerging customary rules.[127] To others, however, unilateral acts and resolutions are self-sufficient law-making processes. Unilateral acts, for instance, are said to bind their authors independently of the response they trigger in others and based only on the principles of good faith, security and predictability in international relations. Unilateral acts, in other words, are not simply implicit agreements. They possess their own logic and dynamic of validity.[128] As for resolutions of international organisations, it is thought that, under certain conditions of form, substance and procedure, they are able to create law in an autonomous and sometimes near-instantaneous fashion.[129] In both cases, these categories of actions are therefore regarded as sources of law proper.

All of this is well known and does not warrant further discussion here. It should be pointed out, however, that unilateral acts and resolutions are far from being the only points of contention regarding the 'other sources' of international law. Similar disputes arise periodically in relation to other acts or categories, without consensus ever emerging on their status as sources of law. One needs only think of state contracts,[130] articles and other texts adopted by the

[126] See, eg, Virally, 'The Sources of International Law', above n 114 at 154–55.

[127] See, eg, Jenning and Watts, *Oppenheim's International Law*, above n 105 at 45–49; Degan, *Sources of International Law*, above n 119 at 194–200; Blaine Sloan, 'General Assembly Resolutions Revisited (Forty Years Later)' (1987) 58 *British Yearbook of International Law* 39, 69. See also *Legality of the Threat or Use of Nuclear Weapons*, 8 July 1996, ICJ Reports (1996) 226, para 70: 'General Assembly resolutions, even if they are not binding, may sometimes have normative value. They can, in certain circumstances, provide evidence important for establishing the existence of a rule or the emergence of an *opinio juris*'.

[128] See, eg, Camille Goodman, 'Acta Sunt Servanda? A Regime for Regulating the Unilateral Acts of States at International Law' (2004) 25 *Australian Yearbook of International Law* 43; Higgins, *International Law and How We Use It*, above n 122 at 35–36. See also *Nuclear Tests Case (Australia v France)* 20 December 1974, ICJ Reports (1974) 253, paras 43–46: 'declarations made by way of unilateral acts . . . may have the effect of creating legal obligations . . . Nothing in the nature of a *quid pro quo* nor any subsequent acceptance of the declaration, nor even any reply or reaction from other States, is required for the declaration to take effect . . . Trust and confidence are inherent in international co-operation . . . Just as the very rule of *pacta sunt servanda* in the law of treaties is based on good faith, so also is the binding character of an international obligation assumed by unilateral declaration'.

[129] See, eg, José Alvarez, *International Organizations as Law-Makers* (Oxford, Oxford University Press, 2005); Erika de Wet, 'The Security Council as a Law-Maker: The Adoption of (Quasi)-Judicial Decision' in Rüdiger Wolfrum and Volker Röben (eds), *Developments of International Law in Treaty Making* (Berlin, Springer, 2005).

[130] The subject of state contracts has known a renewal of interest in light of recent developments in the law of investments. See, eg, Priscilla Leung and Guigo Wang, 'State Contracts in the Globalized World' (2006) 7 *Journal of World Investment and Trade* 829; James Crawford and Anthony Sinclair, 'The UNIDROIT Principles and their Application to State Contracts' (2002) *ICC International Court of Arbitration Bulletin* 57; AFM Maniruzzaman, 'State Contracts in Contemporary International Law: Monist v. Dualist Controversies' (2001) 12 *European Journal of International Law* 309.

International Law Commission,[131] or expert reports such as GATT and WTO panel reports.[132] Much discussion has also taken place around the status of transnational regulatory processes managed by non-state actors in specific sectors of the economy (trade, finance, sport, etc), which work 'like law' (rules are generally obeyed and social mechanisms are in place to sanction disobedience) and which often end up influencing official state-made international law.[133] More provocatively, an author recently argued that states might be assuming international obligations by the mere fact of 'applauding' at official intergovernmental gatherings.[134] Whilst the argument may seem odd, even a little eccentric, it shows how open the question of sources is and how much uncertainty remains with respect to the catalogue of law-making acts and processes in international law.

This first level of uncertainty concerns the *taxonomy* of sources. It is coupled, however, with another type of uncertainty that involves the very definition or criteria of international law sources. The most obvious example of this type of qualitative uncertainty is without a doubt that of customary international law (CIL). In fact, the case of custom is somewhat paradigmatic of the paradoxes of the conventional discourse on formal unity in international law. Indeed, it is often argued that CIL is of primary importance to the unity of international law, for it is the only source capable of producing 'general' law, whereas treaties merely fabricate particular obligations.[135] CIL, in other words, is said to enjoy a

[131] For the view that the work of the ILC goes beyond mere codification and contains elements of law-creation, see eg, Oscar Schachter, 'Recent Trends in International Law-Making' (1992) 12 *Australian Yearbook of International Law* 1, 2–7; Arthur Watts, *The International Law Commission: 1949–1998* (Oxford, Oxford University Press, 1999) 7–9; Robert Jennings, 'Recent Developments in the International Law Commission: Its Relation to the Sources of International Law' (1964) 18 *International and Comparative Law Quarterly* 385. *Contra*, and arguing that the work of the ILC is mostly doctrinal, see eg, Gerhard Hafner, 'The International Law Commission and the Future of Codification of International Law' (1992) 2 *ILSA Journal of International and Comparative Law* 671, 673–75; Donald McRae, 'The International Law Commission: Codification and Progressive Development after Forty Years' (1987) 25 *Canadian Yearbook of International Law* 355; André Oraison, 'La place de la Commission du droit international des Nations Unies au sein de la doctrine des publicistes les plus qualifiés des différentes nations' (1998) 76 *Revue de Droit International, de Sciences Diplomatiques et Politiques* 271.

[132] On this point, see eg, David Palmeter and Petros Mavroidis, 'The WTO Legal System: Sources of Law' (1998) 2 *American Journal of International Law* 398, 400–04; Lanye Zhu, 'The Effects of the WTO Dispute Settlement Panel and Appellate Body Reports: Is the Dispute Settlement Body Resolving Specific Disputes Only or Making Precedent at the Same Time?' (2003) 17 *Temple International and Comparative Law Journal* 221; John H Jackson, *The Jurisprudence of GATT and the WTO: Insights on Treaty Law and Economic Relations* (Cambridge, Cambridge University Press, 2007) 125–29.

[133] See, eg, Janet K Levit, 'A Bottom-Up Approach to International Law-Making: The Tale of Three Trade Finance Instruments' (2005) 30 *Yale Journal of International Law* 125; Eric A Feldman, 'The Tuna Court: Law and Norms in the World's Premier Fish Market' (2006) 94 *California Law Review* 313.

[134] Jordi Sellarés Serra, 'Applause as Unilateral Act (Is an Image Worth a Thousand Words?)' (2006) online paper available at: www.esil-sedi.eu/english/paris_agora_papers.html.

[135] Johathan Charney, 'Universal International Law' (1993) 87 *American Journal of International Law* 529; Josef Kunz, 'The Nature of Customary International Law' (1953) 47 *American Journal of International Law* 662. See also *North Sea Continental Shelf Cases (Federal Republic of Germany*

privileged status in the international order as the only form of global and uniform 'legislation' binding on all nations in the world.[136]

And yet custom remains one of the most enduring mysteries of international law. Though there is near-unanimity on the fact that it represents one of the 'main sources' of obligation in international law, the nature and exact working of custom continues to raise endless questions both in theory and in practice. We know, of course, that custom is different from treaties. It is not 'posited' by way of written agreement but instead arises spontaneously from regular patterns of behaviour which, over time, become legally binding rules of conduct. But when, why and how do regular behaviours become binding rules of conduct? How does one move from that which 'is' to that which 'must be'? These important questions form one of the most important enigmas of international law and, to this day, continue to fuel intense doctrinal interest, controversy and debate. Custom, in a way, seems as indispensable as it is unfathomable.[137]

Of course, a standard definition of custom has emerged over time that presents customary international law as relatively stable process in which rules are created by a combination of two elements: a general and consistent practice (material element) that states follow out of a sense of legal obligation (psychological element).[138] Beyond this point, however, confusion reigns. What, for instance, constitutes 'state practice'? Does practice only consists of material acts, that is, of actual things done by states?[139] Or does it also include declarations, claims and other verbal acts?[140] Do abstentions and omissions 'count' as state practice?[141] Can

v Denmark/Netherlands) 20 February 1969, ICJ Reports (1969) 3, para 63: 'customary law rules . . ., by their very nature, must have equal force for all members of the international community, and cannot therefore be the subject of any right of unilateral exclusion'.

[136] Brigitte Stern, 'Custom at the Heart of International Law' (2001) 11 *Duke Journal of Comparative and International Law* 89; Michael Reisman, 'The Cult of Custom in the Late 20th Century' (1987) 17 *California Western International Law Journal* 133.

[137] On this paradox, see Jack Goldsmith and Eric Posner, 'A Theory of Customary International Law' (1999) 66 *University of Chicago Law Review* 1113; David Filder, 'Challenging the Classical Concept of Custom: Perspectives on the Future of Customary International Law' (1997) 39 *German Yearbook of International Law* 198.

[138] *North Sea Continental Shelf Cases (Federal Republic of Germany v Denmark/Netherlands)* 20 February 1969, ICJ Reports (1969) 3, para 77: 'not only must the acts concerned amount to a settled practice, but they must also be such, or be carried out in such a way, as to be evidence of a belief that this practice is rendered obligatory by the existence of a rule of law requiring it'.

[139] For this argument, see eg, Anthony d'Amato, *The Concept of Custom in International Law* (Ithaca, Cornell University Press, 1971) 88–89; Hugh Thirlway, *International Customary Law and Codification* (Leiden, Sijthoff, 1972) 58; Karol Wolfke, *Custom in Present International Law* (Dordrecht, Martinus Nijhoff, 1993) 42–43.

[140] For this argument, see eg, Michael Akehurst, 'Custom as a Source of International Law' (1977) 47 *British Yearbook of International Law* 1, 3; Maurice Mendelson, 'The Formation of Customary International Law' (1999) 272 *Collected Courses of the Hague Academy of International Law* 165, 204–07; Mark Villiger, *Customary International Law and Treaties* (The Hague, Kluwer Law International, 1997) 20–21.

[141] Most authors take this view. See, eg, Akehurst, 'Custom as a Source of International Law', above n 140 at 10; Rudolf Bernhardt, 'Customary International Law' in Rudolf Bernhardt (ed), *Encyclopedia of Public International Law – Vol I* (Amsterdam, North-Holland, 1992) 900; Kunz, 'The Nature of Customary International Law', above n 135 at 666.

acts *contra legem* form precedents for the purpose of customary law?[142] How general and consistent must state practice be in order to satisfy the custom requirement? According to conventional wisdom, state practice must be widespread, uniform, and must emanate from an active and representative majority of states. But how many precedents are necessary, from how many states, and for how long?[143] Is the practice of some states more significant than that of other states?[144] Does the practice of non-state actors (international organisations, NGOs, individuals) have any impact on the formation of custom?[145] To all these questions, we have no definitive answers.

The notion of *opinio juris* is equally unsettled and paradoxical. For what, exactly, is this subjective or psychological element of conviction? Does it involve a conscientious and intentional act of will, or a more diffuse belief in the existence or the necessity of a rule?[146] If *opinio juris* is an expression of consent, does silence amount to implicit consent or acquiescence?[147] Can *opinio juris* be inferred from the consistent practice of states or from mere declarations?[148] Can

[142] For the argument that they can, see Thirlway, *International Customary Law and Codification*, above n 139 at 98. *Contra*, see Van Hoof, *Rethinking the Sources of International Law*, above n 119 at 277.

[143] The only agreement on this point seems to be that there is no 'statutory' period of time required for the emergence of a new customary norm and that the 'density' of practice matters more than its duration. See *North Sea Continental Shelf Cases (Federal Republic of Germany v Denmark/Netherlands)* 20 February 1969, ICJ Reports (1969) 3, para 74: 'the passage of only a short period of time is not necessarily, or of itself, a bar to the formation of a new rule of customary international law . . . An indispensable requirement would be that within the period in question, short though it might be, State practice . . . should have been both extensive and virtually uniform'.

[144] On this point, see especially Michael Byers, *Custom, Power and the Power of Rules: International Relations and Customary International Law* (Cambridge, Cambridge University Press, 1999).

[145] On this point, see eg, Christiana Ochoa, 'The Individual and Customary International Law Formation' (2007) 48 *Virginia Journal of International Law* 119; Jan Klabbers, 'International Organizations in the Formation of Customary International Law' in Enzo Cannizzaro and Paolo Palchetti (eds), *Customary International Law on the Use of Force: A Methodological Approach* (Leiden, Martinus Nijhoff, 2005).

[146] On *opinio juris* as a form of consent, see Olufemi Elias, 'The Nature of the Subjective Element in Customary International Law' (1995) 44 *International and Comparative Law Quarterly* 501; Gennadii Danilenko, *Law-Making in the International Community* (Dordrecht, Martinus Nijhoff, 1993) 253; Wolfke, *Custom in Present International Law*, above n 139 at 111–13. On *opinio juris* as belief or sense of obligation, see Degan, *Sources of International Law*, above n 119 at 162–64; Malanczuk, *Akehurst's Modern Introduction to International Law*, above n 118 at 44–45; Jennings and Watts, *Oppenheim's International Law*, above n 105 at 27–29.

[147] For the argument that *opinio juris* can be inferred form silence, see eg, Villiger, *Customary International Law and Treaties*, above n 140 at 19–21; Van Hoof, *Rethinking the Sources of International Law*, above n 119 at 219–20; IC MacGibbon, 'Customary International Law and Acquiescence' (1957) 33 *British Yearbook of International Law* 115. *Contra*, see eg, Anthea Roberts, 'Traditional and Modern Approaches to Customary International Law: A Reconciliation' (2001) 95 *American Journal of International Law* 757, 778; Georges Abi-Saab, 'The Democratization of Contemporary International Law-Making – Comment' in Rüdiger Wolfrum and Volker Röben (eds), *Developments of International Law in Treaty Making* (Berlin, Springer, 2005) 36.

[148] For the argument that it can, see eg, Peter Haggenmacher, 'La doctrine des deux elements du droit coutumier dans la pratique de la Cour internationale' (1986) 90 *Revue Générale de Droit International Public* 5; Brownlie, *Principles of Public International Law*, above n 105 at 131–33. *Contra*, see Akehurst, 'Custom as a Source of International Law', above n 140 at 50.

one object to the emergence of a customary rule?[149] In any event, is *opinio juris* a necessary, a sufficient or merely a secondary element of customary law-making?[150] On all these important questions, international law is again largely open and indeterminate.

CIL remains a fundamentally contested terrain. Custom appeals to international lawyers, for it suggests the possibility of creating law without, and perhaps even against, the will of states. Yet custom is a prime example of what Delmas-Marty calls 'fuzzy concepts', that is, concepts which, in spite of well-accepted referential points, lack a fixed, precise meaning (without being altogether meaningless).[151] Although lawyers know how to speak about custom, they struggle to comprehend it fully or to ground it in a stable and coherent theoretical framework. Despite periodic attempts by international law scholars to 'reform' and 're-found' customary international law, or to rescue it from its 'identity crisis',[152] custom is a puzzle made up of scattered and often contradictory doctrinal pieces.

Under these conditions, and absent universally recognised criteria of validity, 'finding' custom remains an uncertain, random, and to some extent intuitive task. It is, at any rate, a controversial enterprise. Nearly every time a judge or an international institution issues a decision based on custom, the same disputes arise. One needs only think of the sort of reactions triggered by the ICJ ruling in the *Nicaragua* case.[153] Despite the importance of the substantive issues raised in this case (use of force, self defence, territorial sovereignty, etc), many commentators focused their attention exclusively on the Court's use of international

[149] For the argument that persistent objection during the emergence of a new customary rule makes that rule inapplicable to the objecting state, see eg, Mendelson, 'The Formation of Customary International Law', above n 140 at 227–44; Villiger, *Customary International Law and Treaties*, above n 140 at 33–37; Wolfke, *Custom in Present International Law*, above n 139 at 66–67; Jennings and Watts, *Oppenheim's International Law*, above n 105 at 29. *Contra*, see eg, d'Amato, *The Concept of Custom in International Law*, above n 139 at 233–63; Ted Stein, 'The Approach of a Different Drummer: the Principle of the Persistent Objector in International Law' (1985) 26 *Harvard International Law Journal* 457; Jonathan Charney, 'The Persistent Objector Rule and the Development of Customary International Law' (1985) 56 *British Yearbook of International Law* 1.

[150] On *opinio juris* as a secondary element, see eg, Mendelson, 'The Formation of Customary International Law', above n 140; and Byers, *Custom, Power and the Power of Rules: International Relations and Customary International Law*, above n 144 (who both take the view that practice is what really matters and that *opinio juris* only serves to identify what does and does not count as 'precedent' for the purpose of custom). For the argument that *opinio juris* may be a necessary and sufficient element of custom, see especially, Bin Cheng, 'United Nations Resolutions on Outer Space: "Instant" International Customary Law?' (1965) 5 *Indian Journal of International Law* 23, 36: 'international law has in reality only one constitutive element, the *opinio juris*'.

[151] Mireille Delmas-Marty, *Le flou du droit – Du code penal aux droits de l'homme* (Paris, PUF, 2004).

[152] See, eg, Andrew Guzman, 'Saving Customary International Law' (2006) 27 *Michigan Journal of International Law* 115; Roberts, 'Traditional and Modern Approaches to Customary International Law: a Reconciliation', above n 147; Posner and Goldschmidt, 'A Theory of Customary International Law', above n 137; Edward Swaine, 'Rational Custom' (2002) 52 *Duke Law Journal* 559; George Norman and Joel Trachtman, 'The Customary International Law Game' (2005) 99 *American Journal of International Law* 541.

[153] *Case Concerning Military and Paramilitary Activities In and Against Nicaragua (Nicaragua v United States of America)* 27 June 1986, ICJ Reports (1986) 14.

law sources, and in particular on its method for proving the 'positivity' of the customary principle of non-intervention.[154] The Court was criticised for its 'revisionist' approach to custom, and for blurring the distinction between practice and *opinio juris*.[155] Some claimed that the Court had 'little idea' of what it was doing and blamed it for 'trashing' customary international law.[156] In any case, international lawyers' attention was directed principally at the criteria of custom as a formal category (that is, at its rule of recognition), rather than at the substance of customary rules.

More recently, the ICRC study on customary humanitarian law has prompted similar debates and reactions.[157] The ICRC study is the product of 10 years of codification. It identifies no less than 161 rules of international humanitarian law which, in the authors' view, have become customary and are therefore binding on all states, regardless of whether they have ratified the core conventions on the law of war (Hague and Geneva Conventions, additional protocols, etc). Yet again, despite the breadth and importance of the study, commentators have focused their attention almost exclusively on the definitions and methods used to prove the customary nature of the 161 rules, rather than on their substance or their consistency with state practice.[158] The study was criticised for oversimplifying custom and reducing it to the somewhat mechanical definition contained in article 38 of the ICJ Statute. Others criticised it for adopting an ambiguous position on some of the 'hard questions' pertaining to custom-formation (persistent objector, inconsistent practice, role of resolutions and of judicial decisions, etc).[159] At stake in these conversations are not the rules, their content, or even the admissibility of the evidence produced to establish their positivity. Instead, discussions invariably concentrate on the rules for recognising a valid rule of customary international law.

[154] See, eg, Wladislaw Czaplinski, 'Sources of International Law in the Nicaragua Case' (1989) 38 *International and Comparative Law Quarterly* 151.

[155] See, eg, Hillary Charlesworth, 'Customary International Law and the Nicaragua Case' (1991) 11 *Australian Yearbook of International Law* 1; PP Rijpkema, 'Customary International Law in the Nicaragua Case' (1989) 20 *Netherlands Yearbook of International Law* 91.

[156] Anthony d'Amato, 'Trashing Customary International Law' (1987) 81 *American Journal of International Law* 101.

[157] Jean-Marie Henckaerts and Louise Doswald-Beck (eds), *Customary International Humanitarian Law – Volume I: Rules* (Cambridge, Cambridge University Press, 2009).

[158] For an analysis focused on the rules themselves, see however, Elizabeth Wilmshurst and Susan Breau (eds), *Perspectives on the ICRC Study on Customary International Humanitarian Law* (Cambridge, Cambridge University Press, 2007).

[159] See, among others, Claude Emanuelli, 'L'étude du CICR sur le droit humanitaire coutumier: la coutume en question' (2006) 110 *Revue Générale de Droit International Public* 435; Yoram Dinstein, 'The ICRC Customary International Humanitarian Law Study' (2006) 36 *Israel Yearbook on Human Rights* 1; John Bellinger and William Haynes, 'A US Government Response to the ICRC Study on Customary International Humanitarian Law' (2007) 89 *International Review of the Red Cross* 443; Michael Cowling, 'International Lawmaking in Action: the 2005 Customary International Humanitarian Law Study and Non-International Armed Conflicts' (2006) *African Yearbook on International Humanitarian Law* 65; Robert Cryer, 'Of Custom, Treaties, Scholars and the Gavel: the Influence of the International Criminal Tribunals on the ICRC Customary Law Study' (2006) 11 *Journal of Conflict and Security Law* 239.

Basdevant wrote in 1936 that 'lawyers' ideas about the character of custom have reached neither unity nor clarity'.[160] More than 70 years later, the epistemological uncertainty that characterises custom has not disappeared. In fact, this uncertainty is so pervasive and enduring that some have started questioning the relevance, or even the possibility, of referring to custom as a source of international law.[161] My intention here is not to advance this type of argument but merely to stress the fact that, despite the permanence of certain themes or concepts (practice, *opinio juris*, persistent objector) and of certain standards (generality, consistency or density of practice), custom is still in search of its rule of recognition. In other words, whilst we may know the basic ingredients of custom, its recipe remains to be found.[162]

The question of sources, as the above demonstrates, forms a contested and indeterminate terrain in which pockets of coherence (law of treaties in particular) cannot hide the vast disagreements that continue to exist, both on the taxonomy and on the test of validity of formal law-making processes. Whether an effective *system* of sources exists in international law therefore remains a controversial matter. The doctrine of sources, it would seem, merely consists in a series of arguments and counterarguments that share a relatively stable conceptual apparatus (treaty, custom, consent, general practice, *opinio juris*, unilateral act, precedent, codification, progressive development, etc) but can hardly be said to form a consistent or coherent normative discourse.

To be sure, certain argumentative patterns or recurrences emerge amid this doctrinal disorder. The doctrine of sources, in particular, is structured by the tension between two principal lines or styles of argument: the 'hard' or 'apologetic' line, which seeks to explain law's bindingness by linking it to the 'consent' of the state; and the 'soft' or 'utopian' line, in which the authority of norms is said to spring from extraconsensual notions of justice or security.[163] Any argument about sources is in some sense an attempt to mediate between these contradictory and conflicting justifications. An argument that grounds custom in patterns of behaviour ('soft' argument) will often be balanced by the notion that a state's persistent objection renders custom inapplicable to it ('hard' argument). A scholar who argues that custom is principally grounded in *opinio juris*, understood as an intentional act of will ('hard' argument) will often concede that this intent need only be present in a majority of states and can in any case

[160] Jules Basdevant, 'Règles générales du droit de la paix' (1936) 58 *Collected Courses of the Hague Academy of International Law* 471, 508.

[161] See, eg, Patrick Kelly, 'The Twilight of Customary International Law' (2000) 40 *Virginia Journal of International Law* 449.

[162] For an analysis of what this uncertainty means for international legal theory as a whole, see Jörg Kammerhofer, 'Uncertainty in the Formal Sources of International Law: Customary International Law and Some of Its Problems' (2004) 15 *European Journal of International Law* 525.

[163] On the tension between 'hard' and 'soft' sources arguments, see David Kennedy, 'The Sources of International Law' (1987) 2 *American University Journal of International Law and Policy* 1. On the oscillation between the 'apologetic' and 'utopian' modes of argument, see Koskenniemi, *From Apology to Utopia*, above n 99.

be inferred from general practice ('soft' argument). An argument about treaty law will typically begin with the notion that states are bound by treaties because they have consented to them ('hard' argument) before observing that states, once bound by a treaty, cannot withdraw their consent, or else security and trust in international relations would be compromised ('soft' argument).

In a way, this dialectical tension between rhetorical modes or strategies gives the doctrine of sources a dynamic structure, that is, a certain form. This ordering of discourse, however, does not mean that a stable set of secondary norms exists in international law. Even if these dialectical regularities are thought of as constituting a form of unity, this type of unity primarily attaches to international law as a discipline or as a field of discourse, not as a legal system in the Hartian sense.[164] The argumentative terrain is in a sense 'bounded' by the hard and soft rhetorical 'poles'. The production of juridical discourse is controlled and policed by the existence of a finite number of argumentative strategies. The practice of argumentation about international law sources is thus, in a way, *disciplined*. But the object and purpose of this practice remain, at their core, highly indeterminate. The question of the validity of international law norms is in no way resolved by these discursive dynamics, however recursive and standardised they may be. The continued and regular movement of the sources debate between the state and the community, consent and justice, normativity and concreteness, does create a sense of 'boundedness' or 'finiteness'. The image is misleading, however. The 'who', the 'what', the 'why' and the 'how' of law-making remain outstanding issues in international law, that is, questions without definitive or unequivocal answers. And it can hardly be otherwise, for whoever *settles* for one or the other mode of argumentation is inescapably exposed to challenges from the other extreme of the argumentative spectrum. A doctrine of sources that grounds validity or authority exclusively in states and what they do or say will be rejected as apologetic. Conversely, a doctrine that locates the source of validity or authority solely in *a priori* normative standards of justice, equity, trust or predictability will be rejected as utopian. To be accepted, or acceptable, any sources argument must therefore remain open and continually navigate along the consent-justice continuum. Consent, in other words, must always be justified by reference to justice, and justice by reference to consent.[165]

International law is thus characterised by the lack of a superior 'meta-law' on sources, that is, a determinate and authoritative account of how, and according to which formal criteria, law is made. This indeterminacy is in fact so inherent to international law that lawyers – who always seek to capture the world around them in finite and rational categories – gave it a name. When referring to this grey area of normativity that lies between evidently valid positive law and that which is categorically non-legal, international lawyers were the first to coin the

[164] See the next chapter on cultural unity.

[165] Koskenniemi, *From Apology to Utopia*, above n 99 at 387.

concept of 'soft law'.[166] My intention here is not to address a concept that others have already debated at length.[167] My point is simply that international law is so replete with acts, categories and processes whose status is tainted by uncertainty that international lawyers have deemed it necessary to develop new concepts to speak about them.

All of this takes us back to the initial suggestion that international lawyers simultaneously know a great deal and very little about sources. This section has shown that uncertainty infuses nearly every level of the sources question. Admittedly, the law of treaties represents a core of certainty, which the Vienna Convention helped to solidify. The conventional tree, however, cannot hide the forest of perennial and unanswered questions that continue to obscure the issue of international law sources. This uncertainty or indeterminacy may not be, as some have suggested, a serious pathology that compromises international law's ability to function as an instrument of social organisation.[168] To be sure, the absence of a binary code of validity/invalidity, or of a rigid and predetermined system of secondary rules of recognition, does raise certain practical issues for the 'consumers' of international law. The indeterminacy of the meta-rules of norm-production makes it more difficult, in particular, for legal subjects to predict with some degree of certainty what legal consequences might ensue from their actions.[169] The fact remains, however, that states continue to communicate, trade and settle their disputes under the rule of international law. If one thing is clear today, it is precisely that states, far from turning their back on international law, increasingly use – some would say abuse – its processes, giving rise to an ever greater number of rules, institutions and tribunals at every level of governance (national, bilateral, regional, international and global). Although this phenomenon of 'legalisation' is not uniform and tends to vary from one sector to another, it suggests that states – international law's main 'consumers' – can live with the practical difficulties posed by the indeterminacy of its formal sources.

Though not insurmountable from a practical perspective, the difficulties posed by indeterminacy are perhaps more serious from a theoretical point of

166 On the intellectual history of soft law and its progressive dissemination outside of the international law domain, see Anna di Robilant, 'Genealogies of Soft Law' (2006) 54 *American Journal of Comparative Law* 499.

167 See, eg, Richard Baxter, 'International Law in "Her Infinite Variety"' (1980) 29 *International and Comparative Law Quarterly* 549; Christine Chinkin, 'The Challenge of Soft Law: Development and Change in International Law' (1989) 38 *International and Comparative Law Quarterly* 850; Jan Klabbers, 'The Undesirability of Soft Law' (1998) 67 *Nordic Journal of International Law* 381; Alan Boyle, 'Soft Law' in Malcolm Evans (ed), *International Law* (Oxford, Oxford University Press, 2006); Jean d'Aspremont, 'Softness in International Law: A Self-Serving Quest for New Legal Materials' (2008) 19 *European Journal of International Law* 1075.

168 See Prosper Weil, 'Towards Relative Normativity in International Law' (1983) 77 *American Journal of International Law* 413.

169 On this point, see eg, Joost Pauwelyn, *Conflict of Norms in Public International Law: How WTO Rules Relate to Other Rules of International Law* (Cambridge, Cambridge University Press, 2003) 91–93; Dupuy, 'L'unité de l'ordre juridique international', above n 68 at 204–05; Koskenniemi, *From Apology to Utopia*, above n 99 at 564–65.

view. In particular, the argument that law is formally unitary 'because it is endowed with a system of secondary norms of production'[170] is not easily won in the field of international law. Certainty and determinacy, of course, are never absolute and are always open to some questioning. Hart himself, it will be recalled, concedes that a 'fringe of vagueness' is bound to exist in any legal system. The fact remains, however, that from a Hartian point of view, a coherent system of secondary rules will only exist if uncertainty is marginal and if secondary rules, in particular rules of recognition, provide clear and accurate answers to the question of validity. Yet what emerges from the above analysis is that uncertainty lies at the very heart of norm-production in international law, not merely at the borderline. The question of where international law comes from and how it is made continues, in the early twenty-first century, to occupy international lawyers' minds with remarkable consistency. A sort of architecture does of course exist within the sources doctrine. But this architecture rests mostly on the fluid dynamics of juridical discourse (that is, of doctrine) rather than on the stability or steadiness of its object (that is, of sources). These internal structures may represent, as will be discussed in the next chapter, elements of what I call *cultural* unity, that is, a sort of unity that attaches to international law as an argumentative practice. This, however, is something fundamentally different from formal unity in the Hartian sense of the term.

My point here is not to rebuff, once and for all, the idea that a stable and coherent system of secondary rules does or can exist in international law. Custom, general principles or unilateral acts may one day reach a degree of determinacy comparable to that which exists in relation to treaties. In fact, one could even argue that the law of treaties is, in and of itself, a sufficiently well-established and determinate 'island of predictability' so as to constitute a source of formal unity in international law. It is in these terms, however, that the question of formal unity ought to be addressed and debated. One cannot simply posit that a system of secondary rules exists in international law, unless of course unity is viewed as an epistemological postulate, that is, as a necessary condition of juridical reasoning that commands to look at all things legal *as if* they were part of a single system. But unity, thus understood, becomes a *principle of interpretation* rather than an empirical fact, and one moves further away from the notion of formal unity as understood by Hart.

Using Hart's theory to debate law's unity therefore requires us to look at the hard issue of determinacy. This is especially true in international law, where this question is exceedingly complex, open and controversial. One cannot simply discard controversies about sources, as suggested by some, as mere 'doctrinal quarrels that have for long hindered reflection on norm-creation in international law'.[171] These controversies, in a sense, make up the doctrine of sources. To ignore them would be to ignore the question of law-making altogether.

[170] See above n 69 and corresponding text.
[171] Dupuy, 'L'unité de l'ordre juridique international', above n 68 at 119.

IV. ISSUES OF ACCEPTANCE: THE INTERNATIONAL ISLAMIC COURT OF JUSTICE AND THE SHARI'A AS THE ULTIMATE RULE OF RECOGNITION

It will be remembered that determinacy is not the only 'hard' question that Hart envisages as part of his theory of the legal system. Even if a legal order is endowed with a fairly stable set of secondary rules of recognition, change and adjudication, Hart insists that it will only be possible to speak of a single and coherent legal system if these rules are generally and uniformly accepted by the system's officials. Here again, this element of acceptance cannot be easily assumed to exist in international law, at least not in the same terms as in domestic legal systems.

This is not to say that the uniform acceptance of secondary rules is a given in domestic systems. But external signs of adherence to secondary rules are abundant and give unity a form of immediateness that is perhaps not present in international law. When the American President takes office, to use a well-known example, he is required under the Constitution to take an oath to 'faithfully execute the Office of President of the United States and . . . to the best of [his] ability, preserve, protect and defend the Constitution of the United States'.[172] Likewise, Federal Judges are required to take an oath of office in which they pledge to 'administer justice . . . and discharge and perform all the duties incumbent upon [them] under the Constitution of the United States'.[173] Similar examples can be found in virtually every legal system in the world. Every time, the system's officials pledge loyalty and allegiance to their people, their sovereign and their constitution.

'Fidelity', 'loyalty' and 'allegiance': the oath of office expresses, in a symbolic and ritualised manner, the adherence of the officials to the Constitution and their acceptance of the secondary rules of the system as official and legitimate standards. The situation is different in international law, however. Oaths and swearing-ins do of course exist at the international level. International judges and civil servants, like their domestic counterparts, usually take an oath when entering into office. International oaths of office, however, do not reflect a level of acceptance comparable to that found in domestic systems. Often, these oaths merely emphasise the independence of international officials vis-a-vis their national governments and contain habitual clauses of impartiality, integrity and confidentiality.[174] When officials do pledge a form of allegiance, it is generally to

[172] Constitution of the United States of America, art II, s 1.

[173] See www.law.cornell.edu/uscode/html/uscode28/usc_sec_28_00000453----000-.html.

[174] See, eg, International Court of Justice: 'I solemnly declare that I will perform my duties and exercise my powers as judge honourably, faithfully, impartially and conscientiously' (Rules of Court, 14 April 1978, art 4); International Criminal Court: 'I solemnly undertake that I will perform my duties and exercise my powers as a judge . . . honourably, faithfully, impartially and consci-

their own particular institution, rather than to the international legal order as a whole (and its secondary rules).[175]

The issue of acceptance, needless to say, is not limited to the symbolic ritual of the oath of office. Acceptance is found, above all, in the continuous and day-to-day attitude of officials towards the system's secondary rules. In international law, the existence of a 'general and uniform acceptance' cannot be taken for granted. International officials do seem to speak the same language of sovereignty and jurisdiction, consent and validity, treaties and customs, etc. But does this common conceptual or grammatical apparatus necessarily signal a shared feeling of belonging to a single system and a shared acceptance of its secondary rules?

This is a very complicated question, the answer to which would demand a systematic examination and interpretation of international officials' practice. For obvious reasons of time and space, this examination cannot be undertaken in the present section. What I shall attempt to do instead is to show, through a concrete example, the type of questions that Hart's theory of acceptance, if taken seriously, raises in an international law context. I shall also seek to show that, despite the presence of many signs of acceptance of public international law's secondary rules, periodic signs of defiance, objection or simply distancing vis-a-vis these rules can also be observed. Whether these signs mean that international law lacks formal unity is of course a subjective and debatable point. But these signals cannot be completely ignored, or discourses on unity risk being biased or hegemonic.

These themes will be explored through an example which, to date, has received virtually no attention in international law scholarship: the constitution of an International Islamic Court of Justice (IICJ).[176] That the IICJ has received little attention is perhaps best explained by the fact that this new tribunal has yet to be formally set up. The IICJ may in fact never see the light of day, or at least not in the near future, due mostly to contradictions inherent in the Organisation of the Islamic Conference (OIC), the IICJ's parent institution. Though not yet in force, the Statute of the IICJ does, however, reveal a particular attitude towards the sources and foundation of international law. The Statute provides, among other things, that the supreme source of validity of international obligations lies in the Shari'a, or Islamic law. Though the practical consequences of this provision

entiously, and that I will respect the confidentiality of investigations and prosecutions and the secrecy of deliberation' (Rules of Procedure and Evidence, 9 September 2002, Rule 5).

[175] See, for instance, the UN Secretary General's oath of office: 'I solemnly swear to exercise in all loyalty, discretion and conscience, the functions entrusted to me as Secretary General of the United Nations, to discharge these functions and regulate my conduct with the interests of the United Nations only in view, and not to seek or accept instructions in regard to the performance of my duties from any government or other authority external to the organisation' (at www.un.org/apps/news/infocusRel.asp?infocusID=122&Body=Ban+Ki-moon).

[176] To my knowledge, the only (descriptive) study published on the IICJ is Michele Lombardini, 'The International Islamic Court of Justice: Towards an International Islamic Legal System?' (2001) 14 *Leiden Journal of International Law* 665.

remain to be seen, the Statute denotes a clear departure from the secular approach prevailing in modern international law. The creation of the Court, if confirmed, may epitomise, if only symbolically, the emergence of a new sphere of normativity, that is, of an Islamic international law applicable between Muslim nations and distinct from public international law as we know it today. To understand this better, it may be useful to situate the genesis of the Court in its wider historical, political and juridical contexts.

A. International law, modernity and secularism

Though international law and religion have historically had a close relationship, this relationship has received little attention from modern legal scholars. This lack of interest may be explained by the lasting influence of classical positivism and its effort to turn international law into a 'science'. Studying law as a science has meant, for most scholars in the nineteenth and twentieth centuries, ridding it of its 'impurities', and most notably of its moral and religious content.[177] But this lack of interest may be due also to the fact that international law's modern history has in large part been the history of its separation from religion.[178] For a long time, the history of international law has been that of European Christianity. This is not to say that no trace of international law could be found before the emergence of Christian Europe. The Egyptian papyruses, the Babylonian tablets or the Laws of Hammurabi teach us that all civilisations have had relations with the outside world and that they have developed rules, customs and standards to regulate their international relations (sanctity of international agreements, protection of diplomats, treatment of prisoners of wars, etc).[179]

It is commonly agreed, however, that most of what we regard as international law today originated in the second half of the Middle Ages, in Christian Europe.[180] During this foundational period, international law was developed under the direct influence of the Catholic Church and natural law theories. Legal discourse was above all a religious discourse. Suarez and Vittoria, the 'founding fathers' of international law, were both theologians. Even Grotius – a jurist, a diplomat and an early 'seculariser' of international law – made ample use of religious sources to

[177] Mark Janis, 'Preface' in Mark Janis (ed), *The Influence of Religion on the Development of International Law* (Dordrecht, Martinus Nijhoff, 1991) xi.

[178] See Leo Gross, *Essays in International Law and Organization* (The Hague, Martinus Nijhoff, 1984) 9–12.

[179] See Serge Koff, 'Introduction à l'histoire du droit international' (1923) 1 *Collected Courses of the Academy of International Law* 5; David Bederman, 'Religion and the Sources of International Law in Antiquity' in Janis (ed), *The Influence of Religion on the Development of International Law*, above n 177.

[180] Jan Hendrik Willem Verzijl, *International Law in Historical Perspective* (Leiden, Sijthoff, 1968) 444.

develop his law of nature and of nations.[181] Traditionally, international law was thus a discipline of canonists and theologians, deeply rooted in religious principles. International law was conceived of as an instrument of Christian unification, as well as being used to regulate the relations between Christian nations and the rest of the world. In any case, religion formed the primary source of inspiration, validity and sanction of international obligations. Treaties, for instance, were regarded as 'binding' because they were concluded under oath, the violation of which constituted perjury liable to divine punishment.[182]

International law as we know it today, however, is different from this law of Christianity. Despite the lack of a universally accepted definition, international law is generally thought of as the set of norms that governs the relations between nation-states, which are understood as unitary, independent and sovereign political entities. At the heart of the modern conception of international law lies the notion that states mutually recognise each other's right to exist as neighbours, partners and full members of the international community, regardless of their political, economic, social or religious systems.[183]

This post-medieval vision of international law owes much to the 1648 Treaties of Westphalia, which ended the Thirty Years War in Europe. The treaties of Osnabrück and Münster contain three cardinal principles that marked international law's entry into modernity: the separation between the domestic and the international spheres, the equal dignity of all nations, and their free exercise

[181] According to Grotius, the basis of international law was to be found in the laws of nature given to men by God. Thus, for Grotius, the reason for international law's binding character was ultimately Divine will: 'we must without exception render obedience to God as our Creator, to whom we owe all that we are and have; especially since, in manifold ways, He has shown Himself supremely good and supremely powerful, so that to those who obey Him He is able to give supremely great rewards . . . Herein, then, is another source of law besides the source in nature, that is, the free will of God, to which beyond all cavil our reason tells us we must render obedience'; Hugo Grotius, *Prolegomena to the Law of War and Peace* (Indianapolis, Bobbs-Merrill Company, 1957) 9. To be sure, Grotius also found that man's sociability and his desire for security were important sources of law. Yet for Grotius, these human instincts were again the product of Divine will: 'the Author of nature willed that as individuals we should be weak, and should lack many things needed in order to live properly, to the end that we might be the more constrained to cultivate the social life'; ibid at 11. On the persistence of theological sources and reasoning in Grotius' work, see William George, 'Grotius, Theology, and International Law: Overcoming Textbook Bias' (1999) 14 *Journal of Law and Religion* 605.

[182] Grotius, *Law of War and Peace*, above n 181 at 423: 'the sanctity of an oath with regard to promises, agreements, and contracts, has always been held in the greatest esteem, in every age and among every people. For as Sophocles has said in his Hippodomia, "the Soul is bound to greater caution by the addition of an oath. For it guards us against two things, most to be avoided, the reproach of friends, and the wrath of heaven". In addition to which the authority of Cicero may be quoted, who says, our forefathers intended that an oath should be the best security for sincerity of affirmation, and the observance of good faith. "For, as he observes in another place, there can be no stronger tie, to the fulfillment of our word and promise, than an oath, which is a solemn appeal to the testimony of God"'.

[183] This principle figures prominently in the Declaration on Principles of International Law Concerning Friendly Relations and Cooperation among States, UN General Assembly Resolution 2625, UN Doc A/8082 (24 October 1970): 'all states enjoy sovereign equality. They have equal rights and duties and are equal members of the international community, notwithstanding differences of an economic, social, political or other nature'.

of territorial sovereignty.[184] The Westphalian project thus stands in stark contrast to international law's medieval past. In a sense, it marks a turn *against* this medieval past. The dominant idea in 1648 was that the political organisation of Europe was prone to conflict and that involving religion in political affairs would inevitably lead to more intolerance, violence and war. The decision was therefore taken to re-found Europe and re-organise it outside of religion. The new *modus operandi* consisted, for the most part, in decoupling international relations from the papacy and the empire. The influence of these two institutions, needless to say, did not dissipate overnight.[185] But in order to free international relations from their old medieval structures, a new entity was consecrated: the nation-state. And this new entity was clothed with an essential attribute: sovereignty, that is, independence from outside interference (including religion).

With the Treaties of Westphalia, international relations were thus understood to operate horizontally between sovereign equals, regardless of their internal constitution.[186] European nations renounced violence among themselves and sought to establish new power equilibriums through dialogue and negotiation.[187] Diplomacy, in a sense, replaced supremacy and international law was no longer perceived as a set of divine natural laws but rather as a system of practices and obligations into which nation-states had freely 'contracted'.[188]

From that point onwards, international law reinvented itself on rational and secular bases. Changes occured slowly and religion was not completely evicted from international relations. European nations, in particular, continued to use religion as a justification for empire and colonialism in the rest of the non-European world. In the European context, however, religion was sent back into the internal sphere of nation-states and international law was no longer

[184] The full text of the Westphalian Treaties is available in Latin, French and English as part of the *Acta Pacis Westphalicae* online project at: www.pax-westphalica.de.

[185] On the persistence, after the Westphalian moment, of a multi-layered system of authority in Europe, see Stephane Beaulac, 'The Westphalian Legal Orthodoxy – Myth or Reality?' (2000) 2 *Journal of the History of International Law* 148.

[186] See Treaty of Osnabrück, art V, 1–2: 'whereas the grievances of the one and the other Religion . . . have been partly the cause and occasion of the present war, it has been agreed and transacted in the following manner . . . That there be an exact and reciprocal equality amongst all the Electors, Princes and States of both Religions . . . so that what is just of one side shall be so of the other, all violence and force between the two parties being for ever prohibited'.

[187] It was all the more easy for European nations to recognise each other's right to sovereign authority that new territories were open to colonial conquest outside of Europe. For a critical analysis of the link between Westphalian sovereignty and the colonial project, see especially Antony Anghie, *Imperialism, Sovereignty and the Making of International Law* (Cambridge, Cambridge University Press, 2005).

[188] Treaty of Osnabrück, art IV, 46: 'Contracts, exchanges, transactions, obligations, and promises illegally extorted, by violence and threats . . . shall be abolished and annulled, so that it shall not be lawful for any person to commence an action or process upon that score'; art VIII, 2: 'each of the estates of the empire shall freely and forever enjoy the right of making alliances among themselves, or with foreigners, for the preservation and security of every one of them, provided nevertheless that these alliances . . . be made without prejudice in every respect to the oath whereby every one of them is bound'.

apprehended as the earthly expression of God's will.[189] International law became a man-made vocabulary of diplomacy used to normalise and standardise the mutual relations between territorial – as opposed to religious – entities.

This is not to say, of course, that modern international law is uninterested in religious matters. For instance, several international instruments do deal with issues such as freedom or religion or the protection of religious minorities.[190] One can also find traces of international law's religious past in recurring themes, principles, categories or even in certain treaty provisions.[191] The fact remains, however, that religion is no longer apprehended as a source and foundation of international law. Or if it is, it is only occasionally and anecdotally, as a background reference, in areas in which positive law is incomplete, or as if to add a little more 'soul' to a discipline which positivism and excessive formalism, according to some, have rendered soulless.[192]

In a sense, the history of international law is thus the history of its disenchantment. Religion, which has for long represented a totalising explanation and an ultimate foundation for all things legal, has been progressively marginalised, privatised and nationalised. International law is no longer the domain of canonists and theologians but has become a discipline of lawyers and diplomats. Neither is it any longer regarded as a branch of natural law. International law has become a technical, rational, man-made tool of social organisation.

This way of telling the history of international law is of course debatable. Sacralising international law as a pure product of reason may, in itself, constitute a new form of theology.[193] The fact remains, however, that departing from

[189] The treaties of Westphalia provide for the free exercise of religion – whether Catholic or Protestant – in all European nations. See Treaty of Osnabrück, art IV, 19: 'those of the confession of Augsburg . . . shall be preserved and maintained in the ecclesiastical state of the year 1624. And it shall be allowable for others who are willing to embrace the exercise of the Augsburg confession, to practice it, as well publicly in the Churches at set hours, as in private in their own houses'.

[190] See, eg, Universal Declarations of Human Rights, UNGA Resolution 217 (III), UN Doc A/810 (10 December 1948), art 18; International Covenant on Civil and Political Rights, 16 December 1966, 999 UNTS 171, art 18; International Covenant on Economic, Social and Cultural Rights, 16 December 1966, 993 UNTS 3, art 2; Convention Relating to the Status of Refugees, 28 July 1951, 189 UNTS 2545, Arts 1 & 4; European Convention on Human Rights and Fundamental Freedoms, 4 November 1950, 213 UNTS 221, art 9; American Convention on human Rights, 22 November 1969, 1144 UNTS 123, art 12; African Charter of Human and Peoples' Rights, 27 June 1981, 1520 UNTS 217, art 8.

[191] The Covenant of the League of Nations, for instance, made reference to the wellbeing and the development of peoples 'not yet able to stand by themselves under the strenuous conditions of the modern world' as forming a 'sacred trust of civilisation' (Covenant of the League of Nations, 28 June 1919, art 22). Similarly, the UN Charter proclaims the 'faith' of its founding members in the dignity and the worth of the human person (Charter of the United Nations, 26 June 1945, preamble).

[192] See, eg, *Case Concerning the Gabcikovo-Nagymaros Project (Hungary v Slovakia)* Separate Opinion of Vice-President Weeramantry, 25 September 1997, ICJ Reports (1997) 88 (in which Justice Weeramantry refers to a number of philosophical, cultural and religious traditions in its finding that 'sustainable development' forms part of customary international law. Weeramantry denounces the 'attitudes of formalism' that prevail in the discipline and that minimise the importance of these traditions as 'legitimate sources for the enrichment of international law').

[193] On this point, see David Kennedy, 'Images of Religion in International Legal Theory' in Janis (ed), *The Influence of Religion on the Development of International Law*, above n 177 at 137–46.

religion has had a defining influence on the modern discipline of international law. This narrative has, at any rate, largely penetrated international lawyers' collective consciousness.

B. Precarious man, postmodernity and the resurgence of religion

In Law as in other social sciences, it has been thought for some time that this movement of secularisation was an irrepressible and irreversible trend. This belief owes much to the great thinkers of modernity, who nearly unanimously prophesised the progressive death of religion in developed, industrialised societies.[194] The religious question, however, may have been forgotten a little too quickly and, since the late 1980s, there are many who speak of a 'resurgence' of religion in the public sphere, both domestically and internationally.[195]

This global resurgence of religion can be observed at nearly every level of society and on the five continents: the Iranian Revolution of 1979; the role of the Catholic Church in the 'third wave' of democratisation in Eastern Europe, Latin-America and Africa; the spectacular rise of evangelical movements in South-America; Hindu and Sikh radicalism in India; Jewish extremism in Israel; the 'Islamisation' of Palestinian nationalism; the assassination of Theo Van Gogh in the Netherlands; Danish cartoons, etc. The resurgence of religion, it must be noted, is not always conflictual or violent. At times, this resurgence is recognised and internalised by secular powers as an ordinary element of the political process (for example, the policy of 'reasonable accommodation' in Canada). Occasionally, the resurgence of religion may even manifest itself in a more positive way, for instance by playing an important role in the resolution of certain disputes (for example, the role of Desmond Tutu in the peace and reconciliation process in South Africa).

Although varied and complex, these examples all demonstrate the refusal of religious movements to see their role limited to the private sphere and to pastoral or spiritual questions. Though far from uniform, the resurgence of religion

[194] Voltaire, Nietzsche, Comte, Durkheim, Weber, Marx or Freud all shared the belief that, in an age of enlightenment, reason would necessarily supplant religion as the foundation of human intelligence and governance.

[195] Scott Thomas, *The Global Resurgence of Religion and the Transformation of International Relations: The Struggle for the Soul of the Twenty-First Century* (New York, Palgrave Macmillan, 2005); David Zeidan, *The Resurgence of Religion: A Comparative Study of Selected Themes in Christian and Islamic Fundamentalist Discourse* (Leiden, Brill, 2003); Jonathan Fox and Shmuel Sandler, *Bringing Religion Into International Relations* (New York, Palgrave Macmillan, 2006); Fabio Petito and Pavlos Hatzopoulos (eds), *Religion in International Relations: The Return From Exile* (New York, Palgrave Macmillan, 2003); David Westerlund (ed), *Questioning the Secular State: The Worldwide Resurgence of Religion in Politics* (London, Hurst & Co, 1996); Emile Sahliyeh (ed), *Religious Resurgence and Politics in the Contemporary World* (New York, SUNY Press, 1990); Martin Riesebrodt, 'Fundamentalism and the Resurgence of Religion' (2000) 47 *Numen* 266; James Rinehart, 'Religion in World Politics: Why the Resurgence?' (2004) 6 *International Studies Review* 271.

is a manifestation of a desire to reaffirm the social role of religion, to reoccupy the public space, and to revisit the delimitation between private and public morality. There is some debate in the literature as to whether this movement represents a genuine re-emergence of religion after a long period of decline, or whether it merely marks a surge of visibility of something that had never quite disappeared.[196] Either way, what seems to be at play is a sort of 'deprivatisation' of religion and a 'desecularisation' of the world.[197] The practical consequences of this movement on the international plane are difficult to predict. It is uncertain, in particular, whether a complete reshaping of world order is underway, in which culture and religion are fuelling new 'clashes of civilisations'.[198] What seems to be clear, however, is that the modernist idea that religion and politics should occupy radically differentiated spheres is increasingly being challenged.

There has been much debate about the causes of this resurgence. To some, the reasons are essentially economic and demographic.[199] Others take the view that religion had never ceased to exert its influence on international relations. Today's sense of resurgence, they argue, merely stems from the historical dominance of Western culture over the discipline of international relations and from the progressive realisation, among Western intellectuals, of the limits of social theories of secular modernity.[200]

There is certainly some truth in this. These reasons, however, do not explain everything. The economic argument, for instance, does not account for the fact that the resurgence of religion is occurring in countries with very different levels of economic development, including in the most advanced industrialised societies. There is something in the resurgence of religion which, ironically perhaps, seems to result from modernity itself, its limits and its disillusions. One thinks, first of all, of the psychological, not to say metaphysical, consequences of the liberal disenchantment. Liberalism has produced a hyper-subjectivised social space in which a certain notion of society as a transcendental force is lost. The rise of communitarianisms, including in countries like France in which the republican ideology has traditionally transcended cultural particularisms, is testament to this.[201] The

[196] See Michael Hoelzl and Graham Ward, 'Introduction' in Graham Ward and Michael Hoelzl (eds), *The New Visibility of Religion: Studies in Religion and Cultural Hermeneutics* (London, Continuum, 2008) 1.

[197] Peter Berger (ed), *The Desecularization of the World: Resurgent Religion and World Politics* (Grand Rapids, Eerdmans Publishing, 1999).

[198] Samuel Huntington, 'The Clash of Civilizations?' (1993) 72 *Foreign Affairs* 21.

[199] See, eg, Pippa Norris and Ronald Inglehart, *Sacred and Secular – Religion and Politics Worldwide* (Cambridge, Cambridge University Press, 2004) (who observe that the most developed societies continue to become more secular, whilst the world in general is becoming more religious).

[200] See, eg, Jonathan Fow and Shmuel Sandler, *Bringing Religion Into International Relations* (New York, Palgrave Macmillan, 2006) (who argue that religion has been one of the most overlooked aspects of international politics due to the Western bias of the discipline of international relations).

[201] See Dominique Schnapper, 'La République face aux communautarismes' (2004) 400 *Etudes* 177; Pierre-André Taguieff, *La République enlisée: pluralisme, communautarisme et citoyenneté* (Paris, Syrtes, 2005).

liberal ideology, by sacralising the individual, has undone traditional hierarchies and allegiances. Modernity has given full powers to individuals and thus ironically produced what Malraux calls 'precarious men', that is, shapeless individuals who live in the 'aleatoire' and cease to construct their existence in relation to something beyond them.[202]

Capitalism, in a more discrete but no less significant way, has contributed to this loss of meaning and direction. Individuals' internalisation of the free market logic has prompted what French psychoanalyst Charles Melman calls a 'new psychic economy' that is no longer centred around desire and its repression but rather around possession, enjoyment and exhibition.[203] The enlightenments substituted the quest for salvation with the quest for happiness. For its part, capitalism proclaims the right not to happiness, but to pleasure, whether actual or virtual, and to its public display. The psychic engine of the modern capitalist man is no longer desire, which is always constructed in relation to a certain ideal, but instead want or envy, which have no other object than the possession of (external) signs of enjoyment. The capitalist man is no longer a desiring machine. He is a wanting machine that navigates only by sight. Without compass or ballast, the capitalist man is less a citizen than a consumer. Summoned to possess and enjoy, he becomes a 'man without gravity'.[204]

The resurgence of religion can certainly be explained by these dislocating and disorientating drifts of modernity. In societies in which authority and knowledge are dissolved, individuals turn to religion for direction and identity. Such is the meaning of Malraux's controversial statement: 'the 21st century will be religious or will not be'. Reintroducing the sacred into the empty sky of modernity is a way for the postmodern man to recover some meaning and a certain vision of humanity, which the civilisation of sciences and machines is unable to provide. That this return to religion should often take place in the context of sectarian or evangelical movements – characterised by the influence of central charismatic figures (gurus and predicators) – is but further evidence of the connection between the resurgence of religion and the demand for meaning and authority.

The resurgence of religion can be explained by political reasons too, most notably the inability of the modern secular state to generate development and democracy in the Third World. Following decolonisation, a number of newly independent states were confronted with a dilemma: should they adopt western political, economical and social structures to gain equality in power, or should they instead affirm the values of their own traditions, even at the price of material weakness?[205] In many countries, this dilemma of identity and development

[202] André Malraux, *L'homme précaire et la littérature* (Paris, Gallimard, 1977).
[203] Charles Melman, *L'homme sans gravité Jouir à tout prix* (Paris, Denoël, 2002).
[204] Ibid at 42–46.
[205] On this dilemma, see Ernest Gellner, *Postmodernism, Reason, and Religion* (London, Routledge, 1992) 18–20.

was resolved by emulating the West. Postcolonial elites in Nehru's India, Nasser's Egypt or Sukarno's Indonesia, largely espoused the mythology of modernity inherited from former colonial powers, based on notions of democracy, secularism and often socialism. These elites took the view that building a strong, centralised, Western-style state system would bring about political stability and economic prosperity, and that this process would be undermined if religion or ethnicity were allowed to dominate politics.[206]

The incapacity of secular nationalist movements to achieve sustained economic development, however, paired with the decline of a number of regimes into corruption and authoritarianism, has prompted popular discontent and a rejection of the postcolonial, secular model of statehood in large portions of the Third World. This double crisis of postcolonial regimes has in turn provoked a phenomenon of identitarian closure, that is, a retreat into local identities and a withdrawal from Western cultural values and models. In this context, religious movements have often been catalysts of popular discontent and have become more political. Religion has filled a void and has positioned itself as an alternative – often the only alternative – to the Western model of governance and development.[207] It is in these circumstances, for instance, that Islamist movements have flourished in a number of countries and have become increasingly perceived as a legitimate form of opposition and resistance to Western hegemony. The resurgence of religion, from this point of view, represents a form of 'indigenisation' of modernity, a counter-project to past and largely unsuccessful attempts at 'modernising' non-Western traditional societies.[208]

C. The resurgence of religion and international law: the OIC and the IICJ

The resurgence of religion has for some time manifested itself in the legal domain. The most visible sign of this is perhaps the multiplication, since the 1970s, of domestic constitutions that recognise the Shari'a as the main and/or ultimate source of law. Islamic constitutions have been adopted, for instance, in Egypt,[209]

[206] Scott Thomas, 'Taking Religious and Cultural Pluralism Seriously: The Global Resurgence of Religion and the Transformation of International Society' (2000) 29 *Millennium: Journal of International Studies* 815, 816–19.

[207] See Francis Fukuyama, *The End of History and the Last Man* (New York, Free Press, 1992) 45 (who argues that, following the collapse of Communism, Islam has become the only viable alternative to the Western liberal model).

[208] On the political dimension of the 'resurgence' phenomenon, see especially, Mark Juergensmeyer, *The New Cold War: Religious Nationalism Confronts the Secular State* (Berkeley, University of California Press, 1993); Jeff Haynes, *Religion in Third World Politics* (London, Open University Press, 1994); David Westerlund (ed), *Questioning the Secular State: The Worldwide Resurgence of Religion in Politics* (London, Hurst & Cie, 1996).

[209] Constitution of the Arab Republic of Egypt, 11 September 1971 (as amended on 22 May 1980), art 2: 'Islam is the Religion of the State. Arabic is its official language, and the principal source of legislation is Islamic Jurisprudence (Sharia)' (www.egypt.gov.eg/english/laws/constitution/default.aspx).

Iran,[210] Pakistan,[211] Sudan,[212] Saudi Arabia,[213] Yemen,[214] Kuwait[215] and Qatar.[216] More recent examples include the new constitutions of Afghanistan[217] and Iraq,[218] both adopted with the blessing of the international community, or the draft Palestinian constitution.[219] The terms of reference vary from constitution to constitution. Reference is made, in some instruments, to the 'principles' of Islamic law whilst other texts mention the 'precepts' or the 'injunctions' of the Shari'a. The spirit, however, remains the same in all Islamic Constitutions: the Shari'a is recognised as the ultimate foundation of positive state law.

To be sure, the practical consequences of these constitutional provisions are far from uniform. It appears, in particular, that in countries where secular institutions continue to exercise important powers, the constitutionalisation of the Shari'a leads only to a marginal Islamisation of the legal order. Such is the case,

[210] Constitution of the Islamic Republic of Iran, 24 October 1979 (as amended on 28 July 1989), art 4: 'all civil, penal, financial, economic, administrative, cultural, military, political, and other laws and regulations must be based on Islamic criteria. This principle applies absolutely and generally to all articles of the Constitution as well as to all other laws and regulations, and the fuqaha' of the Guardian Council are judges in this matter' (www.iranchamber.com/government/laws/constitution.php).

[211] Constitution of the Islamic Republic of Pakistan, 12 April 1973, art 227: 'All existing laws shall be brought in conformity with the Injunctions of Islam as laid down in the Holy Quran and Sunnah, in this Part referred to as the Injunctions of Islam, and no law shall be enacted which is repugnant to such Injunctions' (www.pakistanconstitution-law.com/theconst_1973.asp).

[212] Constitution of the Republic of Sudan, 1 July 1998, art 4: 'God, the creator of all people, is supreme over the State and sovereignty is delegated to the people of Sudan by succession, to be practiced as worship to God, performing his trust, developing the homeland, and spreading justice, freedom and shura in accordance with the Constitution and laws' (www.sudan.net/government/constitution/english.html).

[213] Royal Decree No A/90, 1 March 1992, art 1: 'The Kingdom of Saudi Arabia is a sovereign Arab Islamic state with Islam as its religion; God's Book and the Sunnah of His Prophet, God's prayers and peace be upon him, are its constitution, Arabic is its language and Riyadh is its capital' (www.servat.unibe.ch/law/icl/sa00000_html).

[214] Constitution of the Republic of Yemen, 29 September 1994, art 3: 'Islamic Shari'ah is the source of all legislation' (www.al-bab.com/yemen/gov/con94.htm).

[215] Kuwaiti Constitution, 1 November 1962, art 2: 'The religion of the State is Islam, and the Islamic Sharia shall be a main source of legislation' (www.kuwait-info.com/sidepages/state_constitution.asp).

[216] Permanent Constitution of the State of Qatar, 29 April 2003, art 1: 'Qatar is an independent sovereign Arab State. Its religion is Islam and Shari'a law shall be a main source of its legislations' (www.english.mofa.gov.qa/details.cfm?id=80).

[217] Constitution of Afghanistan, 1 January 2004, art 3: 'In Afghanistan, no law can be contrary to the sacred religion of Islam and the values of this Constitution' (www.mfa.gov.af/Documents/Constitution%20of%20afghanistan.pdf).

[218] Constitution of Iraq, 15 October 2005, art 2: 'Islam is the official religion of the State and it is a fundamental source of legislation: no law that contradicts the established provisions of Islam may be established' (www.portal.unesco.org/ci/en/files/20704/11332732681iraqi_constitution_en.pdf/iraqi_constitution_en.pdf).

[219] Constitution of the State of Palestine – Revised Third Draft, 4 May 2003, reprinted in Nathan Brown, 'The Third Draft Constitution for a Palestinian State: Translation and Commentary' (2003) Palestinian Center for Policy and Survey Research, art 7: 'The principles of the Islamic Shari'a are a main source for legislation. The followers of the monotheistic religions shall have their personal status and religious affairs organized according to their Shari'as and religious denominations within the framework of positive law, while preserving the unity and independence of the Palestinian people (www.pcpsr.org/domestic/2003/nbrowne.pdf).

for instance, in Egypt, where the Constitutional Court has developed a jurisprudence that seeks to reconcile traditional precepts of Islamic law and the liberal rule of law.[220] Nonetheless, these constitutional developments are all important manifestations of the resurgence of religion in the public sphere.

Although less visible than in domestic systems, signs of resurgence can also be found in international law. These include, for instance, the reference to principles or concepts of Islamic law in proceedings before international courts and tribunals.[221] More visible perhaps has been the position taken by some Islamic countries during the negotiation of international human rights law instruments. As is well known, and as well as attempting to redraft or do away with certain treaty provisions,[222] certain Muslim states have made important reservations to human rights treaties, holding that the treaty provisions shall only apply domestically if and to the extent that they are compatible with Shari'a law.[223] Often, these reservations have been objected to by Western nations. Equally, there has been debate in the literature as to whether general and undefined reservations of this type are valid under the law of treaties.[224] Whether admissible or not, however, these reservations do reflect the resurgence of religion in the international public sphere.

[220] See Clark Lombardi and Nathan Brown, 'Do Constitutions Requiring Adherence to Shari'a Threaten Human Rights? How Egypt's Constitutional Court Reconciles Islamic Law With the Liberal Rule of Law' (2006) 21 *American University International Law Review* 379 and Megan McMillan, 'Egypt's Interpretative Incorporation of Human Rights: The Supreme Constitutional Court's Use of International Sources and Prospects for Its Article 2 Analysis' (2007) 16 *Transnational Law and Contemporary Problems* 1089.

[221] See, for instance, *Western Sahara*, 16 October 1975, ICJ Reports (1975), in which Morocco argued that the question of sovereignty over Western Sahara should not be settled on the basis of the criteria traditionally used for establishing sovereignty, but instead in accordance with Islamic concepts of spiritual authority and allegiance. In essence, Morocco argued that the inhabitants of Western Sahara were Muslim and that, as such, they would have recognised their religious ties to the Sultan of Morocco as tantamount to ties of sovereignty (see 'Exposé oral de M. Benjelloun', 12 May 1975, ICJ Pleadings (1975) 4, 194–204). The Court, however, rejected the argument and instead used the traditional notion of 'effective display of authority' to answer the question. The Court's conclusion was that the materials and information presented to it did not establish any tie of territorial sovereignty between Western Sahara and either Morocco or Mauritania (para 163).

[222] When negotiating the Rome Statute on the International Criminal Court, for instance, Muslim states successfully argued for the exclusion of 'lawful sanctions' from the definition of torture under art 7.2(e) so as to exclude certain Islamic forms of punishment from the ambit of the statute. On this point, see Mahnoush Arsanjani, 'The Rome Statute of the International Criminal Court' (1999) 93 *American Journal of International Law* 22, 31.

[223] When acceding to the Convention on the Rights of the Child, for instance, 17 Muslim states issued declarations reserving the right not to comply with provisions of the Convention that are incompatible with Islamic laws and values. The Vatican entered a similar reservation declaring that 'the application of the Convention be compatible in practice with the particular nature of the Vatican City State and of the sources of its objective law'.

[224] See, eg, Ineta Ziemele (ed), *Reservations to Human Rights Treaties and the Vienna Convention Regime: Conflict, Harmony or Reconciliation?* (Leiden, Martinus Nijhoff, 2004); Ryan Goodman, 'Human Rights Treaties, Invalid Reservations, and State Consent' (2002) 96 *American Journal of International Law* 531; Christine Chinkin (ed), *Human Rights as General Norms and a State's Right to Opt Out: Reservations and Objections to Human Rights Conventions* (London, British Institute of International and Comparative Law, 1997); William Schabas, 'Reservations to Human Rights Treaties: Time for Innovation and Reform' (1994) 32 *Canadian Yearbook of International Law* 39.

These examples, to be sure, do not necessarily denote the emergence of an Islamic international law, separate from public international law. After all, Muslim countries that make reservations to human rights treaties do negotiate and often ratify these treaties on the traditional basis of public international law and within the parameters of the law of treaties. One can say, to go back to Hart's terminology, that even though they seek to defend an Islamic point of view on certain human rights issues, Muslim states continue to 'accept', on the whole, the secondary rules of international law. Whilst taking issue with the substance of specific human rights provisions, these states adhere to the general norms and structures of public international law.[225]

However, certain developments within the Organisation of the Islamic Conference (OIC), and more particularly the creation of the International Islamic Court of Justice (IICJ), may reveal something different. What seems to be at play here is no longer simply an attempt to reintroduce a dose of religion into international law but, more significantly perhaps, an attempt to rethink international law, or at least the part of it that applies to Muslim states, as a legal order founded on the Shari'a, that is, on an 'Islamic Grundnorm'. Before considering this point further, a word must be said about the OIC and its purposes.

The OIC is little known to international lawyers and has received limited attention in the literature.[226] This is rather surprising since the OIC, from a quantitative point of view, is among the largest of the world's international organisations, with 57 member states representing more than 1.3 billion people spread over 32 million square kilometres (about 25 per cent of the surface of the earth).

The OIC was established in 1969 in Rabat, at an emergency summit convened in response to the attempted arson in the Al-Aqsa mosque in Jerusalem, Islam's third most important holy place. Although the attack was perpetrated by an Australian evangelical Protestant and not, as was thought for some time, by Zionist entities, many in the Muslim world interpreted this event as evidence of Israel's determination to destroy this Islamic holy place.[227] This explains the primarily defensive vocation of the organisation, whose main purposes are to achieve Islamic solidarity in the economic, social and cultural fields, to safe-

[225] Yadh Ben Achour, 'La civilisation islamique et le droit international' (2006) 110 *Revue Générale de Droit International Public* 19.

[226] See, however, Taoufik Bouachba, 'L'Organisation de la Conférence Islamique' (1982) 28 *Annuaire Français de Droit International* 265; Saad S Khan, *Reasserting International Islam: A Focus on the Organization of the Islamic Conference* (Oxford, Oxford University Press, 2001); Noor Ahmad Baba, 'Organization of the Islamic Conference: Conceptual Framework and Institutional Structure' (1993) 30 *International Studies* 35; Shahram Akbarzadeh and Kylie Connor, 'The Organization of the Islamic Conference: Sharing an Illusion' (2005) 12 *Middle East Policy* 79.

[227] The arsonist, Michael Dennis Rohan, was neither Israeli nor Jewish. He was a follower of an evangelical sect and, by his own admission, hoped to hasten the coming of the Messiah by burning down the Al-Aqsa Mosque. See 'Australian is Seized by Israel as Suspect in Arson at Mosque', *The New York Times* (New York, 23 August 1969).

guard the rights, dignity and religious and cultural identity of Muslim communities, and to support Palestine's struggle for self-determination.[228]

The organisation's material achievements to date have been relatively modest. They include the establishment of specialised institutions (Islamic Development Bank; Islamic Educational, Scientific and Cultural Organisation; Islamic Chamber of Commerce and Industry, etc); the building of universities and cultural centres to encourage the development of Islamic culture and values; the adoption of international conventions in areas such as economic and commercial cooperation, investments protection, civil aviation or telecommunications; and more recently the establishment of a preferential trade system. Politically, however, the organisation has had a rather marginal role. Due to fundamental internal contradictions, the OIC has remained largely unable to articulate a coherent policy agenda on issues as important as the Iran-Iraq war, the Palestinian question or the fight against terrorism.[229]

Although the organisation's operational achievements are modest, the OIC has, since its inception, developed a distinct juridical discourse on international relations among Muslim communities and on the rules that ought to govern these relations. The organisation's normative discourse differs from the traditional structures of public international law in at least two respects. The first concerns the traditionally exclusive position of the state as the fundamental actor in international politics. To be sure, the OIC is formally an inter-governmental organisation and its Charter explicitly provides that it is 'made up of States'.[230] Likewise, one of the main guiding principles of the organisation is that of 'respect for national sovereignty, independence and territorial integrity' of all member states.[231] There is therefore nothing in the OIC Charter that suggests a sharp or radical break with the Westphalian paradigm of statehood.

At the same time, the organisation's institutional discourse does recognise another key entity – the Ummah – alongside the nation-state. The concept of Ummah is far from unequivocal and scholars continue to debate its meaning, history and etymology.[232] It is generally agreed, however, that the concept of

[228] Charter of the Organisation of the Islamic Conference, 4 March 1972, 13039 UNTS 116, art 1.

[229] The OIC counts among its member allies (Turkey, Saudi Arabia) as well as declared enemies of Western powers, most notably of the United States (Iran). On the Palestinian question, some members continue to be in a permanent state of war with Israel (Syria, Iran) whilst others have signed peace agreements with it (Egypt, Jordan). The tension between the Sunni, Shi'a and Wahhabi traditions of Islam explains in large part why the OIC has failed to articulate a coherent notion of Islamic justice and solidarity. On these internal contradictions, see Shahram Akbarzadeh and Kylie Connor, 'The Organization of the Islamic Conference: Sharing an Illusion', above n 226 and Sohail Hashmi, 'International Society and Its Islamic Malcontents' (1993) 13 *The Fletcher Forum of World Affairs* 13, 23.

[230] Charter of the Organisation of the Islamic Conference, art 3.

[231] Ibid at art 2.

[232] See, eg, Abdullah al-Ahsan, 'The Quranic Concept of Ummah' (1986) 7 *Journal of Muslim Minority Affairs* 606; CAO van Nieuwenhuijze, 'The Ummah: An Analytic Approach' (1959) 10 *Studia Islamica* 5.

Ummah in Islam refers to the community of Muslim believers, subjected to God, and united through faith and a common way of life.[233] The Ummah therefore denotes the unity of the Muslim world, over and beyond national borders and political boundaries.

As well as being explicitly mentioned in the OIC Charter, the Ummah has long been part of the organisation's institutional vocabulary. Starting with the third Islamic summit of 1981 in Saudi Arabia, the OIC missions and objectives have been largely defined by reference to the Ummah. The *Mecca Declaration* adopted at the closing meeting of the third Islamic summit illustrates this point:

> [T]he leaders of the Muslim nation [beseech] the Almighty to help them bear the heavy responsibility they have assumed in a world beset by dangers and challenges, and to guide them to the path leading to solidarity, harmony and wisdom. They beseech Allah to help them discard differences and disunity, so that the Muslim nation may once again become the Ummah defined by Allah in His Holy Book as the best Ummah in the history of mankind: . . . an Ummah that has banished enmity and prejudice; an Ummah which sets the scene for a new community in which each Muslim can hope to fulfil his aspiration to dignity and strength and which can achieve for the whole of mankind the desired security, peace and progress[234]

Following the *Mecca Declaration*, reference to the Ummah has become systematic in nearly every instrument adopted by the OIC, whether it be a programmatic, political or legal instrument. Some texts speak of the 'unity and solidarity of the Ummah'.[235] Others refer to the 'progress',[236] the 'prosperity',[237] the 'causes' or 'interests' of the Ummah.[238] Others still mention the 'inalienable right of the Islamic Ummah to develop, acquire and make use of science and technology' or the importance of 'endowing the Islamic Ummah with effective communication instruments facilitating the expressions of its identity and culture'.[239]

The point here is that the concept of Ummah has become an unavoidable reference point in the discourse of the OIC. This does not mean of course that the category of the state has disappeared. OIC texts and instruments continue to refer to the 'member states' of the organisation. Yet at the same time, resolutions, conventions and declarations adopted by the organisation often point to

[233] William Zartman, 'Pouvoir et Etat dans l'Islam' (1979) 12 *Pouvoirs* 5; Frederic Denny, 'The Meaning of Ummah in the Qur'an' (1975) *History of Religions* 34.

[234] Mecca Declaration of the Third Islamic Summit Conference, 28 January 1981, paras 7–8 (www.oic-oci.org/english/conf/is/3/3rd-is-sum.htm).

[235] Tehran Declaration of the Eighth Islamic Summit Conference, 11 December 1997, para 4 (www.oic-oci.org/english/conf/is/8/8th-is-summits.htm#Declaration).

[236] Casablanca Declaration of the Seventh Islamic Summit Conference, 15 December 1994, para 23 (www.oic-oci.org/english/conf/is/7/7th-is-summit.htm#CASABLANCA DECLARATION).

[237] Islamabad Declaration adopted by the Thirty Fourth Session of the Islamic Conference of Foreign Ministers, Doc OIC/ICFM-34/2007/ISLAMABAD-DEC, 17 May 2007, para 2.

[238] Ten Year Programme of Action To meet the Challenges Facing the Muslim Ummah in the 21st Century, 8 December 2005, para 6 (www.oic-oci.org/page_detail.asp?p_id=228).

[239] Tehran Declaration, above n 235 at paras 102 and 112.

the 'leaders of the Islamic Ummah',[240] the 'countries of the Ummah'[241] or the 'peoples of the Ummah'[242] when mentioning the OIC members.

What the above suggests is that, whilst endorsing *étatism* as a sort of 'fait accompli' of international relations, the OIC defines itself and its mission by reference to pan-Islamic ideological premises that posit the existence, beyond nation-states, of a Muslim nation – the Ummah – that rests on religious rather than a territorial, political or ethnic basis.[243] The Muslim nation, to be sure, is more a constitutive myth than a tangible, empirical fact in the modern world. The OIC Secretary General implicitly conceded this point when, in his 2005 Ten-Year Programme of Action, he called upon the members of the organisation to 'revive the Muslim Ummah' and to take joint action to achieve its 'renaissance' as a force for international peace and harmony.[244] This foundational myth, however, does in a sense compete with the myth of the sovereign state. Whilst not radically incompatible with the notion of territorial sovereignty, it challenges – if only at the surface of the institutional discourse – the Westphalian paradigm of the 'anarchical society' in which there is no higher level of authority over nation states.[245] In the Islamic tradition, only God is sovereign and states are mere 'sub-sections of the Ummah',[246] that is, temporary and subsidiary structures enjoying delegated powers.[247] By using as it does the concept of Ummah, the OIC therefore introduces – if only metaphorically or discursively – a notion of divine hierarchy among Muslim communities that is somewhat at odds with the Westphalian concept of absolute sovereign authority.

The second point on which the OIC normative discourse differs from the secular structures of public international law concerns the issue of sources. The members of the organisation have long expressed the view that obligations among Muslim nations find their source in the Shari'a. This notion is reflected in a number of international instruments adopted by the organisation, such as the *Cairo Declaration on Human Rights in Islam*, adopted by the Islamic

[240] Final Communiqué of the Third Extraordinary Session of the Islamic Summit Conference, 8 December 2005, preamble (www.oic-oci.org/ex-summit/english/fc-exsumm-en.htm).

[241] Resolution No 5/6-C (IS) on Cooperation in the Field of Youth and Sports, 11 December 1991, preamble (www.oic-oci.org/english/conf/is/6/6th-is-sum(cultural).htm#05).

[242] Resolution No 3/34-E on the Activities Related to Economic Assistance to Member States and Non-OIC Countries and Muslim Communities, 17 May 2007, para 57 (www.oic-oci.org/34icfm/english/resolution/34ICFM-ECO-RES-FINAL-ENG.pdf).

[243] Naveed Sheikh, *The New Politics of Islam: Pan-Islamic Foreign Policy in a World of States* (London, Routledge, 2003) 20–42.

[244] Ten Year Programme of Action, above n 238 at para 1.

[245] Hedley Bull, *The Anarchical Society – A Study of Order in World Politics* (New York, Columbia University Press, 1977).

[246] Dakar Declaration of the Eleventh Session of the Islamic Summit Conference, 14 March 2008, at 7: 'Africa's situation . . . has drawn our attention because the problems of poverty besetting the continent should give rise to a solidarity drive among the other sections of the Ummah' (www.oic-oci.org/is11/english/DAKAR-DEC-11SUMMIT-E.pdf).

[247] On the Islamic theory of the state, see Majid Khadduri, *War and Peace in the Law of Islam* (Baltimore, The John Hopkins Press, 1955) 3–18.

Conference of Foreign Ministers in 1990.[248] Although formally non-binding, the Cairo Declaration represents the closest approximation of an 'Islamic approach' to human rights.[249] Its preamble presents human rights as 'binding divine commandments' the violation of which constitutes an 'abominable sin'. Further, nearly every provision of the Declaration confirms the religious foundation of human rights: article 2 provides that 'life is a God-given gift' and its preservation a 'duty prescribed by Shari'a'; article 7 provides that 'parents are entitled to certain rights from their children, and relatives are entitled to rights from their kin, in accordance with the tenets of the Shari'a'; article 12 holds that 'every man shall have the right, in accordance with the Shari'a, to free movement'; article 22 mentions 'the right to express [one's] opinion freely in such manner as would not be contrary to the principles of the Shari'a' and so on.

Islamic law, according to the Declaration, is thus more than a simple background for human rights. The Shari'a is properly *constitutive* of the rights and obligations contained in the Declaration. It represents their primary source and foundation. In fact, the Declaration goes further by stating that 'all the rights and freedoms stipulated in this Declaration are subject to the Islamic Shari'a' and that 'the Islamic Shari'a is the only source of reference for the explanation or clarification of any of the articles of this Declaration'.[250] Shari'a law is therefore regarded as the *sole* and *exclusive* source of validity for human rights in Islam.

Other texts adopted by the OIC make reference to the Shari'a as the 'source of justice'[251] or as a 'source of friendly relations among Islamic countries'.[252] The notion that law among Muslim nations has its source in the Shari'a is best epitomised, however, by the establishment of the International Islamic Court of Justice. The idea of setting up a permanent court to settle disputes between Islamic states was prompted primarily by the Iran-Iraq war. Resolution 11/3-P, adopted at the height of the war, is the first instrument to mention the establishment of an Islamic Court of Justice 'as an arbiter, judge and umpire in all conflicts that may arise between Islamic States'.[253] In 1983, and on the basis of this resolution, the Secretary General of the OIC mandated a group of experts to draw up the Statute of the Court. In January 1987, after several years of negotiations, the Statute of the Court was finally adopted by the group of experts. That same year, the Fifth Islamic Summit adopted Resolution 13/5-P, in which

[248] Cairo Declaration on Human Rights in Islam, 5 August 1990 (www1.umn.edu/humanrts/instree/cairodeclaration.html).

[249] The Cairo Declaration was presented by the Saudi foreign minister at the 1993 World Conference on Human Rights in Vienna as representing the 'consensus' of Muslim nations on rights issues. See Ann Elizabeth Mayer, *Islam and Human Rights: Tradition and Politics* (Boulder, Westview Press, 1998) 22.

[250] Cairo Declaration on Human Rights in Islam, arts 24–25.

[251] Mecca Declaration of the Third Islamic Summit Conference, above n 234.

[252] Tehran Declaration of the Thirtieth Islamic Conference of Foreign ministers, 30 May 2003, preamble (www.oic-oci.org/english/conf/fm/30/declaration.htm).

[253] Resolution No 11/3-P (IS) on the Establishment of an Islamic Court of Justice, 28 January 1981 (www.oic-oci.org/english/conf/is/3/3rd-is-sum(political).htm#11).

the members of the organisation, 'desirous of establishing a principal judicial organ for settling disputes in accordance with the Islamic Shari'a', formally approved the draft Statute of the Court and annexed it to the OIC Charter.[254]

The uniqueness of the IICJ Statute rests in the fact that it considers the Shari'a as the primary applicable law. Article 27 of the Statute – the clause of applicable law – provides that 'a) the Islamic Shari'a is the fundamental law of the International Islamic Court of Justice; b) the Court may draw inspiration from international law, bilateral or multilateral international conventions, international customary law, general principles of law or from the judgements pronounced by international tribunals'.

According to the Statute, the law applicable to disputes between OIC members is therefore 'fundamentally' religious. To be sure, this applicable law – whose 'inalienable' source is the Shari'a[255] – possesses several points of contacts with public international law. Article 27 does indeed refer to the classical categories of international law: treaties, custom and general principles. However, whilst the Shari'a is regarded as the fundamental law of the Court, these classical sources of international law are referred to as optional and secondary sources, from which the Court 'may' draw inspiration. The letter of the Statute does therefore suggest a certain degree of 'acceptance' of the secondary rules of public international law. But this acceptance is conditional and qualified, for treaties, custom and general principles are ultimately subordinated to the Shari'a.

The Statute of the Court, it is worth recalling, has not yet entered into force. Under article 49, the Statute shall enter into force after ratification by two thirds of the member states and, to date, only 10 states have ratified the Statute.[256] Among them, however, are some of the most influential members of the organisation, including Egypt, Saudi Arabia and Pakistan. By adopting resolution 13/5-P, all members of the organisation have also accepted the principle of settling their disputes on the basis of religious norms. The *idea* of international Islamic justice based on a religious rule of recognition is therefore in some sense in operation within the OIC.

Whether this idea will ever materialise and give rise to an autonomous, self-contained Islamic legal order, separate from public international law, is uncertain. The point here is simply that a group of 57 states exists today that shares a particular worldview and that this worldview, in two respects at least, is at odds with the classical structures of public international law. This group of states does not reject the whole of public international law. It does in fact routinely

[254] Resolution No 13/5-P (IS) on the Establishment of the International Islamic Court of Justice, 29 January 1987 (www.oic-oci.org/english/conf/is/5/5th-is-sum(political).htm#13).

[255] Statute of the International Islamic Court of Justice, art 1.

[256] These are: Kuwait, Saudi Arabia, Jordan, Libya, Bahrain, Qatar, Egypt, The Maldives, Pakistan and Sudan. See Reports of the Secretary General on Legal Affairs Submitted to the Thirty-Third Session of the Islamic Conference of Foreign Ministers, Doc OIC/33-ICFM/2006/LEG/SG-REP, 21 June 2006, 1.

adopt its key categories (the state) and its main normative instruments (treaties). But this adoption takes place in very particular terms. The state is apprehended as part of a broader community, the Ummah, which transcends it in time and space. Treaties, customs and general principles are regarded as applicable law among Muslim nations, but only to the extent that they comply with the Shari'a, the inalienable and fundamental source of law in Islam. What emerges from this is thus a re-enchanting narrative that somewhat displaces the secular, sovereign state from the centre stage of international politics and refocuses the perennial problem of sources and foundation around an 'Islamic Grundnorm', presented as the focal point of explication and interpretation of international law.

It may well be that this narrative merely represents a form of postmodern or postcolonial identitarian grievance, a form of rhetorical resistance to Western hegemony, whether real or perceived, which public international law somewhat personifies. It may also be that this effort from Islamic countries to re-appropriate international law for themselves and on their own terms will only marginally affect the substance of international law. Yet to return to Hart, the OIC and the IICJ do raise a number of questions regarding international law, secondary rules and their 'general and uniform acceptance'. The most elementary structures of international law – those concerning its subjects and its sources – are internalised by OIC members in distinctive terms that suggest a different 'internal point of view' regarding law's nature, foundation and validity.

These developments are not, in and of themselves, problematical or pathological. Neither do they necessarily compromise one's ability to speak of international law as a formal order. If one takes the increasingly popular view, for instance, that a multicultural society should make room for recognising the worth of distinctive cultural traditions,[257] then one could imagine that the differentiation of a group of states and the recognition of an alternative sphere of justice may paradoxically provide greater inclusion and integration for Muslim nations in the world community.

My main point, however, is somewhat different. The IICJ and most of the normative developments within the OIC reveal a particular *attitude* toward international law's secondary norms and in particular its rules of recognition. They reveal the aspiration of a group of states to be governed by a special system that is somewhat different from the dominant, secular legal order. Whether this alternative system of law and justice actually exists is almost irrelevant for the purpose of Hart's theory of acceptance. The point here is simply that the project of an IICJ with the power to settle disputes under Islamic law *raises the question of pluralism in international law* in very much the same way as the

[257] On the 'politics of recognition' in multicultural societies, see in particular Charles Taylor, *Multiculturalism and the Politics of Recognition* (Princeton, Princeton University Press, 1992); Iris Young, *Justice and the Politics of Difference* (Princeton, Princeton University Press, 1990); Nancy Fraser and Axel Honneth, *Redistribution or Recognition? A Political-Philosophical Exchange* (New York, Verso, 2003).

project of establishing Shari'a courts to settle marital or financial disputes in Ontario once raised the question of pluralism in Canadian law. To assume or posit, as a sort of evidence, that the secondary rules of international law are uniformly accepted therefore obfuscates part of the reality of international relations, as if to force international law into a pre-determined (Western) theoretical framework. The discourse then becomes ideological and hegemonic and not, as it purports to be, analytical or descriptive.

V. INTERMEDIATE CONCLUSIONS

Deleuze used to speak of concepts as 'thicknesses', that is, as volumes which can be examined from different points of view and which possess different levels of expression, projection and manifestation.[258] My aim in this chapter has been to identify and explore the conceptual thickness of the notion of formal unity in international law. I have attempted to show, first of all, that the constitution of a set of norms into a unitary system rests on a complex web of structuring dynamics. In other words, there is no single and exclusive law of organisation which, by itself, can explain the unity of the legal order. Instead, a variety of principles of unity can be considered, which all explain in their own way how order is produced and maintained among juridical norms. Three main dynamics of formal unity have been explored: the institutional, the inter-normative and the interpretative or hermeneutic dynamics. Of course, the list is not exhaustive. It does show, however, that formal unity in law can mean very different things depending on one's point of view and that different models are available, that is, different ways of thinking about the relations of dependence and composition that unite different 'parts' of a legal 'whole' together.

To speak of formal unity from an institutional perspective is to consider, first of all, the social universe in which the system operates. It implies asking, for instance, whether international law is embedded in a concrete, stable and permanent social structure – that is, in an institution capable of expressing a coherent 'social consciousness' – or whether the social structure that underpins the international legal order is fragmented into distinct social sectors (the society of merchants, the society of environmentalists, the society of humanitarians, etc), each generating its own law according to its own rationality and preferences (market, technology, science, dignity, security and so on). If the society in which law operates is indeed fragmented, the question then becomes whether there is an authority that can organise the relation between the social fragments and, where conflicts arise, resolve them. Either way, the decisive criterion of unity

[258] 'A philosophical idea, a philosophical concept, is always a thickness, a volume. You can take it at one level, then at another level, and at another level still, it never contradicts itself. But these are different levels nonetheless' (author's translation), La voix de Gilles Deleuze en ligne – Cours du 10 novembre 1981 (online audio recordings of Deleuze's lectures at University Paris VIII, Vincennes-Saint-Denis: www2.univ-paris8.fr/deleuze/article.php3?id_article=17).

concerns the social basis of the law. The question, in short, is whether *one* community generates *one* set of laws to resolve *one* set of problems, or whether law is produced by a plurality of collectivities, all engaged in separate governance projects.

To speak of formal unity from the inter-normative perspective is to consider the relation between different classes of norms and in particular whether the legal order is equipped with a system of second-degree rules that control how law is created, transformed and implemented. International law will be said to be one if it is endowed with a complete and coherent set of systemic rules (rules on norm-creation and responsibility in particular) that form a normative framework common to all international norms or norm-complexes. International law will be fragmented, on the other hand, if this normative framework is indeterminate, incomplete or contested, or if alternative frameworks emerge in particular areas of the law, that is, if special branches develop their own system of sources and responsibility. Looking at frameworks means looking beyond (primary) rules of conduct and considering the 'background' norms that act as a sort of systemic genome, that is, as the genetic code that contains the instructions for building, running and maintaining the system.

Lastly, to speak of formal unity from the interpretative or hermeneutic perspective is to consider the relations between legal norms and law-appliers, whether immediate law-appliers (states) or second-degree law-appliers endowed with the power to interpret the law in their name (judges and arbitrators). To think of formal unity from this point of view will mean, for instance, asking whether judges interpret legal norms hermetically or whether they seek to establish a form of semantic solidarity among norms or norm-complexes. Are judges engaged in a common hermeneutic activity? Do they seek harmony between their interpretation and that of other courts and tribunals? Do they search for common principles behind the text of individual rules? Do they see their decisions as isolated, one-off events or as chapters in an ongoing normative story? Formal unity, in this perspective, does not rest on the existence of an *a priori* framework that remains in the background of the system. It involves a collective practice of mediation, that is, the fact for the interpretive community to create, through interpretation, relationships between norms or groups of norms.

In the second part of the chapter, I have emphasised Hart's theory of unity and its use in the fragmentation debate. Here again, I have sought to do justice to the thickness and complexity of Hart's theory of secondary rules. I have tried to show, in particular, that international lawyers tend to adopt a rather short and at times simplistic reading of this theory. Often, international lawyers regard the existence of a 'certain number' of secondary rules as a necessary and sufficient condition of formal unity, whereas Hart regards it as a mere starting point.

My re-reading of Hart's *Concept of Law* has served to highlight the fact that secondary rules are merely the 'raw material' of his systems theory. If one is to speak of a single system of law, Hart argues, these rules must be both determinate and uniformly accepted by the system's officials. Yet absent the hierarchical and integrating structures that give domestic systems a certain immediate and palpable unity, one cannot simply assume that these two conditions exist in international law. On the contrary, my analysis of the sources question and of the IICJ has served to show that – save for a limited number of key concepts and categories – secondary rules in international law are open, controversial, and the source of polemical debates. And the existence of a uniform point of view on issues as fundamental as international law's primary subjects or its rule of recognition cannot be taken for granted.

This does not mean that we should renounce analysing international law as a system. All of this may only be the passing symptom of a state of transition, the symbol of a legal order that is looking for its forms in a complex and changing environment. The fact remains, however, that if Hart's theory of the legal system is adopted as an analytical framework, one cannot simply ignore the difficult questions of determinacy and acceptance. Doing so would turn Hart's complex and sophisticated theory into a mere normative postulate, that is, an *a priori* statement of what the law should be, the truth of which must be accepted without question.

In the end, the present chapter has served two main purposes. First, it has suggested a more complex understanding of formal unity in law, one that reflects the plurality of forces or dynamics that can account for law's unity as a system. Second, it has examined the conditions under which Hart's dominant model of formal unity can be used in the context of international law, insisting in particular on the two hard questions of determinacy and acceptance.

One last conclusion emerges from this discussion. The difficulties posed by the questions of determinacy and acceptance in the field of international law, as well as being indicative of the limits or specificities of international law, may signal the limits of Hart's theory itself. Perhaps Hart's theory is simply inapplicable to the international legal order. We know, for instance, that Hart's concept of law is based on a key distinction between the sovereign and its subjects, mere citizens and officials, the government and the populace.[259] The *Concept of Law* is of course a critique of Austin's theory of law as sovereign commands, backed by a threat of sanction. Hart views this definition as doubly restrictive, for its places the sovereign 'above the law' and it does not account for rules that have nothing to do with orders or commands.[260] Yet Hart maintains the distinction between the sovereign and its subjects as a central and essential element of his theory of the legal system. In fact, this distinction underpins the one that he draws between primary rules (which impose duties on legal subjects) and secondary rules (which confer powers on sovereign authorities).

The problem of course is that this distinction, by definition, does not operate in international law. States are simultaneously the acting subjects, the operators

[259] Hart, *The Concept of Law*, above n 26 at 49–76 (Ch IV: 'Sovereign and Subject').
[260] Ibid at 26–33 and 64–69.

and the agents (of creation, interpretation and application) of the law. The distinction between citizens and officials, which is rather simple and straightforward in domestic systems, simply does not work on the international plane. Those who hold the authority to make and implement the law are also subject to it. For this reason, it is difficult, perhaps even impossible, to distinguish the state-as-subject from the state-as-authority in international law.

Hart, to be sure, acknowledges the possibility of law without a sovereign. This, it will be recalled, is what he calls 'primitive' law. Hart takes the view, however, that 'only a small community closely knit by ties of kinship, common sentiment, and belief, and placed in a stable environment' can live successfully by such a regime.[261] And even where these conditions are met, Hart considers that 'the rules by which the group lives will not form a system', but merely a set of separate standards.[262] This begs the question of whether international law is not excluded *ex hypothesi* from Hart's concept of the legal system.[263]

This basic discrepancy between the premises of Hart's concept of law and the nature of the international order suggests two things. The first is that, even if one seeks to analyse international law as a formal legal order and if one does not disqualify Hart's theory from the outset as fundamentally at odds with the international order, the theory of secondary rules cannot explain, on its own, the formal unity of international law. It sheds light on only one aspect of the legal order and does so in terms that exclude, *ab initio*, many of the distinctive features of international law. This is but another reason not to use the Hartian paradigm as an exclusive paradigm of unity and to consider other theories, explanations or dynamics of unity, whether institutional or hermeneutical.

But the basic inadequacy of the Hartian framework may also suggest the need for a more radical break from purely formal approaches to unity in international law. It may well be the case that the very idea of legal order sits uneasily with international law. If this is true, it becomes necessary to consider other levels of analysis, other frameworks that take into account other objects and criteria of unity besides legal norms, their compatibility or their formal arrangement. The last two chapters of this book intend to do just that.

[261] Ibid at 89.

[262] Ibid at 90.

[263] For a more in-depth critique of Hart's definition of the legal system and its application to international law, see Jason Beckett, 'The Hartian Tradition in International Law' (2008) 1 *Journal of Jurisprudence* 51.

6

Cultural Unity

THE PREVIOUS CHAPTERS have shed light on the complexity of the unity question. Unity emerges in its multiplicity, as a thick concept that can be approached from many different angles and at different levels. Up to this point, however, the analysis has remained primarily concerned with the substantive point of view. Whether material or formal, unity has thus far been conceptualised from the standpoint of substantive norms and the way in which they interact or are assembled together. If the analysis were to stop here, the deconstruction of the concept of unity would be incomplete. This is not to say that conceptualising international law as rules and institutions is wrong or uninteresting. Article XI of the GATT, the twelve miles rule, the France-Argentina bilateral investment treaty, the principle of good faith or the case law of the ICTY: all of this constitutes international law. But it would be simplistic to limit the analysis of international law, of its identity and unity, to the question of rules.

International law, beyond rules and institutions, is made up of men and women who think about the world around them, speak a certain language, defend certain ideas, pursue projects of criticism and reform, and make decisions for themselves or for others. International law is also a craft and a profession, made up of teachers, legal advisers, civil servants, activists, arbitrators and so on. Finally, international law is a normative enterprise, that is, a system that is aimed at the realisation of certain ends and values, and not simply a technique of regulation and dispute settlement. International law, in sum, is as much a system of rules and institutions as it is a system of thought, communication and values.

Thinking of unity as a complex object requires looking beyond substantive norms, considering other levels of analysis and contemplating the possibility that the unity of international law may reside elsewhere than in its rules and institutions. It also means developing new conceptual tools and frameworks to deal with these non-substantive forms of unity and considering what these may signify in the context of the fragmentation debate. This is what I endeavour to do in the rest of this book.

In the present chapter, I start by looking at what I shall term 'cultural unity'. This concept, as will be seen below, refers to the internal structures of international law as an intellectual and professional discipline. Before considering this notion further, I must begin by considering what it means to think of international law as a discipline, as well as justifying my choice to use the concept of 'culture' to speak of its unity. At the outset, one caveat is in order. As in the rest of this book, my main concern in this chapter is not to suggest or prove that cultural unity actually exists in international law. My aim here is simply to shake things up, open up new theoretical avenues and consider what *it can mean* to think of unity from a cultural point of view. What follows therefore is not a complete or coherent theory of cultural unity but rather an invitation to think outside the box and explore other possibilities of discourse on international law's unity. That said, I now turn to the first question in this chapter: what does it mean to think of international law, not as rules and institutions, but as a discipline?

I. INTERNATIONAL LAW AS AN INTELLECTUAL AND PROFESSIONAL DISCIPLINE

International law is above all an intellectual discipline. This proposition can be understood in a number of ways. That international law is predominantly an intellectual discipline means, first of all, that perhaps more than any other branch of the law, it is a 'lawyer's law'. Disciplines like administrative law or contract law are developed almost exclusively through legislation and precedent. Historically, however, international law has had very little of either and, as a result, has had to rely extensively on the teachings of experts and scholars for its development. This may be less true today, with the proliferation of treaties, the progressive codification of customary law, and the slow emergence of what some call an 'international common law' through the incremental decision-making of international tribunals.[1] Absent a world legislator with a universal *juris dictio*, however, international law does depend, to some extent at least, on what international lawyers think and make of it.[2] This does not mean that international law is only this. But part of international law's distinctiveness resides in the importance of doctrine and scholars in formalising and interpreting its rules.[3]

[1] Andrew Guzman and Timothy Meyer, 'International Common Law: The Soft Law of International Tribunals' (2009) 9 *Chicago Journal of International Law* 515.

[2] Martti Koskenniemi, *From Apology to Utopia: The Structure of International Legal Argument* (Cambridge, Cambridge University Press, 2005) 615.

[3] One of the best illustrations of this is the fact that most histories of international law are in fact histories of international law's great scholars and schools of thought. For a recent and characteristic example, see Stephen Neff, 'A Short History of International Law' in Malcolm Evans (ed), *International Law*, 2nd edn (Oxford, Oxford University Press, 2006). For a critical discussion of the notion that legal scholarship 'makes' international law, see Jörg Kammerhofer, 'Law-Making by Scholarship? The Dark Side of 21st Century International Legal Methodology' in James Crawford et al (eds), *Select Proceedings of the European Society of International Law – Vol 3* (Oxford, Hart Publishing, 2011).

To say that international law is an intellectual discipline also refers to the fact that it has always been more than a simple collection of rules, institutions and doctrines, that is, more than a formal technique of regulation and dispute settlement. Since the eighteenth century and under the indelible influence of Kantian critique, international law has represented a form of *philosophical enquiry*, a metaphysics of humanity. International law, to be sure, *can* be described as a set of formal concepts and categories (principles, rules, standards and so on). But international law is also, and perhaps more fundamentally, a *mode of thought* about the world and how order, peace and progress can be achieved within it. International law is an inquiry into the genesis of the international society: how can humanity move out of the state of nature? How can the community of sovereign nations be organised under the rule of law? In this process, what relationship does international law maintain with other spheres of normativity (morality, religion, domestic law and so on)? Is international law universal? Should it be? In some sense, international law is a speculation about society and its 'possible futures', and a conversation about the role of law in accomplishing these imagined futures.[4]

The overwhelming influence of positivism since the second half of the nineteenth century has somewhat altered this image of international law as a philosophical inquiry. Positivism seeks to exclude ethical, moral and philosophical questions from the legal discipline. In a sense, it has therefore developed *against* the notion of international law as a speculative utopia. International law itself has also undergone profound transformations since the nineteenth century. What used to be perceived as a primitive set of diplomatic doctrines and practices has become a highly complex system of rules and institutions governing nearly every aspect of international relations, from the exploitation of the deep sea-bed to the use of extra-atmospheric space, from consular relations to the free movement of goods, and from the prosecution of torturers to the protection of sea turtles.[5]

This new scope, depth and complexity have led some to the conclusion that international law's metaphysical age is over and that the discipline has entered a 'post-ontological era'.[6] International lawyers, they argue, should no longer feel the need to justify and prove the existence of their law: international law exists and is everywhere to be found.[7] With the reality and positivity of international

[4] On the concept of international law as a 'vision' and as a process of mental construction of the international society, see Philip Allott, *The Health of Nations: Society and Law Beyond the State* (Cambridge, Cambridge University Press, 2002). See also Stephen Toope, 'The Roles of International Law and International Lawyers' in Hugh Kindred et al (eds), *International Law Chiefly as Interpreted and Applied in Canada*, 7th edn (Toronto, Edmond Montgomery Publications, 2006).

[5] Philip Sands, 'Turtles and Torturers: the Transformation of International Law' (2001) 33 *New York University Journal of International Law and Politics* 527.

[6] Thomas Franck, *Fairness in International Law and Institutions* (New York, Oxford University Press, 1995) 6.

[7] Prosper Weil, 'Le droit international en quête de son identité' (1992) 237 *Collected Courses of the Hague Academy of International Law* 9, 47 ('le droit international existe, je l'ai rencontré').

law as an accepted proposition, international lawyers can move away from the big cosmological questions regarding the nature and foundation of international law and focus on what Foucault used to call the 'flat little empirical question':[8] what happens and how does it work?

There is truth, of course, in this statement. In a world where norms and institutions proliferate at every level and in every direction, the classical questions about international law's existence and reality lose some of their original meaning and importance. The 'too much' of one thing clearly does not raise the same questions as the 'too little'. It does nevertheless raise important questions. Whilst the 'reality' of international law may no longer be a pressing question today,[9] international lawyers have recently turned their attention to the issue of obedience to international rules, as demonstrated by the burgeoning literature on 'compliance theories'.[10] More significantly perhaps, the proliferation of regimes has raised important questions about the *general direction* of modern international law: is international law today primarily about sovereignty or human rights, trade or the environment, security or democracy? How do these different regimes interact with one another and how should one resolve tensions or conflicts among them? The old questions about international law's reality are thus replaced by equally existential questions about its meaning and purpose.[11]

Changes in international law's social environment have also raised new questions. From the seventeenth to the nineteenth centuries, 'classical' international law developed within Westphalian parameters, in a European context marked by political, cultural and economic homogeneity. These classical parameters have, since then, undergone a triple transformation. International law is no longer, first of all, the public law of Europe but rather a truly international law, applicable to the entire planet and therefore to a radically more diverse community. International law is also no longer the exclusive preserve of sovereign states. It is increasingly relevant to, and sometimes made by, non-state actors like international organisations, transnational corporations, NGOs, national liberation movements and so on. Finally, international law no longer operates in a context of relative power equality (that is, among European nation-states) but in a world

[8] Michel Foucault, 'Deux essais sur le sujet et le pouvoir' in *Dits et écrits*, Tome IV (Paris, Gallimard, 1994) 233.

[9] This recurring question has not disappeared, however. See, for instance, the theme of the American Society of International Law's 2009 meeting: 'International Law as Law' (www.asil.org/pdfs/AnnualMeetingTheme2009.pdf).

[10] See, eg, Beth Simmons (ed), *International Law – Part 3: Institutions and Theories of Compliance* (London, Sage, 2008); Asher Alkoby, 'Theories of Compliance with International Law and the Challenge of Cultural Difference' (2008) 4 *Journal of International Law and International Relations* 151; Christof Häfner, 'Theories of Compliance with International Law' (2007) 45 *Archiv des Völkerrechts* 597; Rudolf Avenhaus (ed), *Verifying Treaty Compliance: Limiting Weapons of Mass Destruction and Monitoring Kyoto Protocol Provisions* (Berlin, Springer, 2006); Markus Burgstaller, *Theories of Compliance with International Law* (Leiden, Nijhoff, 2005).

[11] See, on this theme, Marti Koskenniemi, 'What is International Law For?' in Malcolm Evans (ed), *International Law* (Oxford, Oxford University Press, 2003); Emmanuelle Jouannet, 'What is the Use of International Law? International Law as a 21st Century Guardian of Welfare' (2007) 28 *Michigan Journal of International Law* 815.

of mice and elephants in which world 'superpowers' and 'failed states' live side by side. This triple revolution again raises fresh and important questions about the possibility of law in a heterogeneous and hegemonic world.[12]

In the end, and despite a 'pragmatic' or 'bureaucratic' turn since the end of the Second World War, international law continues to be more than a mere body of rules. International law is fundamentally a discipline of anticipation, a mode of thought and an idea of humanity as a society governed by law.[13]

International law, however, is not simply an intellectual discipline. It is also a professional discipline, that is, the common practice of men and women who share a particular expertise and are engaged in personal, professional or political projects, communicate with each other, defend ideas, practices or doctrines, and produce normative discourse in stylised and ritualised modes for a particular audience (academics, students, clients, judges, policy-makers, media and so on). In a sense, international law can be described as a series of professional performances, from the 1934 mock trial of Adolf Hitler in New York, to the *amici curiae* submitted by environmental NGOs before the WTO Appellate Body; from the *French Doctors* preaching the right of humanitarian intervention, to the Bush Administration lawyers re-writing the laws of war to justify Guantanamo's legal black-hole; from the Simma-Cassese debate about NATO bombings in Kosovo, to feminist lobbies advocating the reform of European Union legislation in Brussels. Taken from this point of view, international law is not simply an intellectual terrain in which 'imaginary forces' ponder over the constitution of a legal community.[14] It is also an argumentative terrain, that is, a rhetorical and polemical field within which individuals express their fears, desires, ambitions and utopias, and within which they pursue projects using a common professional vocabulary.[15]

[12] On the heterogeneity theme, see for instance, Hélène Ruiz-Fabri, Rüdiger Wolfrum and Jana Gogolin (eds), *International Law in a Heterogeneous World – Select Proceedings of the European Society of International Law* (Oxford, Hart Publishing, 2008). On the hegemony theme, see in particular, Michael Byers and Georg Nolte (eds), *United States Hegemony and the Foundations of International Law* (Cambridge, Cambridge University Press, 2003); Gerry Simpson, *Great Powers and Outlaw States – Unequal Sovereigns in the International Legal Order* (Cambridge, Cambridge University Press, 2004); Detlev Vagts, 'Hegemonic International Law' (2001) 95 *American Journal of International Law* 843; Martti Koskenniemi, 'International Law and Hegemony: a Reconfiguration' (2004) 17 *Cambridge Review of International Affairs* 197; Nico Krisch, 'International Law in Times of Hegemony: Unequal Power and the Shaping of the International Legal Order' (2005) 16 *European Journal of International Law* 369; Thomas Franck, 'The Power of Legitimacy and the Legitimacy of Power: International Law in an Age of Power Desequilibrium' (2006) 100 *American Journal of International Law* 88; Peter Fitzpatrick, '"Gods Would be Needed . . .": American Empire and the Rule of (International) Law' (2003) 16 *Leiden Journal of International Law* 429.

[13] See Boutros Boutros-Ghali, 'Le droit international à la recherche de ses valeurs: paix, développement, démocratisation' (2000) 286 *Collected Courses of the Hague Academy of International Law* 9, 20: 'le droit international est, par essence, un droit d'imagination et un droit d'anticipation'.

[14] Mireille Delmas-Marty, *Les forces imaginantes du droit – Le relatif et l'universel* (Paris, Seuil, 2004) 8–9.

[15] My approach to international law as a discipline draws extensively on David Kennedy's writings. See, in particular, David Kennedy, 'My Talk at the ASIL: What is New Thinking in International Law?' (2000) 94 *American Society of International Law Proceedings* 104; 'When Renewal Repeats: Thinking Against the Box' (2000) 32 *New York University Journal of International Law and Politics*

To think of international law as a disciplinary field is to think of it as something more than a static edifice of formal concepts, ideas, doctrines and institutions. International law as a discipline is a space for the circulation of ideas about the world, a mode of communication, a collective experience and expertise. Again, this does not mean that rules do not matter. The point is simply that there is more to international law than rules. In a sense, one could say that reducing international law to positive rules would be like reducing theatre to the writings of Racine, Shakespeare, Molière or Brecht. Theatrical texts are of course an integral part of theatre. But theatre is above all a spectacle, that is, a process that always begins with a director using a text to make a statement about the world around him. Theatre is also the intervention of a *dramaturge* who works on the meaning of the play, explores its deep structure, and reveals its subtext in a way that will guide everything that follows, from acting to costumes and set-design. Theatre is of course actors, who give characters a face and a voice. And theatre, to finish, is a place of physical action, a place where roles are played out and stories are told. Theatre, in the end, is more than a literary form. It is about representations, plays and performances, as much as it is about texts. Theatre is also a social space and a cybernetic machine, that is, a machine used to fabricate and communicate messages.

International law, like theatre, cannot be reduced to text (that is, to the text of positive norms). International law is a social space, a place for the production of arguments and messages, a process involving different roles and professions (judges, legal advisers, activists, academics, etc). International law is a cybernetic machine too, a stylised and normative language in which different sensibilities, ideologies and interests are described, defined and justified.[16]

As soon as international law is understood not as rules and institutions, but as an intellectual universe, a field of knowledge and an argumentative practice, the unity question takes on a very different appearance. The question is no longer whether rules are compatible or whether they are assembled together to form a system. Instead, it becomes whether regular patterns can be observed in the way in which lawyers think and speak of international affairs, and whether mental or discursive structures exist that give international law its identity and unity as an autonomous discipline. In what follows, I shall refer to these patterns and structures as *cultural* unity. Before considering what cultural unity might look like, however, I must say something about the notion of legal culture itself.

335; 'The Disciplines of International Law and Policy' (1999) 12 *Leiden Journal of International Law* 9.

[16] On international law as a stylised mode of communication, see in particular, Ed Morgan, *The Aesthetics of International Law* (Toronto, University of Toronto Press, 2007). For a more classical formulation, see eg, Robert Jennings, 'International Courts and International Politics – Josephine Onoh Lecture 1986' in David Freestone et al (eds), *Contemporary Issues in International Law: A Collection of the Josephine Onoh Memorial Lectures* (The Hague, Kluwer Law International, 2002) 26: 'in this culturally, ideologically, and economically divided world, it is international law itself which provides a common language, the language in which these very differences are described and defined, explained, and the different aspirations propagated'.

II. THE CONCEPT OF LEGAL CULTURE

The concept of culture has several meanings and the relationship between these various definitions is not always simple.[17] In its first and widest meaning, the concept of culture covers everything that separates human from animal existence, or humanity from nature. Understood as such, culture is the symbolic marker of civilisation, the sum of all faculties, functions and practices that characterise men as rational beings.[18] Culture, in other words, is that which distinguishes *homo sapiens* from other animal species.

Culture in its second, anthropological meaning refers to that which expresses the characteristic genius of a given population at a particular time in its history. Culture is here understood as the system of shared beliefs, values, customs, behaviours and other habits that characterise the members of a particular group.[19] Culture, from this point of view, is not that which separates mankind from nature but rather that which distinguishes the members of one human group from those of another.

In a third, more classical definition, culture refers to the taste or aptitude in the 'things of the mind' like arts, poetry, literature, sciences or philosophy, and knowledge of the specific language in which these are expressed. Culture, in this perspective, is not that which characterises a particular community or group but the process of cultivation or improvement of the individual. Culture is here understood as education or erudition.[20]

One can already observe a certain tension between the traditional meanings of culture. Culture, at times, refers to a totalising philosophical object. At other times, it refers to a set of distinctive human features. At other times still, it refers

[17] In a study published 1952, Kroeber and Kluckhohn identified no less than 164 possible definitions of the concept of culture in the social sciences. See Alfred Kroeber and Clyde Kluckhohn, *Culture: A Critical Review of Concepts and Definitions* (Cambridge, Harvard University Press, 1952).

[18] It is in this sense that Kant, for instance, understands the term *Kultur*. See, eg, Immanuel Kant, 'Toward Perpetual Peace: A Philosophical Sketch' *in Toward Perpetual Peace and Other Writings on Politics, Peace and History* (Yale, Yale University Press, 2006) 92–95 (in which Kant defines culture as the characteristic trait of civilised peoples, ie, nations seeking to extricate themselves from the state of nature); and more generally *Critique of Judgement* (Oxford, Oxford University Press, 1978) 319 (in which Kant defines culture as the key attribute of men as rational beings).

[19] The foundational definition of culture in anthropology was given by Edward Tylor in *Primitive Culture* (New York, Harper, 1871) 1: 'culture is that complex whole which includes knowledge, belief, art, morals, law, custom, and any other capabilities and habits acquired by man as a member of society'.

[20] Culture, in this classical sense, resembles Cicero's *cultura animi*, ie, the culture of the mind 'which plucks up vices by the roots; prepares the mind for the receiving of seeds; commits them to it, or, as I may say, sows them, in the hope that, when come to maturity, they may produce a plentiful harvest' (Cicero, *Tusculan Disputations: On the Nature of Gods, and on the Commonwealth* (New York, Cosimo Classics, 2005) 69). The concept of culture as instruction also bears resemblance to what the Greeks, before Cicero, called *paideia*, ie, the process of educating humans to their true and fullest potential, as citizens or as kings. On the Greek concept of culture, see Werner Jaeger, *Paideia: The Ideals of Greek Culture* (Oxford, Oxford University Press, 1986).

to an intellectual process or to the finished product of that process. And depending on the perspective held, culture may be understood at the level of humanity as a whole, at the group level, or at the individual level.

The concept of culture resists easy definition. This definitional problem has become more acute still since the 'cultural turn' that has swept across the social sciences and humanities since the end of the 1970s. The term 'cultural turn' has been used to describe a fundamental shift in emphasis away from positivist, utilitarian and materialist epistemologies. Largely influenced by postmodern and poststructuralist theories, this paradigmatic shift has taken two main forms: that of a re-examination and that of a re-discovery. It has prompted, first of all, a re-examination of the role of the state as the sole entity from which to establish classifications and anatomies of power.[21] But the cultural turn has also meant the re-discovery of culture as a key structuring factor in constituting social relations and identities, on equal footing with socio-economic factors.[22] One important consequence of this has been the expansion of the concept of culture beyond anthropology into nearly every branch of the social sciences: sociology, history, geography, economics, linguistics, political sciences and, more recently, legal studies.[23]

The dissemination of the concept of culture has had two consequences. First of all, it has led to a proliferation of the loci, scales and layers of culture. The social space has become saturated with cultural forms and references. Each segment of society, each class, each generation now has its own culture: working-class culture, bourgeois culture, capital culture, provincial culture, black culture, pop culture, geek culture and so on. Even brands and companies have come to be presented as particular forms of culture: Pepsi culture versus Coke culture; Mac culture versus PC culture, etc.[24]

The dissemination of the concept of culture across the social sciences has also resulted in a proliferation of theoretical approaches. One important aspect of this has been the reconsideration of the concept of culture as a given that is

[21] The influence of Foucault and his analysis of 'micro-power' structures were decisive in this regard. See, among other writings, Michel Foucault, *Discipline and Punish: The Birth of the Prison* (New York, Vintage Books, 1979); *The Will to Truth* (New York, Tavistock Publications, 1980).

[22] See, eg, Fredric Jameson, *The Cultural Turn: Selected Writings on the Postmodern 1983–1998* (London, Verso, 1998); David Chaney, *The Cultural Turn: Scene-Setting Essays on Contemporary Cultural History* (London, Routledge, 1994); Kate Nash, 'The "Cultural Turn" in Social Theory: Towards a Theory of Cultural Politics' (2001) 35 *Sociology* 77; Nancy Armstrong, 'Who's Afraid of the Cultural Turn?' (2001) 12 *Differences* 17.

[23] See, in particular, Paul Kahn, *The Cultural Study of Law* (Chicago, Chicago University Press, 1999).

[24] See Adam Arvidsson, *Brands: Meaning and Value in Postmodern Media Culture* (New York, Routledge, 2006). On a lighter note, see Umberto Eco's essay, *Comment voyager avec un saumon* (Paris, Librairie Générale Française, 2000) in which he takes the view that the world is now divided between Mac and PC users and compares the division between them to the schism between Catholics and Protestants: 'the Macintosh is Catholic and the PC is Protestant. Indeed, the Macintosh is . . . cheerful, friendly, conciliatory, it tells the faithful how they must proceed step by step . . . It is catechistic . . . The PC is Protestant . . . it allows free interpretation of scripture, demands difficult personal decisions, imposes a subtle hermeneutics upon the user . . . to make the system work you need to interpret the program yourself: a long way from the baroque community of revelers, the user is closed within the loneliness of his own inner torment'.

'already there' and is simply passed on to us, that is, as a mere environment in which individuals are born, live their lives and die, like in a home.[25] Culture is no longer regarded as a neutral background or surrounding. It is increasingly recognised as an active force that shapes social relations. To some, culture is primarily a source of conflict.[26] Others regard it as a source of creativity, progress and development.[27] Either way, culture is regarded as a driving force that plays an active role in society, and not simply as a context or habitat. Increasingly, and more importantly perhaps, culture is no longer regarded as a primitive, intangible and objective factor. From Bourdieu's *Esquisse*[28] to Said's *Orientalism*,[29] culture is understood as a socially constructed object, shaped by power relations and involved in the (re)production of symbolic and social hierarchies. More recently, culture has also been reinterpreted as an object of rights, whether it be the right to culture (that is, the right to access and participate freely in cultural life) or the right to have one's culture respected and protected.[30]

The concept of culture, as the above demonstrates, is as central as it is ambiguous. Its spread across the social sciences has been accompanied by a semantic dispersion, from the infinitely big (culture as the invention of mankind 'to make the world a viable place')[31] to the infinitely small (Mac's apple logo), so much so that some have started to question the usefulness of a concept whose meanings are so multiple, shifting, slippery and dissonant.[32] For my part, I shall endorse

[25] On this notion of culture as a '*donné déjà-là*' (a given-already-there), see Danièle Letocha, 'Entre le donné et le construit: le penseur de l'action. Sur une relecture du *Lieu de l'homme*' in Simon Langlois and Yves Martin (eds), *L'horizon de la culture Hommage à Fernand Dumont* (Québec, Presses de l'Université Laval, 1995) 29.

[26] Samuel Huntington, 'The Clash of Civilizations?' (1993) 72 *Foreign Affairs* 21, 22: 'it is my hypothesis that the fundamental source of conflict in this new world will not be primarily ideological or primarily economic. The great divisions among humankind and the dominating source of conflict will be cultural'.

[27] See, for instance, the approach to culture taken in the UNESCO Convention on the Protection and Promotion of the Diversity of Cultural Expressions, 20 October 2005, preamble: 'cultural diversity creates a rich and varied world which . . . is a mainspring for sustainable development . . . culture [i]s a strategic element in national and international development policies, as well as in international cooperation development'.

[28] Pierre Bourdieu, *Outline of a Theory of Practice* (Cambridge, Cambridge University Press, 1977) (in which Bourdieu highlights the importance of 'cultural capital' in the legitimisation and the reproduction of social hierarchies). See also Pierre Bourdieu, *Distinction – A Social Critique of the Judgement of Taste* (Cambridge, Harvard University Press, 1987) (in which Bourdieu argues that cultural practices and preferences can be mapped to social class and profession).

[29] Edward Said, *Orientalism* (New York, Vintage Books, 1979) (in which Said argues that Western culture has constructed a constellation of false assumptions and prejudicial stereotypes about the non-Western world which has served as an implicit justification for European and American colonial and imperial ambitions).

[30] For a general overview, see eg, Francesco Francioni and Martin Scheinin (eds), *Cultural Human Rights* (Leiden, Martinus Nijhoff, 2008).

[31] 'La culture c'est tout ce que l'homme a inventé pour rendre le monde vivable et la mort affrontable', Aimé Césaire, 'Entretien avec Maryse Condé' *Lire* (Paris, June 2004) 114.

[32] See, eg, Robert Brightman, 'Forget Culture: Replacement, Transcendence, Relexification' (1995) 10 *Cultural Anthropology* 509; Nicholas Garnham, 'Reaching for my Revolver: Problems with the Concept of Culture' (2001) 9 *European Review* 413; Melvin Lasky, 'The Banalization of the Concept of Culture' (2002) 39 *Society* 73.

Zigmunt Bauman's position that the plasticity of the culture concept is what makes it useful as a cognitive or analytical tool.[33] As will be discussed below, it is that plasticity that enables us to integrate under a single term a diversity of elements that are not covered by competing notions like tradition or ideology. Before taking this point further, however, I must clarify the general sense in which I am using the term culture in the present chapter.

By culture, I shall be referring to what Geertz calls 'webs of significance', that is, the system of symbols, representations, values, as well as the learned ways of thinking, feeling and acting, which are common to a social group.[34] Understood in this generic sense, culture refers to the particular configuration of assumptions or understandings, the cognitive structures and the logical frameworks, which control the way in which ideas and statements are produced, validated and communicated within a given group. These webs of significance, it must be noted at the outset, are less explicit than latent structures that govern the production, contestation and transformation of *meaning* by the members of the group. Culture, in other words, is the underlying system of conceptions and behaviours by which members of a group communicate, perpetuate and develop their knowledge about and attitude toward the world around them.[35]

In the legal field, the concept of culture may have two different meanings. These are what Lawrence Friedman call 'external' and 'internal' legal culture.[36] External legal culture, according to Friedman, is the legal culture of the general population: how do people feel about the legal system and its institutions? When are they willing to use courts and do they think that these courts are fair? What part of the law do they consider legitimate? What do they know about the law in general? Internal legal culture, on the other hand, refers to the attitudes, values, ideologies and principles of legal professionals, that is, lawyers, judges, academics and others who work 'within the magic circle of the legal system'.[37] Internal legal culture, in other words, refers to the specific parameters within which juridical thought and discourse operate. It is to this type of internal legal culture that I shall refer in the rest of this chapter.

Before considering in further detail the concept of cultural unity, I must say a few words about my reasons for speaking of culture in lieu of other, perhaps less debatable notions. Given culture's instability as a concept, it may have been easier to use similar concepts with less contested meanings. One such concept may have been, for instance, the concept of 'legal tradition', as developed in particular by H Patrick Glenn in his *Legal Traditions of the World*.[38] There are several parallels between the concept of tradition and the idea of culture. Glenn

[33] Zygmunt Bauman, *Culture as Praxis* (London, Sage Publications, 1999) xiv.

[34] Clifford Geertz, *The Interpretation of Cultures* (New York, Basic Books, 1972) 5.

[35] Ibid at 89.

[36] Lawrence Friedman, *The Legal System: A Social Science Perspective* (New York, Russel Sage Foundation, 1975) 193–94.

[37] Ibid.

[38] Patrick Glenn, *Legal Traditions of the World – Sustainable Diversity in Law*, 3rd edn (Oxford, Oxford University Press, 2007).

conceives of tradition as that which gives a group its coherence and identity. Like Geertz in relation to culture, Glenn defines tradition in terms of 'webs' of information, beliefs and values – whether implicit or explicit – that shape our vision of the world and our behaviour.[39]

There are therefore obvious similarities between the concepts of culture and tradition, something that Glenn readily admits. Why, then, choose one concept over the other? Glenn offers two justifications for his own preference for tradition. He takes the view, first of all, that the notion of culture is inappropriate because it is primarily a Western construct.[40] I shall not address this justification in too much depth here. Besides the fact that Glenn himself relies almost exclusively on Western thinkers to develop his theory of tradition (Burke, Popper, Locke, Kuhn, Rorty, etc), the argument does not in itself decide the issue. The mere fact that a concept is the product of Western thought does not make it improper or unsuitable, unless of course it can be proven that the concept does indeed reflect a particular ideology or agenda which, in turn, leads to bias in the analysis.

Glenn's second justification for discarding the concept of culture is perhaps more compelling and refers to the concept's ill-defined and ambiguous nature. As previously mentioned, there is obvious truth in this statement. Despite this, however, the concept of culture seems better suited to speak of the unity of international law as a discipline for one essential reason. Tradition, in Glenn's theory, is defined as the 'continued presence of the past'. This definition revolves around the key notion of *continuity*:

> [T]radition involves the extension of the past to the present . . . Another dimension of tradition . . . is found in the necessity of tradition having been continuously transmitted . . . Absent historic continuity, reaching down to present adherents, all traditions appear as strange ones and all adherents to them appear as different people[41]

Without continuity, tradition loses its intrinsic quality as a controlling element in determining social identity. Glenn, of course, is aware that traditions change and that they always comprise a plurality of voices.[42] However, he treats these tensions, these conversations or these controversies as mere elements of 'variance' or 'dissidence', which only marginally affect what he calls the 'primary' or 'principal' version of tradition, that is, the version that is accepted as 'true' by the greater number.[43]

The problem with this way of thinking is that it risks confining the analysis to what Foucault calls 'the form of the same' (la forme du même).[44] This approach

[39] Ibid, ch 1: 'A Theory of Tradition: The Changing Presence of the Past'.

[40] Ibid at 154. Glenn develops his critique of the concept of legal culture in 'Legal Cultures and Legal Traditions' in Mark Van Hoecke (ed), *Epistemology and Methodology in Comparative Law* (Oxford, Hart Publishing, 2004).

[41] Ibid at 12.

[42] Ibid at 14.

[43] Ibid at 37.

[44] Michel Foucault, *The Archaeology of Knowledge* (London, Routledge, 2002) 23.

invites us to think about unity and identity within a group in terms of permanence, continuity and stability. By doing so, it seems to exclude *ex hypothesi* the possibility that controversies and dialectics may themselves be elements of unity/identity. Tradition is understood as a continued relationship to the past. Culture, on the other hand, is constructed through a dialectical relationship to the past *and* the future. Culture involves both the presence of the past and its constant re-writing, as a way of projecting oneself into the future. For this reason, the concept of culture is better suited to integrate notions of discontinuity, rupture, threshold, dispersion, series or transformation. It allows us, in other words, to grasp more fully the inner economy of a discipline in its dynamic and perhaps even contradictory character. This is why I shall use the concept of culture, and not tradition, to think about the unity of international law as a discipline.

Thus far, I have shown that international law, beyond its rules and institutions, can be thought of as an intellectual and professional discipline. I have also justified my choice to speak of 'legal culture' to talk about its cognitive, semantic and discursive structures. What remains to be seen is what the unity of international law as a cultural system might actually look like.

III. THE UNITY OF INTERNATIONAL LAW AS A CULTURAL SYSTEM

It is not uncommon to hear that international lawyers have more in common with their foreign peers than with domestic lawyers within their own jurisdiction. At first glance, this proposition might seem rather odd. Internationalists can hardly be said to form a tight and homogeneous group. International law professions are far more diverse than domestic legal professions (lawyers, judges and teachers for the most part). The 'college' of international lawyers comprises an infinite variety of roles, from legal advisers at the White House to ICRC delegates in Gaza, prosecutors in war crime tribunals, legal officers at the European Commission, judges at the Law of the Sea Tribunal, professors of international environmental law, diplomats, activists and so forth. Moreover, there is no single 'curriculum' in international law. Each international lawyer is educated in their own national academic system, in their own language, and according to particular intellectual cultures and traditions. Neither is there an 'international bar' that controls education, training and practice within the international law professions. All of this means that the teaching and practice of international law are far less integrated than the teaching and practice of, say, French law, where nearly all lawyers receive the same training in the same universities before joining the same professional schools, taking the same competitive examinations (bar, *magistrature*, *agrégation*) and becoming members of the same professional associations. What, then, do an investment arbitrator, a professor of international environmental law at the University of Yaoundé, the Canadian ambassador to the UN and an Indian lawyer working to promote women's rights in Asia all have in common?

The main argument of the present chapter is that what unites these different professionals, what enables communication between them, what makes it possible for them to understand each other (without necessarily agreeing with one another), might be the fact that they share a common *culture* of international law. To date, this notion of cultural unity has received very little attention in the literature, if any at all.[45] In what follows, I shall therefore only attempt to lay the groundwork for a theory of cultural unity, set down a few theoretical markers and consider what shape the analysis of international law as a cultural system might take.

In doing so, I shall draw a distinction between two levels of analysis which, although not mutually exclusive, involve different aspects, criteria and logics of unity. The first level of analysis takes as a starting point the notion of international law as a mental universe, that is, as a set of worldviews, a symbolic apparatus and a system of thought. The second level of analysis, for its part, considers international law not as a mode of thought but rather as a mode of expression or a form of argument. In what follows, my aim is not to synthesise these two levels of analysis into a full or coherent theory of cultural unity. Neither is it to show that either form of unity actually exists in international law. More modestly, my purpose is to set out the main problems and to open up possible avenues of thought on the largely ignored question of cultural unity.

A. International law as a mental universe: *esprit de corps* and collective consciousness

The first way to think about cultural unity is to consider the mental structures that underpin and define international law as an intellectual field.[46] The term 'mental structure', of course, can be understood in many different ways and at different levels. In what follows, I shall focus on two types of mental structures, which refer to the notions of '*esprit de corps*' and 'collective consciousness' respectively.

The most obvious form of intellectual solidarity among the members of a group can be found in the existence of a common project, that is, of a collective goal that unites disparate desires, energies and practices or a central question that defines the boundaries of a given discipline. To speak of a federating

[45] When the notion of cultural unity is mentioned, it is generally in passing, indirectly or implicitly. See, eg, Jean-Paul Jacqué, 'Pratique et doctrine' (2005) 51 *Annuaire Français de Droit International* xv, xvii: 'doctrine and practice are above all the product of men who share a common language. All have been trained in the same mould, that of the teaching of international law . . . We are all immersed in the same culture. We practise the same art in different contexts' (author's translation).

[46] By intellectual field, I mean an area of structured, socially patterned activity organised around certain themes and problems and in which conceptions, knowledge and ideas are produced and communicated according to specific rules and forms of authority. This notion of intellectual field is borrowed from Pierre Bourdieu, 'Champ de pouvoir, champ intellectuel et habitus de classe' (1971) 1 *Scolies* 7.

project does not mean, of course, that all the members of the group have to experience the project or associate with it in the same way. Within a single discipline, there are always utopians and realists, optimists and sceptics, apologists and critics. Beyond the diversity of experiences, sensibilities and practices, however, the unity of a discipline may nonetheless rest on a common, defining project, a cause that acts as a principle of collective emulation: diagnostic and cure for medicine; mapping the laws of nature for physics; maximising sales for marketing and so on. Whether real or imaginary, this type of common project can constitute a centre of gravity, a focal point around which diverse disciplinary theories and practices coalesce.

What is true of medicine, physics or marketing may also be true of international law. It may be that international law's autonomy and identity as a cultural system rest on the existence of a federating project or ethos, what Bourdieu calls the '*esprit de corps*' of a discipline.[47] Bourdieu, it must be noted, views *esprit de corps* primarily as an exclusionary device. *Esprit de corps* allows one to differentiate between those who are worthy of admission to the group and those who are not, those who are 'in' and those who are 'out'. In Bourdieu's view, *esprit de corps* is thus instrumental in producing and reproducing social elites.[48] However, this notion of corporate self-consciousness can also be used more inclusively as something that refers to a common mindset or a core of shared assumptions generating a form of moral unity among the members of a professional group, beyond the diversity of their social practices. *Esprit de corps* is also the visceral form of recognition of that which constitutes the essence of the group, its identity and its truth.[49]

One might argue, then, that the unity of international law finds its source in a sort of cosmopolitan *esprit de corps*, a shared intellectual sensibility that underpins the 'invisible college' of international law and produces a form of intellectual solidarity among the members of the discipline. This notion of an *esprit d'internationalité* acting as a ferment of disciplinary unity has scarcely been made in the literature. It is implicit, however, in some recent works on the history of ideas in international law, and most notably in Martti Koskenniemi's writings on the international law tradition and its intellectual trajectories.

In his *Gentle Civilizer of Nations*, Koskenniemi tells the story of what he considers to be the 'golden age' of modern international law, its 'heroic period' between 1870 and 1960.[50] Koskenniemi puts forward two main hypotheses. The first hypothesis is that modern international law was not born, as the doctrinal orthodoxy has it, in Westphalia or in Vienna but at the end of the nineteenth century, in the corridors of the *Institut de Droit International* and in the pages

[47] Pierre Bourdieu, *Homo Academicus* (Paris, Editions de Minuit, 1984) 80–81.

[48] Pierre Bourdieu, *The State Nobility: Elite Schools in the Field of Power* (Stanford, Stanford University Press, 1996).

[49] Bourdieu, *Homo Academicus*, above n 47 at 80.

[50] Martti Koskenniemi, *The Gentle Civilizer of Nations: The Rise and Fall of International Law, 1870–1960* (Cambridge, Cambridge University Press) 2002.

of the *Revue de droit international et de legislation comparée*. The birth of the modern discipline of international law, Koskenniemi argues, was the product of a small group of liberal lawyers committed to reinventing international law as an instrument of political reform and progress, and not simply as a set of diplomatic techniques and procedures.[51] Koskenniemi is aware, of course, that elements of international law existed before 1870. He does, however, regard these elements as part of the 'prehistory' of international law and takes the view that modern international law, as a profession united by common liberal ideas, only truly came to life under the influence of the 'men of 1871'.[52]

Koskenniemi's second hypothesis is that the history of international law as a civilising mission came to an effective end sometime around 1960, when the vision of the 'international' as a integrated social space gave way to a kaleidoscopic representation of the world calling for new, technical, specialised and functional types of knowledge and leading to the progressive atomisation of international law into separate spheres of legality (trade, environment, communications, human rights and so on) all operating in isolation from one another. Since then, he argues, international law has become depoliticised, marginalised and has turned into a technical instrument for the advancement of particular interests and powerful actors.[53]

These hypotheses are of course open to debate. Koskenniemi, for instance, centres his argument on a small community of cosmopolitan lawyers, a very tight, self-proclaimed and self-reproducing European elite claiming to represent the 'legal conscience of the civilised world'. One may question whether this essentially local history can be universalised and whether Koskenniemi's tale of the rise and fall of the 'spirit of 1871' can be generalised to the discipline as a whole. For our purposes, however, what matters is Koskenniemi's general approach and his conception of international law as an intellectual tradition, a political project – one could almost say a personal *epic*. The story told by Koskenniemi is not one of great diplomatic conferences, great treaties, great cases and great wars. It is, instead, a story of great men, moved by a common reforming sense, a common belief and, in a sense, a common trust in international law as an emancipatory promise, as a rational, scientific and secular instrument for the propagation of modern, liberal ideals.

Koskenniemi, to be sure, insists that this common project had its ups and downs, its periods of crisis, its paradoxes and ambiguities.[54] His central claim, however, is that in this golden age of internationalism, international law's autonomy as a discipline was built upon a professional ideology, a mobilising ideal, a *cause commune* to which the different advocates of international law –

[51] Ibid at 3–4.

[52] Martti Koskenniemi, 'International Law and Raison d'Etat: Rethinking the Prehistory of International Law' in Benedict Kingsbury and Benjamin Straumann (eds), *The Roman Foundations of the Law of Nations: Alberico Gentili and the Justice of Empire* (Oxford, Oxford University Press, 2010).

[53] Koskenniemi, *Gentle Civilizer of Nations*, above n 50 at 413–509.

[54] Ibid at 98–178 (on the ambiguous relation of the men of 1871 to colonialism).

whether politicians, philosophers, activists, diplomats or scholars – subscribed. The central idea that underpins Koskenniemi's two hypotheses is therefore that the identity of international law as an intellectual and professional discipline rested, at least in part, on a common historical project, a cosmopolitan ethos made up of a number of federating *mots d'ordre*: critique of sovereignty, peaceful settlement of disputes, religious tolerance, individual freedoms, free trade, contact between peoples and so on.[55] Implicit in Koskenniemi's argument is the notion that the unity of international law is somewhat linked to the spirit or legal consciousness of international lawyers (and that today's fragmentation stems from the progressive dissolution of that common spirit or consciousness).

Here is therefore a first proposition, a first possibility of discourse: the cultural unity of international law refers to the existence of a common project or intellectual sensibility that unites at least the majority of international lawyers across their personal, national, institutional or political allegiances.[56] Whether this historical project has actually ever existed and if it has, what remains of it today, are beside the point. The argument is simply that it is *possible* to think of cultural unity as something that refers to this sort of common sense or consciousness.

Other principles of cultural unity can be envisaged, however. It may be, for instance, that the unity of international law as a discipline refers, not so much to a positive and explicit ideology but instead to more diffuse ways of thinking, to a mix of images and ideas that form a sort of latent cognitive frame and informs the experience, perception and interpretation of international lawyers. In this perspective, the cultural unity of the discipline does not denote an internationalist *esprit de corps*, a concept that implies the existence of a common programme or common values. Rather, cultural unity refers to the notion of 'collective consciousness', as understood by Durkheim, that is, the range of beliefs and sentiments common to average members of a group and that constitutes the group's 'social psyche'.[57]

The logic is slightly different here. The identity of the profession is no longer understood in terms of common goals and purposes, that is, as something that is to come. Instead, cultural unity is understood in terms of *a priori* representations of self and society, that is, in terms of certain forms of cultural capital that are already there and are transmitted from generation to generation.

That being said, what might 'collective consciousness' look like in a discipline like international law? Needless to say, this is a vast and complex question and it would take more than this chapter to provide definitive answers. However, I shall make four suggestions here, to open up the debate and start giving shape to the notion of cultural unity. There are, I submit, four types of knowledge,

[55] Ibid at 11–97.

[56] For a similar argument, see Guillaume Sacriste and Antoine Vauchez, 'The Force of International Law: Lawyers' Diplomacy on the International Scene in the 1920s' (2007) 32 *Law and Social Inquiry* 83, 92–97.

[57] Emile Durkheim, *The Division of Labor in Society* (Glencoe, The Free Press, 1947) 79–80.

beliefs or representations, in other words four forms of cultural capital that underpin the collective consciousness of a professional discipline like international law: a recurring question; a history/geography; canonical truths; and exemplars.

1) A discipline is constituted, first of all, by reference to a recurring question, a fundamental enigma, which all the members of the group seek to resolve collectively. This fundamental question acts as a sort of point of presence or, as Lacan would have it, a *point de capiton* (anchoring or 'quilting' point), that is, a point of convergence around which meaning is distributed, disseminated and stabilised, and that enables everything that happens in a particular discourse to be situated retroactively and prospectively.[58]

   The question of 'life', for instance, constitutes biology's *point de capiton*. Everything in biology, any knowledge or discourse can be traced back in some way to the question of life: where does life come from? How did it first appear? According to which laws did life develop? Under which forms does it currently exist? Similarly, one could consider that a discipline like international law is constructed and unified by a central question, a grand federating theme, something like 'ordering the world under the rule of law'. Every argument, every doctrine or theory of international law is more or less directly related to this fundamental question: how to civilise the relations of sovereign states? On what foundations can an international rule of law be established among them? What are the best techniques for bringing order, stability and progress in the international community?

   International lawyers, to be sure, relate to these foundational questions from different point of views and with different sensibilities. Some are committed and confident. Others are pessimistic or cynical. Most are somewhere in between.[59] But whether they are enthusiasts, sceptics or critics, international lawyers are all engaged in a reflection and conversation on the possibility, the forms and the means of controlling or organising power on the international plane.
2) The identity and autonomy of a discipline can also be analysed from the point of view of its history/geography. Let us be clear at the outset that what matters here is not so much the 'true' history of a discipline as its 'reconstructed' history, that is, the sort of history which involves a judicious selection of events, myths, legends and heroes that form part of the group's 'collective memory'.[60]

[58] Jacques Lacan, *The Seminar of Jacques Lacan – Book III: The Psychoses, 1955–56* (London, Routledge, 1993) 267–68.

[59] See Martti Koskenniemi, 'Between Commitment and Cynicism: Outline for a Theory of International Law as Practice' in UN Office of Legal Affairs (ed), *Collection of Essays by Legal Advisers of States, Legal Advisers of International Organizations and Practitioners in the Field of International Law* (New York, United Nations, 1999).

[60] On the importance of 'reconstructed' histories in the identity of academic disciplines, see Tony Becher and Paul Trowler, *Academic Tribes and Territories*, 2nd edn (Buckingham, Open University Press, 2001) 48–50.

A discipline's history/geography revolves, first of all, around seminal dates, events and moments. In the field of medicine, for instance, one thinks about the first anaesthesia by chloroform; the first human vaccination; the discovery of X-rays; the discovery of aspirin and penicillin; the discovery of DNA; the first heart transplant; the first cloned mammal and so forth. In the field of international law, one thinks about the publication of Grotius's *De Jure Belli Ac Pacis*; the peace of Westphalia; the Congress of Vienna; the two World Wars; the creation of the UN; the Nuremberg trials; the great 'decade of codification'; the fall of the Berlin Wall; the two Gulf Wars; the NATO bombings in Kosovo; the establishment of the ICC and so on.

There are also the great figures and the great heroes of a discipline – the founding fathers, the great 'knowledge conveyors' (*passeurs de savoir*) and 'knowledge breakers' (*casseurs de savoir*): Einstein, Planck, Oppenheimer, etc for the physicists; Weber, Marx, Durkheim, etc for the sociologists; Grotius, Vattel, Kelsen, etc for the internationalists. And there is, to conclude, the particular geography of a discipline, its symbolic places of knowledge, power and glory, the points of passage and pilgrimage. In international law, one would think, for instance, about The Hague (the 'capital' of international law), Geneva, New York or Heidelberg.

History and geography are critical elements of a discipline's culture and folklore. They convey founding myths, tales and stories that act as agents of socialisation within the group. This is most evident in the field of international law, where the reconstructed history of the discipline conveys the image of a slow but steady progress of law against power, reason against passion, and order against chaos.[61]

This narrative is well known to international lawyers. Once upon a time, the story goes, the world was in a state of nature in which force, power, politics and anarchy reigned. Then came the state system, Westphalia and the end of the religious wars in Europe. International law progressively emerged as a new form of organisation among sovereign entities. For 250 years, lawyers have worked hard to elaborate the great doctrines of the law of peoples, seeking both to consolidate and control sovereignty. Then a new problem surfaced: this law of peoples was too philosophical and too remote from the political and diplomatic realities of the world. International law had to reinvent itself to become modern. It turned its back on the abstract philosophical considerations of the 'traditional' system of international law and entered the pragmatic era of treaties and institutions. Since then, and despite occasional crises, international law won a series of decisive victories: the dismantling of colonial empires; the liberalisation of world trade; the recovery of the hole in the ozone layer; the prosecution of war criminals and so on.[62]

[61] On the vocabulary of progress in international law, see Thomas Skouteris, *The Notion of Progress in International Law Discourse* (The Hague, TMC Asser Press, 2010).

[62] On the structure of this familiar narrative, see David Kennedy, 'The Disciplines of International Law and Policy' (2004) 12 *Leiden Journal of International Law* 9, 91–93. On the role of 'crises' in

A double tale of progress emerges from this official history. The first is a narrative of progress *through law*. International law is depicted as a modernising and progressive instrument that has enabled the international community to escape the state of nature and thereby move from a world dominated by power and interests to a world governed by universal standards of law and justice. The second is a narrative of progress *in the law*. International law is presented as a dynamic discipline that has successfully managed to reinvent and modernise itself, moving from a primitive and fuzzy set of doctrines and customary principles to a highly sophisticated system of treaties, institutions and tribunals. That these stories are not historically accurate is almost irrelevant for my purposes.[63] The point is that this type of disciplinary romance creates a sense of origin and provenance. It also acts as a sort of programme for the future, if only by identifying common enemies (politics, religion, ideologies and so on). In any event, these tales of escape, progress and renewal *produce* disciplinary identity.

3) The third type of cultural capital that makes up the identity and unity of a discipline is that which concerns 'canonical truths', that is, the symbolic generalisations, the facts, objects, propositions or axioms that are uncontroversial among the members of the group. It may be, in the pure sciences for instance, a set of physical laws or mathematical formulae, such as Newton's motion laws or Ohm's laws of resistance in physics. In the social sciences, canonical truths instead take the form of concepts, models or theories whose truth is regarded as highly probable, like the law of supply and demand in economics.

These types of fundamental laws or general theorems are rather rare in the field of international law. The discipline does have its share of metaphors and images, however, which are almost universally used and accepted. The most obvious examples here are of course the metaphor of the state as a 'legal person' endowed with its own capacity, or the metaphor of the 'international community'.[64] More importantly perhaps, canonical truths often take the form of *canonical oppositions*, that is, oppositions between pairs of specific opposites that define the space of discussion within a field.[65] A discipline like psychology, for instance, is replete with canonical oppositions, between the learned and the innate, the ego and the superego, the conscious and the sub-conscious. In international law too, discourse-production is largely structured by these types of canonical oppositions: public/private,

international law's representation of itself, see Hilary Charlesworth, 'International Law: A Discipline of Crisis' (2002) 65 *Modern Law Review* 377.

[63] As noted by Kennedy (ibid at 91), there were elements of law before 1648 and the years 1648–1914 saw a range of extremely diverse ideas about the universality of international law, sovereignty, the relationship between law and morality, the status of violence and so forth.

[64] See René-Jean Dupuy, *La communauté internationale entre le mythe et l'histoire* (Paris, Economica, 1986).

[65] On the concept of canonical opposition, see Pierre Bourdieu, *Pascalian Meditations* (Stanford, Stanford University Press, 2000) 100–01.

law/politics, national/international, monism/dualism, binding/non-binding, individual/state, theory/practice and so forth.

4) Lastly, the collective consciousness of a discipline can be regarded as resting on what Thomas Kuhn calls *exemplars*. Exemplars are standard examples of resolved enigmas, exemplary cases of successful application of the discipline's laws and theories, which are regarded as paradigmatic.[66] Exemplars are concrete instances of problem-solving with which everyone in a discipline is familiar and which communicate knowledge about the discipline. All physicists, for example, begin by learning physics through a series of classical experiments or exemplars: the inclined plane, the conical pendulum, the rolling balls and so forth.

   In international law, as in any other legal discipline, exemplars mainly take the form of *precedents*. One very important aspect of becoming an international lawyer – of acquiring the culture of international law – lies in becoming familiar with its 'great cases', not so much as sources of law, but as classical instances of problem-solving, as examples of proper legal reasoning, one could almost say as *literary texts* that illustrate the particular language, form of argument and 'style' of the discipline.[67]

I have, up to this point, considered two perspectives from which to look at the question of cultural unity in international law. The first perspective refers to the idea of an *esprit d'internationalité*, a collective project or professional ethos that unites international lawyers across their personal allegiances or preferences. The second perspective, for its part, looks at the various forms of cultural capital – the recurring questions, the reconstructed histories, the symbolic generalisations and the exemplars – which act as a latent cognitive frame for the members of the international law profession and define the boundaries, both internal and external, of the discipline. Both perspectives, however, have one thing in common. They think of unity as something that lies primarily within international law's mental structures, whether explicit or implicit. In what follows, I want to consider another perspective altogether and suggest that unity may also reside in what could be called international law's *grammatical* structures, that is, its internal configuration as a discursive formation.

B. International law as a discursive formation: syntax and grammar

International law is not only a mindset, a worldview or a mode of thought. It is also a universe of discourse. This is true, first of all, of legal rules themselves.

[66] Thomas Kuhn, *The Structure of Scientific Revolutions* (Chicago, University of Chicago Press, 1986) 187.

[67] On the role of 'style' in the symbolic autonomisation of the juridical field, see Pierre Bourdieu, 'The Force of Law: Toward a Sociology of the Juridical Field' (1986) 38 *Hastings Law Journal* 805, 815–17.

Law cannot function properly as a social-control mechanism unless it can communicate meaning effectively to its subjects and, to do so, it necessarily takes the form of a normative discourse. This normative discourse can be verbal or gestural or a combination of the two (one thinks, for instance, of certain military orders). It can be written or unwritten (treaty/custom). Either way, rules are inescapably discourse-dependent.[68]

In international law, as in any normative space, there is also the grand mass of juridical discourse that *surrounds* rules, both upstream and downstream. There is, first of all, the pre-legislative discourse, that is, everything said during the law-making process, at the negotiating or drafting stage. A legal text is always the culmination of a long period of gestation – parliamentary debates in domestic law; diplomatic negotiations in international law – during which different options, propositions and arguments are weighed and compared with one another. The *travaux préparatoires* are nothing but the meticulous account of this pre-legislative discursive activity. That the *travaux* are used as a means of interpreting international treaties is testimony to the fact that rules are only the visible tip of the iceberg, the more or less finite and formalised synthesis of a long accumulation of discourse produced on a given topic or problem.[69]

In addition to this pre-normative discourse that *leads* to rules, there is also all the 'downstream' discourse that is *derived from* rules. The most evident form of derivative juridical discourse is of course judicial discourse: the written submissions of the parties, the pleadings, the courts' decisions, the judges' opinions and so forth. But derivative juridical discourse also includes many other types of discourse, like bureaucratic discourse – the directives, resolutions, decisions, declarations and other texts adopted by international organisations – or diplomatic discourse, that is, the discourse produced by states to defend and justify their interests, actions or policies (justification of the use of force, reasons for not ratifying a treaty, etc). And then there is of course doctrinal discourse, which maps the discipline, develops theories and projects of reform, and evaluates the three other types of discourse (case commentaries, survey of international practice, analysis of state rhetoric, etc).[70]

International law is the vocabulary in which all this discourse is formulated, a machine for the production of statements, propositions and arguments. It

[68] André-Jean Arnaud, *Critique de la raison juridique* (Paris, LGDJ, 1981) 454–58.

[69] *Vienna Convention on the Law of Treaties*, 23 May 1969, art 32.

[70] In addition to these various forms of *juridical* discourse on rules and institutions, there also exists a *non-juridical* discourse on the law: the representations, opinions and attitudes of the public at large (citizens and media) generally known as 'external' or 'popular' legal culture. On the representation of law in popular media (literature, newspapers, television, films, etc), see the burgeoning 'law and pop culture' literature: Michael Freeman (ed), *Law and Popular Culture* (Oxford, Oxford University Press, 2005); Michael Asimow and Shannon Mader, *Law and Popular Culture: a Course Book* (New York, Peter Lang, 2005); Richard Sherwin, *Popular Culture and Law* (London, Ashgate, 2006); *When Law Goes Pop: the Vanishing Line Between Law and Popular Culture* (Chicago, University of Chicago Press, 2002); Steve Greenfield, Guy Osborn and Peter Robson, *Film and the Law* (London, Cavendish, 2001); Austin Sarat (ed), *Law on the Screen* (Stanford, Stanford University Press, 2005).

represents, in other words, a vast and complex *discursive formation*, as understood by Foucault.[71] One of Foucault's major contributions to the study of discourse has been to show that discursive formations are not random accumulations of statements (*énoncés*). A discipline is not simply the sum of everything said about a particular object or question (for example, botany is not simply the sum of all things said about plants). A discursive formation is characterised above all by the rules that govern the production and dispersion of statements within it.[72]

For a proposition to belong to botany, or to international law, it must always meet certain conditions, certain standards of acceptability required for statements to be admitted as being 'within the true' (*dans le vrai*) of a discipline. A proposition that is objectively 'true' (for example, the earth is round) can be rejected as unacceptable or alien to a discipline (for example, alien to astronomy) if it does not comply with its rules of discourse-production or is located within a theoretical perspective that is totally unfamiliar to the discipline. These are what Foucault calls 'non-disciplined truths' (*vérités non-disciplinées*). Conversely, a statement can be objectively 'wrong' (for example, the earth is flat) and yet be universally accepted if it is located within the 'order of truth' of the discipline, that is, if it obeys its regime of truth production. These are what Foucault calls 'disciplined errors' (*erreurs disciplinées*).[73]

Discourse is thus never a small, private affair. It is always located within an 'order of discourse', which controls and polices the production of statements. To understand this point better, let us consider the story of Semmelweis, which Louis-Ferdinand Céline recounted in his medical dissertation.[74] Semmelweis was a Hungarian physician working at the Vienna General Hospital who discovered that hand-washing could drastically reduce the number of women dying of puerperal fever (postnatal infection). In the late 1840s, he hypothesised that puerperal fever was caused by 'cadaverous particles' transmitted to women at the time of childbirth and that doctors themselves carried on their hands from the autopsy room to the obstetrical clinic. Semmelweis was the first to recommend the use of prophylactic procedures ('scrubbing up' with a solution of chlorinated lime) to prevent the spread of germs and to stop the possibility of infection at the source.

Yet despite the publication of clinical trials showing that hand-washing reduced postnatal mortality from 30 per cent to below 1 per cent, Semmelweis's theory was entirely rejected by the medical establishment. His findings were ignored, even ridiculed. He was dismissed from his hospital and harassed by the medical community in Vienna. His findings were extreme and went against the

[71] On the concept of discursive formation, see Michel Foucault, *The Archaeology of Knowledge* (London, Routledge, 2002) 34–35.

[72] On the notion of discourse as a regulated universe, see Michel Foucault, *L'ordre du discours* (Paris, Gallimard, 1971).

[73] Ibid at 35–37.

[74] Louis-Ferdinand Céline, *Semmelweis* (London, Atlas Press, 2008).

dominant scientific opinion of the time. His theory lacked a full-fledged scientific explanation (he was unable to *prove* that puerperal fever was caused by the absorption of cadaveric material or other particles). The medical community was also very reluctant to admit that doctors themselves might be causing so many deaths. In a sense, Semmelweis was a 'true monster' (*un monstre vrai*).[75] He discussed objects, employed methods and placed himself within a theoretical perspective totally alien to the medical profession of his time. He spoke the truth but was not 'in the truth' of the medical field. His discourse remained trapped in a sort of wild exteriority until, years after his death, Pasteur's germ theory finally proved him right and made him a true pioneer of antisepsis.

A discursive formation, as the story of Semmelweis shows, cannot be reduced to a mere accumulation of practices, theories and statements. At a more fundamental level, a discipline is characterised by its 'discursive policies', the rules of formation that control the production of discourse and define its order of truth, its domain of validity, normativity and actuality.[76] These rules and policies, in a sense, constitute the syntax and the grammar of the discipline, the rules of language that every proposition or statement must reactivate to be accepted as valid, comprehensible or respectable (that is, to be 'within the true').

The unity of international law as a discursive formation may indeed lie in these grammatical structures, in the conditions and constraints under which legal arguments are formulated, selected and organised. What remains to be seen, however, is what these grammatical rules might actually be in the field of international law. As in the rest of this book, I shall only suggest possible avenues of thought on this point. To do so, I shall begin by considering Foucault's four general propositions in *The Archaeology of Knowledge*. In this essay, Foucault addresses the issue of the unity of discourse and does so by rejecting, at the outset, the notion that discourse can be unified by reference to a single speaking subject or a historico-transcendental teleology. This approach is well suited to the study of international law for this discipline by definition, lacks a legislator, a supreme court or a government, that is, a single speaking subject to which the totality of juridical discourse can be attributed or attached.

Foucault, then, begins by asking a simple question: on what is the unity of disciplines like medicine, linguistics or political economy based? Why is it that we regard these disciplines as distinct, autonomous and sovereign fields of discourse? What sort of links can validly be recognised between all the statements that form these disciplines? Foucault considers four possible answers, four different rules of formation that represent the elementary grammar of discursive formations.

First rule of formation: a group of statements, different in form and dispersed in time, is unified by the reference to one and the same object.[77] Thus, one could

[75] Semmelweis, it turns out, died a reviled and outcast man. Following his rejection by the medical community, he suffered a nervous breakdown and was committed to a mental institute, where ironically he died of septicemia, at age 47.

[76] Foucault, *L'ordre du discours*, above n 72 at 37.

[77] Foucault, *Archaeology of Knowledge*, above n 71 at 35–36.

say that statements belonging to the field of medicine form a coherent group because they all refer to the object 'disease' or that statements belonging to psychopathology are unified by their common reference to the object 'madness'. Likewise, one might say, in the legal field, that statements belonging to comparative law all refer to 'legal tradition' or that statements belonging to private international law refer to the object 'conflict' (of laws or jurisdiction). From this point of view, the first grammatical rule of public international law might be that, in order to be in the truth of the discipline, a statement must refer to a specific range of objects, something like 'the legal relations among states'.[78]

Second rule of formation or hypothesis: it might be possible to establish groups of statements by identifying the system of permanent and coherent concepts involved.[79] For example, one could say that the unity of linguistics is based on the fact that it rests on a definite number of concepts whose content and usage have been definitively established: the concept of judgement, the concepts of subject and predicate, the concepts of word, verb, signifier, logical copula, etc. Or one might argue that the medical discourse uses a fairly stable stock of notions to describe pathologies and their symptoms: irritation, inflammation, infection, rash, somatisation, latency, degeneration, deficit, recession, antecedent, malign, benign, chronic, clinical, endogenous, etc. The unity of international law, from this point of view, might be said to emanate from the existence of a well-defined alphabet of legal notions and concepts: state, territory, population, effectiveness, treaty, ratification, immunity, jurisdiction, recognition, succession and so forth.

Third rule of formation to regroup the statements and account for the unitary form under which they are presented: the identity and persistence of certain themes.[80] Despite the controversies, the diversity of philosophical or ethical options, a discipline like economics, for instance, might be said to receive its coherence from the central importance of certain themes, like the Physiocractic theme, that are capable of linking and animating a group of discourses. Similarly, one could perceive unity in biology from the grand unifying theme of evolution which, from Buffon to Darwin and Monod, has directed research and structured the discipline. In international law, one could likewise think of the identity and individualisation of the field by reference to the permanence or the recurrence of certain themes that animate the discipline from within and form a

[78] Whilst some international lawyers might reject the notion that modern international law is primarily concerned with the relations among states, nearly everyone in the discipline will agree on the historical importance of the figure of the state. This is generally regarded as the basic defining feature of international law (what, in the main, makes it distinct from other disciplines). On this point, see Pierre-Marie Dupuy, 'L'unité de l'ordre juridique international' (2002) 297 *Collected Courses of the Hague Academy of International Law* 9, 93: 'What gives the general international legal order . . . its formal unity? To this question, there is a simple answer: the State. Since the beginning . . . this original legal order owes its unity to the particular nature of its primary subjects' (author's translation).

[79] Foucault, *Archaeology of Knowledge*, above n 71 at 38–39.

[80] Ibid at 39–40.

common theoretical horizon, like the themes of international law's 'reality', 'primitiveness', 'foundation' or 'effectiveness', or more recently perhaps the themes of unity and fragmentation.

Lastly, a fourth rule of formation to define a group of relations between statements: their form and type of connection, a certain constant manner of making statements.[81] The principle of unity, in this perspective, lies in the presence of argumentative routines, of rhetorical modes or sequences in which statements are habitually made and combined together. For instance, although we do not really know where to 'find' international law, a valid statement about the binding nature of a rule is one that normally takes the form of a 'sources' rhetoric. Although we do not really know what the sources of international law are, arguments about the nature and typology of sources will typically take article 38 of the ICJ Statute as a starting point. And although we do not know what custom really is, legal arguments characteristically rely on the two elements of practice and *opinio juris* as prerequisites to treating a mere habit as binding law. In sum, although lawyers might disagree on the nature, function and substance of international rules, they all rely on established and ritualised chains of argument and evidence. The unity of international law, from this point of view, is not so much a matter of recurring objects, concepts or themes as it is a matter of 'style' or discursive 'habitus', to use Bourdieu's terminology.[82]

Like any discursive formation, international law therefore possesses a number of rules that 'police' the production of discourse within its domain. To be 'in the truth' of international law, that is, to be validated by the members of the 'invisible college', a statement must refer to a full, tightly packed, continuous, geographically well-defined field of objects; it must use a well-defined alphabet of notions; it must be located within a recognisable thematic horizon; and lastly, it must adhere to a certain aesthetics of argument (that is, a certain 'style').

These discursive policies – one could perhaps say *protocols* – define international law's domain of validity and actuality. They set out the criteria according to which the 'truth' or 'falsity' of a statement is to be tested. They delineate a world of common sense – a common atmosphere – within which meaningful analysis and argument can take place. In other words, these policies *set parameters for* the production, the dispersion and the validation of juridical discourse. From a grammatical point of view, cultural unity is just that: the discursive closure and the relative autonomy of international law as a generative language, that is, as a symbolic medium of communication and knowledge, a collective system of cognition, classification and production of legal arguments, which is at once structur*ed* – by the patterned social forces that produce it – and

[81] Ibid at 36–37.

[82] Bourdieu defines habitus as the systems of durable, transposable dispositions that function as 'structuring structures', ie, as principles that generate and organise practices and representations within a group or discipline. See Pierre Bourdieu, *The Logic of Practice* (Stanford, Stanford University Press, 1990) 52–65.

structur*ing*, since it gives form and coherence to the practices and activities of those who use it.[83]

C. Static and dialectical unity: folded international law

Thus far, I have considered cultural unity from the point of view of the permanent structures, the patterned and regular modes of thought and argument that characterise a discipline like international law. Whilst already opening up a new field of research and investigation, this approach has its own limits. One problem with this approach is that it equates unity with resemblance, with the common traits of discourse, with the identity and the stability of the representations, concepts and thematics that underpin its production. Though this approach is valid, it does somehow overlook the plural, changing and contradictory nature of discursive formations and fails to consider the possibility that the identity of a discipline may equally well reside in its movements, breaks, thresholds and discontinuities.

It is on this point that Foucault makes his most innovative contribution in *Archaeology of Knowledge*. Foucault, to be sure, does not reject the analysis of unity from the point of view of discursive policies. The fields of objects, recurring themes, conceptual frameworks and styles of arguments are, for Foucault, useful starting points from which to think about the order of discourse. But Foucault immediately sees a series of problems: objects are never 'given' to discourse in the most definitive way, they do not exist 'outside' discursive practices. Instead, discourse systematically creates the objects of which it speaks. Concepts and notions are too numerous and too diverse to fit within the unity of a logical architecture. Thematics give rise to various strategic possibilities that point in different directions. And the normative types of statements are too heterogeneous to simulate, from one period to another, a sort of great uninterrupted text.[84]

Hence Foucault's idea of describing these dispersions and discontinuities themselves; of discovering whether order could perhaps be discovered in these very tensions and contradictions. The question is no longer whether permanent structures operate under the surface of discourse, but rather to examine the field of strategic possibilities that the discourse leaves free, to consider how one

[83] This is not to say that this discursive closure is absolute and that international law is radically autonomous, self-sufficient and self-validating. My argument is simply that legal routines/habitus are elements – among others – of international law's autonomy as an intellectual discipline. For a similar argument about law's autonomy, see Roger Cotterrell, *Law's Community: Legal Theory in Sociological Perspective* (Oxford, Clarendon Press, 1995) 42–49. For a doctrine of radical closure, see the autopoiesis theory developed in relation to law by Niklas Luhmann and Gunther Teubner: Niklas Luhmann, *A Sociological Theory of Law* (London, Routledge, 1985); Gunther Teubner (ed), *Autopoietic Law: a New Approach to Law and Society* (Berlin, W de Gruyter, 1988). In the field of international law, see Anthony D'Amato, 'International Law as an Autopoietic System' in Rüdiger Wolfrum and Volker Röben (eds), *Developments of International Law in Treaty Making* (Berlin, Springer, 2005).

[84] Foucault, *Archaeology of Knowledge*, above n 71 at 40–42.

order of discourse makes it possible, from a particular set of concepts or objects, to play different games. This type of analysis does not seek to isolate and identify islands of coherence in order to describe their internal structure. It sets itself the task of describing the inner economy of a discipline from a dynamic point of view, by shedding light on the dialectical tensions that arise between different statements or groups of statements.[85]

This approach to unity enjoins us to think of disciplines not as flat, seamless terrains but as wrinkled, discursive fabrics, that is, as complex systems in which discourse constantly folds and unfolds. The goal is not to flatten contradictions in order to bring out discursive similarities or regularities. On the contrary, it is to take contradiction as an intrinsic element in the discipline's identity and unity. The aim is thus to 'take the fold' (*prendre le pli*) of discourse, as Deleuze might have put it, that is, to examine the ebb and flow of discourse and to identify, in this movement, the principles of dispersion and articulation of arguments.[86]

A concrete example might help us understand the meaning of this difference of approach. In the previous chapter, it has been shown that the doctrine of sources represents a complex, open and indeterminate set of often contradictory propositions. On what basis, then, does the autonomy of the sources discourse rest? What forms of unity can one find in this compound of juridical statements?

The first way to consider this question and to think of the cultural unity of international law on this point is to say that 'competent' sources arguments – that is, arguments admitted as being 'in the truth' of the sources discourse – are all based on a well-defined field of objects, on a well-defined alphabet of notions and on definite, normative types of statements. A source argument typically refers to article 38 of the ICJ Statute; it uses the vocabulary of treaties, custom or general principles; it seeks to establish the generality of practice or the existence of *opinio juris* and so forth. In short, a competent sources argument involves an agreed upon and well-honed grammatical system.

This type of unity, however, essentially remains at the surface of discourse. It basically concerns the more or less generalised use of certain juridical *words* and grammatical constructions. It may thus be useful to think of other, more fundamental or deeper forms of unity. Rather than insisting on the permanence of themes and concepts, one might consider whether a certain type of order does not in fact lie in the recurring tensions that structure the sources rhetoric.

I had already begun to identify these tensions earlier. It will be recalled that, as a rule, statements about the binding nature of legal instruments follow two basic rhetorical modes or styles – two mutually exclusive strategies of argument. The 'hard' line of argument seeks to explain or justify the 'bindingness' of the law by reference to state consent. The 'soft' line of argument, on the

[85] Ibid at 44–78.

[86] Gilles Deleuze, *Le pli: Leibniz et le baroque* (Paris, Editions de Minuit, 1998).

other hand, relies on extraconsensual notions of justice, security or predictability.[87] These 'hard' and 'soft' lines of argument represent the two primary axes of discourse, the two points of choice around which sources arguments are produced, articulated and distributed.

For example, when a state invokes a treaty against another state before a tribunal, experience shows that parties systematically use certain types of arguments that always follow the 'hard' and 'soft' lines of discourse:

A: State B is bound by the treaty because it consented to it (hard).

B: I only consented to the treaty under specific conditions and reservations and/or I have, since then, withdrawn my consent (hard).

A: State B's reservation does not apply to me since I have objected to it (hard). In any case, a state cannot unilaterally withdraw from a treaty as this would compromise the security and predictability of legal relations among states (soft).

B: I did consent to the treaty but have, since then, been freed from my obligations due to exceptional circumstances – *rebus sic sanctibus*, force majeure, necessity, etc (soft).

This whole panoply of 'hard' and 'soft' arguments can be found at play in the *Gabcikovo Nagymaros* case, for example.[88] In this vast and complex dispute, Slovakia claimed that Hungary had breached its obligations under a bilateral treaty concluded in 1977 by unilaterally suspending a joint project for the construction and operation of a system of locks on the river Danube (hard). Hungary, for its part, argued that it was no longer bound by the 1977 treaty as it had been lawfully terminated in 1992 (hard) and that, in any case, its responsibility was not engaged due to the material breach of the treaty by Slovakia itself, the occurrence of a fundamental change of circumstances, and the existence of a state of ecological necessity (soft).

The *Gabcikovo* case is interesting not simply because of the panoply of arguments used by the parties, but also because the decision itself epitomises the tension between the 'hard' and 'soft' points of choice and the attempt by the judge – to deliver justice – to reconcile these two opposite strategic possibilities. Whilst finding that the 1977 treaty was still in force and that Hungary was not entitled to suspend and subsequently abandon the joint project,[89] the Court did accept, albeit implicitly, some of Hungary's arguments. The Court took the view, in particular, that ecological necessity, although not rendering the 1977 treaty inoperative, became part of the 'territorial regime' established by the treaty and that parties should consequently 'restore' this regime in a way that

[87] David Kennedy, 'The Sources of International Law' (1987) 2 *American University Journal of International Law and Policy* 1, 20–24; Koskenniemi, *From Apology to Utopia*, above n 2 at 307–25.

[88] *Case Concerning the Gabcikovo-Nagymaros Project (Hungary v Slovakia)* 25 September 1997, ICJ Reports (1997) 7.

[89] Ibid at para 155.

takes account both of the initial purposes of the treaty and of environmental considerations.[90] Similarly, whilst rejecting the fundamental change of circumstances argument, the Court felt compelled to note that parts of the 1977 treaty 'have been overtaken by events' and thus concluded that parties should resume cooperation on the joint project in an 'equitable and reasonable manner', keeping in mind 'its impact upon, and its implications for, the environment'.[91]

The ICJ judgment in this case exemplifies how the juridical discourse constantly oscillates between consent (the 1977 treaty) and justice (environmental considerations) and how the discourse of the judge seeks to reach a form of reasonable and pragmatic accommodation among them. What we find here is a sort of three-step rhetorical waltz. First step of the waltz: a state that has ratified a treaty is bound by certain obligations (consent). Second step of the waltz: consensual law must not be conceived of as an absolute. It must be interpreted dynamically so as to take account of its changing normative environment (justice). Third step of the waltz: parties must therefore negotiate (consent) so as to implement the treaty in a reasonable and equitable manner (justice).

What is true of judicial discourse is of course true of other forms of juridical discourse, and in particular of doctrinal discourse. There again, similar tensions arise between consensual and extra-consensual strategies of argument, and doctrinal discourse is always seeking to find a form of dynamic equilibrium between them. This is most evident in relation to custom. The question of the binding nature of custom, as has already been demonstrated, is one of the most recurring and controversial questions in international legal theory. Yet doctrinal discourse on this point is structured by the tension between two fundamental rhetorical options. The first option – objectivism – seeks to explain the binding nature of custom in relation to an order of reference situated beyond the state and its consent, whether this be history, social necessity, elementary considerations of humanity or natural law. The second option – voluntarism – explains or justifies the binding nature of custom by reference to the state and its consent, whether explicit or implicit.[92] Any doctrine, to be admissible, must necessarily employ, in one way or another, these two points of choice simultaneously. A theory of custom that rests exclusively on sociological or humanitarian considerations will be rejected as abstract and utopian. A theory of custom that rests exclusively on state practice and consent runs the risk of being rejected as non-normative, as a mere description of what is 'already there'.

Hence the necessity to continuously engage with these two modes of argument. For example, a doctrine that posits that custom springs from general and consistent practice (soft) will often concede that, in order to select what 'counts' as practice and what does not, one must look at what states say and think of it

[90] Ibid at paras 142–47.
[91] Ibid at paras 136 and 140.
[92] Brigitte Stern, 'Custom at the Heart of International Law' (2001) 11 *Duke Journal of Comparative and International Law* 89, 91–93.

(hard).[93] Conversely, a doctrine that posits that the main source of custom is *opinio juris*, understood as the external acceptance by states that a particular behaviour is commanded by law (hard) will generally admit that *opinio juris* does not simply 'lend itself' to easy detection and must therefore often be inferred from state practice (soft).[94] Here again, juridical discourse is 'bounded' by the consensual and extra-consensual poles of argument, and the back-and-forth movement of discourse between these two points of choice constitutes a primary principle of distribution of statements in the sources doctrine.

Some authors have attempted to map the entire discipline of international law from the point of view of these recurring and dialectical tensions between opposing argumentative trajectories. Often, they have argued that these tensions can be traced back to one, fundamental ideological contradiction that underpins the discipline as a whole and explains its inner structure.[95]

My point here is slightly different, however. I am merely interested in showing that from a theoretical point of view it is possible, and certainly desirable, to couple the analysis of static unity with an analysis of dialectical unity. I have attempted to show what this second type of analysis might look like. It consists, for the most part, in looking for unity not so much in the permanence and stability of the objects, concepts and themes of discourse as in the systematically different (different but systematic) ways of dealing with these objects, themes and concepts. On this issue, my analysis remains essentially archaeological, as defined by Foucault. My argument is not that there is, underneath these recurring contradictions of discourse, and at a more fundamental level, a secret principle of organisation that must be identified to capture the unity and autonomy of a discipline. Instead, my point is that these dispersions of discourse are worth describing and analysing in themselves. International law is a space within which arguments encounter one another and combine to form islands of coherence. But it is also an area of systematic disagreement and contradiction, a field of strategic possibilities. To grasp something of the argumentative architecture of this field of discourse, attention must be paid to its points of diffraction, to its lines of dispersion, or to its 'lines of flight' (*lignes de fuite*), as Deleuze might have said. These lines, too, make up in their own way the cultural unity of the discipline.

[93] See, eg, Michael Akehurst, 'Custom as a Source of International Law' (1977) 47 *British Yearbook of International Law* 1, 10 and 39; Maurice Mendelson, 'The Formation of Customary International Law' (1999) 272 *Collected Courses of the Hague Academy of International Law* 165, 226.

[94] See, eg, Andrew Guzman, *How International Law Works – A Rational Choice Theory* (Oxford, Oxford University Press, 2008) 203–04; Mark Villiger, *Customary International Law and Treaties* (The Hague, Kluwer Law International, 1997) 27–29.

[95] David Kennedy, *International Legal Structures* (Baden-Baden, Nomos Verlagsgesellschaft, 1987); Koskenniemi, *From Apology to Utopia,* above n 2.

IV. INTERMEDIATE CONCLUSIONS: THE INVISIBLE HAND OF LEGAL CULTURE

International law is not simply a set of formal rules and institutions. It is also a cultural system. The main proposition of the present chapter is in fact rather simple: the culture of international law can be studied and analysed like any other culture. Like any other culture, international law has its histories, its founding myths, its beliefs and its own ways of seeing, thinking and communicating. To grasp international law in its individuality (that is, in its unity) is also to grasp something about these cultural forms. Naturally, there are many ways in which to study a culture. This chapter offers no complete or coherent methodology in this regard. It does, however, suggest certain points of reference and thereby opens up two broad theoretical avenues.

The first approach looks at international law as a site for the production of discourse, as a formal and ritualised language in which officials, diplomats, lawyers and other international law professionals identify problems, propose solutions and put forward justifications. To study the culture of international law, from this point of view, is to study the grammatical rules that structure this professional language. Again, there are many ways in which to study grammar. I have suggested, however, that the grammar of international law, like that of any discursive formation, can be usefully analysed by considering four types of discursive policies: a geographically well-defined field of objects; a well-defined alphabet of notions; a common theoretical or thematic horizon; and a certain aesthetic of argument (that is, a certain 'style').

These grammatical policies, however, do not completely enable one to grasp the inner dynamics of a field of discourse, that is, the way in which statements are systematically scattered, distributed and how they respond to one another. Hence the necessity also to consider the rules of dispersion of discourse, that is, the constant and patterned ways in which the same objects give rise to different rhetorical strategies. The cultural unity of international law, as a professional language, can therefore mean two different things. From a static point of view, cultural unity refers to the existence of a set of grammatical rules that any statement must observe to be 'within the true' of discourse, that is, within the discipline's order of truth and validity. From a dialectical point of view, cultural unity refers to the systems of dispersion of discourse, that is, the distribution of statements along recurring (and often competing) strategic lines of argument.

But there is more to the culture of international law than these grammatical rules. A language is not simply a sum of its words, or a vocabulary used to communicate ideas in recognisable and established grammatical forms. A language is always more than this. A language conveys images, ideas, representations and symbols. As Umberto Eco pointed out, 'any language is a prison, for it always imposes a certain vision of the world'.[96] If international law is a professional

[96] TV interview with Bernard Pivot, *Double je*, TV5, 25 July 2005 (author's translation).

language, then it too must impose a certain vision of the world. Therefore, to think about the culture of international law is also to think about this symbolic baggage, this mental universe, the intellectual schemes in which the social reality of international lawyers is constructed.

But here again, this question can be approached from two different points of view. International law's 'vision of the world' can be understood, first of all, as a federating project, a common sense shared by international law professionals. This is the 'strong' version of cultural unity, which presupposes the existence of a well-defined professional ideology to which the majority of international lawyers subscribes. Some have spoken of an internationalist spirit which, they argue, drove the discipline in its early, foundational years. As pointed out earlier, it is uncertain that this sort of *esprit de corps* has ever existed and, if it has, what remains of it today. The points remains that it is *theoretically possible* to think of the culture of international law in terms of its specific ethos, its cosmopolitan ideals or universal *mots d'ordres* (peace through law, human rights, rule of law, etc). But the international law 'vision' can also be conceived of in a looser way, as something that refers to more diffuse forms of cultural capital. I have mentioned four such forms in this chapter: a recurring professional question; a history/geography; canonical truths; and exemplars. The list is of course not exhaustive. It does, however, illustrate the various forms of knowledge and the types of representation that constitute the 'collective consciousness' of a discipline like international law, the sort of latent cognitive frame that is not explicitly recorded but which underlies the law's explicit functioning.

All of this may appear both familiar and strange. Familiar because legal culture is something in which we, as lawyers, all bathe, an 'atmosphere' in which we are all situated.[97] But also strange because it is never easy to objectivise the latent structures of one's own intellectual mental universe, of one's own social milieu. The fact remains, however, that these cognitive and discursive structures act as a sort of 'invisible hand' that establishes between simultaneous or successive phenomena a community of meaning, symbolic links, an interplay of resemblance and reflection. Earlier, I asked what an international arbitrator, a professor of environmental law, a UN ambassador and a human rights activist all have in common. Why is it that, despite such different lives and practices, we regard them as belonging to the same 'college' of international lawyers? The cultural approach offers one type of answer: despite different and sometimes contradictory agendas, these professionals fight different wars but on the same battlefield, they use similar rhetorical strategies, position themselves at the same level or at the same distance from their object, and share essentially the same semantic apparatus. This may constitute a weak form of unity. But it is unity nonetheless.

[97] Outi Korhonen, *International Law Situated: an Analysis of the Lawyer's Stance Towards Culture, History and Community* (The Hague, Kluwer Law International, 2000) 49–50.

7

Logical Unity

THE CULTURAL APPROACH presented in the previous chapter already represents a step in a genuinely new theoretical direction. Whilst doctrinal orthodoxy looks at unity from the point of view of formal rules and institutions, I have suggested looking at an entirely different field of objects, and imagining new forms and criteria of unity. This new field of objects, first of all, moves beyond rules and institutions and looks at international law as an intellectual field and as a discursive formation. But it is also necessary to consider new forms and criteria of unity too, which refer to the grammatical structures and the visions, the modes of thought and argumentation of international law.

Cultural unity, however, does not represent the end-point of the present study. The conceptual deconstruction of unity can be pursued and other perspectives can be considered. In the present chapter, I look at one last 'family' of unity, which I shall call 'logical' unity. As will soon become clear, the notion of logical unity covers a range of different ideas and realities. In one perspective, logical unity is understood as a mere postulate or principle of interpretation. I shall call this type of unity *epistemo*-logical unity. In another perspective, logical unity refers to the normative tension of the law towards certain superior values. This is what I call *axio*-logical unity.

Although these perspectives are different, they share a common denominator: both consider unity in relation to elements of transcendence that 'sublimate' the plurality and complexity of positive law. In one case, this sublimation is rational, abstract and postulated *a priori*. In the other, it is material, concrete and reconstructed *a posteriori*. In both instances, however, unity involves a form of surpassing of the immediate, empirical reality of the law. This is why I shall speak of these forms of unity under the same umbrella notion of 'logical' unity.

I. EPISTEMO-LOGICAL UNITY: AH! IN THE HYPOTHESIS!

LOGICIAN: [to the OLD GENTLEMAN] Here is an example of a syllogism.
The cat has four paws. Isidore and Fricot have four paws.
Therefore Isidore and Fricot are cats.

OLD GENTLEMAN: [to the LOGICIAN] My dog has got four paws.

LOGICIAN: [to the OLD GENTLEMAN] Then it's a cat . . .

OLD GENTLEMAN: [to the LOGICIAN] So then logically speaking, my dog must be a cat?

LOGICIAN: [to the OLD GENTLEMAN] Logically, yes. But the contrary is also true . . .

OLD GENTLEMAN: [to the LOGICIAN] Logic is a very beautiful thing . . .
LOGICIAN: [to the OLD GENTLEMAN] Another syllogism. All cats die. Socrates is dead. Therefore Socrates is a cat.

OLD GENTLEMAN: [to the LOGICIAN] And he's got four paws. That's true. I've got a cat named Socrates.

LOGICIAN: [to the OLD GENTLEMAN] There you are, you see . . .

OLD GENTLEMAN: [to the LOGICIAN] So Socrates was a cat, was he?

LOGICIAN: [to the OLD GENTLEMAN] Logic has just revealed the fact to us . . . Let's get back to our cats . . . The cat Isidore has four paws.

OLD GENTLEMAN: [to the LOGICIAN] How do you know?

LOGICIAN: [to the OLD GENTLEMAN] It's stated in the hypothesis.

OLD GENTLEMAN: [to the LOGICIAN] Ah! In the hypothesis!

Eugène Ionesco, *Rhinoceros*[1]

Logical unity can be thought of, first of all, as a simple dogma of legal reason, that is, as a normative postulate. By normative postulate, I mean an *a priori* proposition, the truth of which is required to be accepted without proof, and which states the conditions under which an object – in our case a legal object – is to be understood and interpreted. To speak of epistemo-logical unity, in this sense, is therefore to conceive of unity not so much as an empirically verifiable reality – as the fact, for instance, that norms do not conflict – but rather as a methodological requirement or a principle of cognition.[2]

A. Hermeneutic presumption, entitlement and constraint

For the legal theorist, unity as a normative postulate represents both a presumption and a principle of action: a presumption, first of all, that behind the complexity and the diversity of legal phenomena lies a number of objectifiable laws; but a principle of action too, according to which the role of legal science is to identify these laws, formulate general concepts and principles, establish logical relations among them, until some form of coherent and consistent system can

[1] Eugène Ionesco, *Rhinoceros and Other Plays* (New York, Grove Press, 1960) 19–20.

[2] Claus-Wilhelm Canaris, *Systemdenken und Systembegriff in der Jurisprudenz: entwickelt am Beispiel des deutschen Privatrechts* (Berlin, Duncker & Humblot, 1969) 16–17. See also Michel Van de Kerchove and François Ost, *The Legal System Between Order and Disorder* (Oxford, Oxford University Press, 1994) 7–9.

finally be said to exist. To say 'international law is unitary', from this point of view, does not signify 'international law presents itself to me as a coherent whole that I can describe as a unity'. Rather, it signifies 'my purpose as a legal scientist is to understand and analyse international law as a singular object. To do so, I must eliminate its uncertainties and ambiguities, put it in order, and reveal the laws to which all legal objects and phenomena are subject. Therefore, I presume that some form of unity must exist in international law and, from there, I construct a logical system that sustains that idea'. Unity, as a function of juridical reason, is simply a principle of organisation of knowledge, an *a priori* condition of judgement, which requires placing the emphasis on elements of order and certainty, disambiguating, clarifying, distinguishing and hierarchising legal phenomena.

For the law-applier, on the other hand, unity acts as a hermeneutic constraint and as an enabling clause. A constraint, first of all, that places judges under the obligation to interpret rules in relation to other rules and principles, and to establish if and to what extent these other rules or principles affect their validity, their meaning or their scope. The unity postulate, in this first perspective, simply means that rules must not be read in 'clinical isolation' from their broader normative environment. Rules must be interpreted as 'parts' of a bigger 'whole'. This principle is known as the principle of 'systemic integration'.[3]

But the unity postulate also acts as an enabling clause that gives the judge the power to resolve conflicts, fill the gaps in the law, and act 'as if' the legal order were complete and coherent. The unity postulate acts as a double fiction here. A fiction of coherence, first of all, according to which a single coherent legislative will lies behind the multiplicity of norms. It is presumed that the law has been produced and developed according to a single, rational plan, and that the law-maker cannot have intended for one thing to be at once legal and illegal. If two norms conflict, it can therefore only mean one of two things: either the law-maker intended to repeal one norm by adopting the other; or it had a certain normative hierarchy in mind. The role of the judge, under this presumption, is to discover and interpret this legislative will and to resolve the apparent contradictions in the law by establishing relations of primacy or priority among rules.[4]

[3] See above n 44 of the introduction.

[4] On the presumption of coherence (also known as the presumption against conflict), see eg, Joost Pauwelyn, *Conflicts of Norms in Public International Law: How WTO Rules Relate to Other Rules of International Law* (Cambridge, Cambridge University Press, 2003) 240 ('Every new norm of international law is created within the context of pre-existing international law and the presumption is that this new norm, much like new legislation enacted by the same legislator, builds upon and further develops existing law'); Wilfried Jenks, 'The Conflict of Law-Making Treaties' (1953) 30 *British Yearbook of International Law* 400, 427 ('It seems reasonable to start from a general presumption against conflict'); Michael Akehurst, 'The Hierarchy of the Sources of International Law' (1974) 47 *British Yearbook of International Law* 273, 275 ('just as there is a presumption against the establishment of new customary rules which conflict with pre-existing customary rules, so there is a presumption against the replacement of customary rules by treaties and vice versa'); Max Sorensen, *Les sources du droit international* (Copenhague, Einar Manksgaard, 1946) 226–27 ('le texte est considéré comme partie du système global du droit international et

The unity postulate also acts as a fiction of completeness, according to which there are no gaps in the law, no question to which the legal order does not provide an answer. Even in the absence of direct or explicit rules, it will be presumed that the legal order provides implicit solutions to all problems. The role of the judge under this presumption is to discover – through a process of analogy and deduction – the general principles and the underlying norms applicable to a dispute.[5] In both instances, the unity postulate acts as a logical fiction, which underpins and justifies the judge's interpretation of the law, a presupposition that requires the judge to build systemic relationships between norms.[6]

The International Law Commission (ILC) explicitly adopted this epistemological or axiomatic approach to unity in its fragmentation report. By mandating the Commission to study the fragmentation phenomenon, the UN General Assembly placed the ILC in a rather delicate position. Fragmentation, unlike the law of treaties or state responsibility, is not really a 'codifiable' question. In fact, many within the Commission have questioned whether the ILC was indeed the appropriate forum to deal with fragmentation.[7] How should the ILC approach fragmentation? How should it go about studying the question and what contribution should it make? Should the ILC provide a historical or sociological

l'interprétation se propose de la mettre en harmonie avec la réglementation générale de celui-ci. La présomption sur laquelle se base cette méthode d'interprétation est que les contractants, en rédigeant le traité, sont partis de certaines données qu'il n'était pas besoin de reproduire dans le texte, et auxquelles ils se sont référés tacitement'). See also *Case Concerning Right of Passage Over Indian Territory (Portugal v India)*, Preliminary Objections, 26 November 1957, ICJ Reports (1957) 125, 142: 'it is a rule of interpretation that a text emanating from a Government must, in principle, be interpreted as producing and as intended to produce effects in accordance with existing law and not in violation of it'.

[5] Hans Kelsen, *Principles of International Law* (New York, Holt, Rinehart and Winston, 1966) 439–40 ('Existing international law can always be applied to a concrete case . . . If there is no norm of conventional or customary law imposing upon the state the obligation to behave in a certain way, the subject is under international law free to behave as it pleases; and by a decisions to this effect existing international law is applied to the case'); Hersch Lauterpacht, *The Function of Law in the International Community* (Oxford, Clarendon Press, 1933) 392 ('The absence of direct regulation of a particular matter is the result of the determination, or at any rate the acquiescence, of the community in the view that, in the particular case, the needs of society and the cause of justice are best served by freedom from inference. To that extent it may correctly be said that the absence of explicit legal regulation is tantamount to an implied recognition of legally protected freedom of action'); Prosper Weil, 'The Court Cannot Conclude Definitively . . . Non Liquet Revisited' (1998) 36 *Columbia Journal of Transnational Law* 109, 110 ('there is no room for *non liquet* in international adjudication because there are no lacunae in international law. According to this view, the absence of *non liquet* in international adjudication is a consequence of the completeness of the international legal system').

[6] See Eyal Benvenisti, 'The Conception of International Law as a Legal System' (2008) 50 *German Yearbook of International Law* 393, 397–99.

[7] Report of the International Law Commission on the Work of its Fifty-fourth Session, UN GAOR, 57th Sess, Supp No 10, ch IX, UN Doc A/57/10, paras 495–99: 'one of the main questions that the Study Group considered was whether the topic of fragmentation of international law . . . was suitable for study by the Commission. [T]here appeared to be considerable uncertainty, at least initially, about the potential scope of the topic and the substance and format of a possible final result of the Commission's work . . . Some members questioned whether the topic fell within the Commission's mandate'.

account of fragmentation? Or should it engage more actively in the resolution of norm conflicts and actually settle the tension between special regimes?

Among these possible approaches, the Commission opted for a rather technical and pragmatic 'analytical study'. Historical, sociological and institutional questions were left largely unanswered. Neither did the ILC offer direct solutions to normative conflicts. Instead, the Commission decided to provide a conceptual 'toolbox' to be used by lawyers dealing with problems of fragmentation, which would enable them to reach a reasoned decision in a legal-professional way.[8] The accent was thus put on techniques and methods of interpretation necessary to deal with rules or rule-complexes that point in different directions. The ILC report is mostly interested in legal reasoning, understood as a purposive activity that seeks to establish meaningful relationships between rules and principles.[9]

But speaking of 'meaningful relationships' between rules and principles of international law is situating legal reasoning, at the outset, in the context of a 'system'. The Commission does recognise this point explicitly in its final conclusions, the first of which is that:

> International law is a legal system. Its rules and principles (i.e. its norms) act in relation to and should be interpreted against the background of other rules and principles. As a legal system, international law is not a random collection of such norms. There are meaningful relationships between them[10]

Whilst embracing the notion that international law is a system, the Commission does make it clear, however, that 'this cannot be understood as reaffirming something that already "exists" before the systemic effort itself'.[11] Systematicity is created by legal reasoning and interpretation. It is these two processes that establish systemic relationships between norms. The systematicity of international law (that is, its unity) is therefore a logical construct, which is 'stated in the hypothesis', to paraphrase Ionesco's logician. Everything happens *as if* rules, decisions and principles were 'the operation of a whole that is directed toward some human objective'.[12] It must be *presumed*, says the Commission, that states have not intended to create conflicting norms or norm-systems. In case of conflict, the judge is therefore entitled to give priority to one norm. In fact, the Commission speaks of a 'political obligation' on the part of law-appliers to take account of the preferences and expectations of the community whose law they administer and to build logico-systemic relationships between rules or regimes.[13] Presumption, entitlement and hermeneutic constraint: we are clearly within the confines of the 'unity-as-postulate' theory.

[8] ILC Fragmentation Report, paras 18–20.
[9] Ibid.
[10] ILC Fragmentation Conclusions, para 1.
[11] ILC Fragmentation Report, para 34.
[12] Ibid.
[13] Ibid at para 35.

It is clear, then, that the Commission conceives of unity not so much as an empirically verifiable fact, as a requirement or condition of legal reason. It should be noted, however, that the Commission, whilst embracing the unity postulate, does not *justify* it. The Commission simply notes that 'there is seldom disagreement' that law is a system and that 'systemic thinking penetrates all legal reasoning'.[14] The attitude of the Commission is understandable. In order to facilitate discussion and provide practical recommendations, it was probably necessary, from a strategic point of view, to leave complex normative or theoretical questions aside.[15] Nonetheless, the Commission's position is not self-evident. Systemic thinking has not always penetrated legal disciplines. One need only think about the Common Law tradition, which has long remained an empiricist and pragmatist tradition, relatively hostile to formal systematisation projects. Things, of course, have changed. But even in the modern era, the systemic approach is far from uncontested. Movements such as American realism, Marxism, existentialism or, more recently, legal pluralism have all challenged the notion that law necessarily exists as a formal, systemic and unitary order.

Where, then, does the 'law-as-unity' postulate come from? Since when and for what reasons do most lawyers presume the logical unity (that is, the systematicity) of things legal? There is of course no obvious answer to these questions. The idea of law's systematicity did not simply appear one day out of the cultural blue. Law's progressive systematisation has been a long process, the distant origins of which probably lie in the rediscovery of Roman law and of Aristotelian logic in the twelfth century. In this long process, however, two elements have played a decisive role: Kantian critique and the subsequent development of German 'legal science' (*Rechtswissenschaft*) in the nineteenth century.

B. Kantian critique and unity as a regulative principle

Kant was critical in at least two respects. He was decisive, first of all, by reason of his philosophy of knowledge. One of the great questions of Kantian philosophy concerns the conditions of possibility of knowledge. How and under what conditions is knowledge formed within our consciousness? What is the scope and value of our knowledge? What roles do experience, reason, doubts and intuitions play in the formation of knowledge? Others before Kant, from Descartes to Locke, Leibniz, Berkeley or Hume, studied the question of knowledge. But Kant developed a radically new philosophy according to which the formation of knowledge always involves elements that do not come from experience itself, but rather from *a priori* principles without which knowledge is quite simply impossible.

[14] Ibid.

[15] Ibid at paras 484–85 (where Koskeniemmi – while conceding that the Commission's approach 'may seem unsatisfactory or at least inconclusive' since fragmentation requires 'a legislative, not a legal-technical response' – argues that leaving aside political and theoretical questions was the only way to conduct the study 'within the confines of the ILC' and to make a 'constructive contribution').

Kant tells us that we can only apprehend reality under its phenomenal form. We perceive things through the *a priori* forms of sensibility, in time and space. The ultimate being of things – their nature – radically escapes our intelligence. The 'noumenon' – the 'thing-in-itself' – eludes our grasp and remains beyond our rational understanding. Noumena only manifest themselves to us in changing and uncertain phenomenal forms. At the same time, Kant claims that the idea of the being-in-itself is indispensable to escape the radical relativism of phenomenal reality. To move beyond the multiplicity, diversity and complexity of the world, and grasp an object in its essence and singularity, we are compelled to presuppose that this object exists as a thing-in-itself. The unity of the object is inaccessible to us. Yet the *idea* of its unity enables us to surpass our unstable and uncertain empirical knowledge of the world. At the very heart of human reason is therefore what Kant calls the 'regulative principle of unity':

> [T]he regulative principle of systematic unity prescribes that we should study nature as if systematic and purposive unity, combined with the greatest possible manifoldness, were everywhere to be met with, in infinitum. For although we may succeed in discovering but little of this perfection of the world, it is nevertheless required by the legislation of our reason that we must always search for and surmise it[16]

This *a priori* principle of unity is a defining feature of Kant's philosophy as a whole, and in particular of his thinking on cosmopolitan law. The question of legal unity in Kant's philosophy manifests itself at the junction of three interrelated notions: cosmopolitanism, perpetual peace and universal History. And these three notions, in turn, lead to a single idea: the idea of a 'universal state of peoples' (*Allgemeiner Völkerstaat*). But Kant, needless to say, would have been unable to ground the unity of cosmopolitan law in political or historical experience. Everywhere around him, Kant found the division of states, peoples and cultures, the reign of force and violence. Kant saw no common reason or perpetual peace at play in the real world. Only divisiveness and war: 'despite the occasional semblance of wisdom to be seen in individual actions, [the world is] made up, by and large, of foolishness, childish vanity, and, often enough, even of childish wickedness and destructiveness'.[17]

Kant's idea of the unity of cosmopolitan law is thus inaccessible to human perception. In the Kantian system, unity is a 'pure idea of reason', without which cosmopolitan law cannot be imagined, let alone realised. Unity is a requirement of human intelligence, a condition of possibility. The unity postulate, as a regulative principle of thought, is above all the logical expression of a system of truth production about law, that is, of a legal epistemology.

In this sense already, Kant is decisive. He makes unity a condition *sine qua non* of reason, in general, and of juridical reason, in particular. But Kant is also decisive in a second manner, which concerns legal theory more directly. At a

[16] Immanuel Kant, *Critique of Pure Reason* (New York, St Martin's Press, 1965) 568.

[17] Immanuel Kant, *Toward Perpetual Peace and Other Writings on Politics, Peace, and History* (New Haven, Yale University Press, 2006) 4.

time when Western legal tradition was largely influenced by natural law theories, Kant suggested a theoretical break and methodological move that paved the way for the development of a more 'scientific' legal science. Until the mid-eighteenth century, the natural law tradition – from Hobbes and Grotius to Spinoza, Pufendorf or Leibniz – presented itself as an amalgam of diverse elements: ethics and law, positive law and natural justice, observation and speculation. For Kant, this *mélange des genres* led to methodological confusion. He thus suggested drawing a series of new disciplinary distinctions.

First of all, he proposed drawing a distinction between the domain of virtue and the domain of law, which both refer to different kinds of duties. The domain of law, he claimed, involves 'duties of right' (*Rechtspflichten*), that is, duties promulgated by some form of external legislation (positive law) and which must be enforced because other persons have a right to their fulfilment. By contrast, the domain of virtue involves 'duties of virtue' (*Tugendspflichten*), that is, general maxims imposed by a form of internal legislation (reason itself) and which need not be the object of external enforcement, for they are not connected to correlative rights. On the one hand, then, are duties to others and on the other are duties to oneself: legality on one side and morality on the other.[18]

Kant was also critical of the natural law tradition for not maintaining a clear distinction between two types of legal analysis: the description of positive law (that is, the knowledge of actual rules laid down by law) and the question of whether what positive law prescribes is right or wrong. Kant, as mentioned earlier, argued that knowledge gained through experience, and knowledge acquired through the application of pure reason, are fundamentally different. For Kant, analysing what our experience tells us is already enforced as law, and analysing what our reason tells us should be enacted as law, are therefore two very different kinds of analysis. Both are possible, and equally worthwhile. But these two types of analysis perform very different functions and, according to Kant, should be kept separate.

For all these reasons, Kant argued for the deconstruction of the natural law tradition and a new division of juridical labour between separate disciplines, with distinct methods and goals. A new division, first of all, between law and virtue, the first being concerned with juridical laws (external laws) and the second with ethical laws (internal laws). But a new division also *within* the domain of law between the metaphysics of law (the province of the philosopher searching for ideal standards *through the application of pure reason*) and the science of rights (the province of the professional lawyer examining actual rules *revealed by experience*).[19] On the one hand, then, is positive science, which is purely empirical. And on the other hand is legal philosophy, which is purely rational.

[18] Immanuel Kant, *The Metaphysics of Morals* (Cambridge, Cambridge University Press, 1996) 16–19.

[19] Immanuel Kant, *Metaphysical Elements of Justice – Part I of the Metaphysics of Morals*, 2nd edn (Indianapolis, Hackett, 1999) 28–30.

Kant, it must be noted, was very clear that one should always accompany the other. In particular, he took the view that a positive science of law should always be informed or 'enlightened' by the lights of pure reason: 'although the empirical knowledge of these actual laws can provide us with helpful clues, a purely empirical theory of justice and Law, like the wooden head in Phaedrus fable, is very beautiful, but, alas, it has no brain!'.[20] The fact remains, however, that Kant suggested nothing less than a fundamental methodological break between the philosophical and the scientific analysis of law. This distinction was later endorsed by Hegel in his own philosophy of law.[21] It soon became a commonplace of juridical science in the early nineteenth century and paved the way for the era of legal positivism.

What remained to be seen, however, was how empirical knowledge of the law could be turned into a 'science'. On this point, Kant and Hegel gave little by way of practical guidance. Both were legal philosophers, not jurists. Kant was concerned with categorical imperatives, and Hegel with the theory of the state. Both agreed, however, that the development of a 'scientific' science of rights should follow two broad principles or directions. First, in order to avoid the speculative drifts of the natural law tradition, juridical science should focus its attention entirely on positive law, in other words, on the actual law of the land, and its methodology should therefore be strictly empirical. Second, the science of rights, to become truly 'scientific', should seek to discover the inherent structure of its subject, its immutable laws and principles, and present its analysis in the form of a systematic knowledge.[22]

C. *Rechtswissenschaft* and the development of a 'scientific' jurisprudence

Kant's programme of turning the science of rights into a genuine empirical science was pursued in its most systematic and comprehensive manner by nineteenth-century German jurists. German lawyers began to use the concept of *Rechtswissenschaft* at the turn of the nineteenth century, and it is fairly clear that what they had in mind was the development of a legal science in the limited Kantian sense, that is, a science of positive law. Whilst the form and purpose of *Rechtswissenschaft* gave rise to heated methodological debates, there seems to have been widespread agreement among nineteenth-century German lawyers that the intellectual dignity of the discipline would be a measure of its scientific character (that is, its *Wissenschaftlichkeit*).[23]

[20] Ibid at 29.

[21] Georg Wilhelm Friedrich Hegel, *Philosophy of Rights* (Oxford, Clarendon Press, 1942).

[22] Immanuel Kant, *The Philosophy of Law – An Exposition of the Fundamental Principles of Jurisprudence as the Science of Right* (Edinburgh, Clark, 1887) 43–45. On the nature and structure of legal science according to Kant, see Simone Goyard-Fabre, *La philosophie du droit de Kant* (Paris, Vrin, 1996) 61–78.

[23] Mathias Reimann, 'Nineteenth Century German Legal Science' (1989) 31 *Boston College Law Review* 837, 847–48.

In its search for a new legal science, German jurisprudence began by turning away from its traditional veneration of abstract deductive logic, and started looking at law as a historical phenomenon.[24] Gustav Hugo, one of the founders of the historical school of jurisprudence, is representative of this new trend. For Hugo, the purpose of legal science is to identify the reasons that lie behind positive rules, and these reasons can be either philosophical or historical. History, according to Hugo, 'represents half of law's scientific part'.[25] What Hugo means by this is that the role of the lawyer cannot be limited to asking whether rules are reasonable. Lawyers must set themselves the task of revealing how law came to be what it is (how it became law) by reason of experience and human action. This is what Hugo calls 'chronological jurisprudence', a type of jurisprudence that seeks to establish how principles of positive law arose, and how they developed over time.[26] Hugo's chronological jurisprudence follows Kant in his emphasis on positive law and his rejection of metaphysical speculation. It is not fully 'scientific', however, since it does not explore the inner structure of its subject, that is, its systematicity. But in one respect at least, Hugo goes beyond Kant: he identifies history as the primary data of an empirical legal science.

What Hugo does not say is how to build a system out of this historical material. On this point, Feuerbach and Thibaut were the first to suggest organisational methods and criteria. According to them, *Rechtswissenschaft* has to serve two purposes: reducing the mass of empirical data collected by chronological jurisprudence to general principles; and building a rational system out of these general principles. For Feuerbach, legal science has to construct legal concepts with 'exact certitude, acute precision and lucid clarity'. It must reveal the 'internal coherence' of legal rules, and establish the 'systematic coherence' of legal dogmas.[27] Similarly, Thibaut defines legal science as the 'systematic sum total of laws'.[28]

However, despite these efforts to make legal science more empirical, precise and coherent, early nineteenth-century German legal science remains largely influenced by the natural law tradition and legal philosophy. Hugo, for instance, regards philosophy as 'a distinct branch of jurisprudence considered as a science' from which chronological jurisprudence ought to draw 'value judgments' about historical facts and material.[29] Feuerbach and Thibaut also consider philosophy a necessary component of legal science, needed to evaluate historical facts in the light of reason: 'empirical knowledge gives to jurisprudence its body, philosophical knowledge gives it its spirit'.[30] This continued influence of

[24] Ibid.

[25] Gustav Hugo, *Histoire du droit romain* (Paris, Librairie de Jurisprudence et d'Administration d'Antoine Bavoux, 1825) i.

[26] Ibid at ii–iii.

[27] Johann Paul Anselm Feuerbach, *Theorie der erfahrung in der rechtswissenschaft*, cited by Reimann, 'Nineteenth Century German Legal Science', above n 23 at 849.

[28] Anton Friedrich Justus Thibaut, *System des Pandektenrechts* (Stockstadt, Keip & von Delft, 1999) 4 ('Ein systematischer Inbegriff von Gesetzen').

[29] Hugo, *Histoire du droit romain*, above n 25 at xxvi–xxvii.

[30] Feuerbach, *Theorie der erfahrung in der rechtswissenschaft*, cited by Reimann, 'Nineteenth Century German Legal Science', above n 23 at 851.

philosophy is easily explained. After centuries of metaphysical speculation about law and justice, nineteenth-century lawyers are understandably reluctant to exclude *all* thinking about the 'ought' and limit their discipline strictly to the question of the 'is'. The fact remains that in the early nineteenth century, legal science is as much about empirical knowledge of the law as it is about normative thinking and critical evaluation.

German legal science, however, takes a new turn under the influence of Savigny and his disciples. Savigny firmly rejects his predecessors' belief in philosophical reason as an important element of legal science. For Savigny, half-historicism means half-scientificity. Kant, he argues, must be taken seriously and legal philosophy must be left to philosophers. Legal science should abandon normative speculation once and for all and establish a modern *Rechtswissenschaft* based strictly on historical grounds.[31]

Savigny regards law as the customary expression of the 'spirit of the people' (*Volksgeist*).[32] Law, like language, reflects a nation's folklore, its indigenous culture. Law has no separate existence. It is above all a cultural product, not a philosophical or a rational idea.[33] Savigny's approach to legal science is in turn largely informed by this cultural vision of law. For Savigny, legal science can only operate by combining the historical and the systemic method. Historical investigation is necessary to reveal the general principles of positive law. But the study of the past is only a tool, a starting point for what Savigny regards as the true purpose of legal science: detecting the innermost principles of the system and revealing the system's internal coherence, that is, the ways in which individual legal concepts and rules are 'united into one great whole'.[34] From a methodological point of view, this means that the role of the legal scientist is to reduce the empirical-historical pluralism of law to its inherent unity.

Savigny is generally remembered for his historical approach to law. Yet it is the systematic element of his *Rechtswissenschaft* that actually left the most profound mark on German legal science, and on legal science more generally. This can be seen in the work of some of Savigny's disciples, in particular in that of Puchta and Jhering, the founders of the '*Begriffsjurisprudenz*', or conceptual jurisprudence. The work of Puchta, Savigny's immediate successor at the University of Berlin, demonstrates a progressive dismissal of the historical method and the will to take the systematic method to new logical extremes.[35] For Puchta, the 'system' has a more essential meaning than for Savigny. The system is not simply an image or a metaphor reflecting the connections that exist between the different parts of the law. For Puchta, law is *quintessentially*

[31] Joachim Ruckert, 'The Unrecognized Legacy: Savigny's Influence on German Jurisprudence after 1900' (1989) 37 *American Journal of Comparative Law* 121, 130–34.

[32] Friedrich Carl von Savigny, *System des heutigen römischen rechts* (Berlin, Veit, 1840) xiv.

[33] Friedrich Carl von Savigny, *The Vocation of Our Age for Legislation and Jurisprudence* (New Jersey, The Lawbook Exchange, 2002) 24–26.

[34] Savigny, *System des heutigen römischen rechts*, above n 32 at xxxvi.

[35] Reimann, 'Nineteenth Century German Legal Science', above n 23 at 860–62.

systemic.[36] Puchta thus proposes a fundamental change of perspective. Systematicity is no longer a distant goal or a hidden characteristic of the law, which legal science must reveal through historical investigation. Systematicity is the logical premise, the starting point from which legal science must construct a complete, coherent and hierarchical order of juridical concepts, creating a sort of 'pyramid of concepts in which all parts are logically interconnected'.[37]

Equally important is Puchta's belief that the system itself is capable of generating new law. Puchta is aware that an important part of the law emanates directly from the people (*Volksrecht*), a point on which he is in agreement with Savigny. For Puchta, however, law emanates from other sources too, whether it is legislated law (*Gesetzesrecht*) or the law of the jurists (*Juritzenrecht*). Thus the system is not only a principle of organisation. It itself is a source of law, a principle of production and reproduction of legal norms.[38]

Two decades after Puchta, the work of Jhering accentuated the distancing of conceptual jurisprudence from the historical method and further radicalised the systematic logic.[39] Jhering was important for two reasons. He insisted, first of all, that legal science should be liberated once and for all from the legacy of Roman law. Jhering acknowledged the historical importance of Roman law, but only as an 'element of civilisation', or a model of inventiveness and intellectual rigour. Thus, whilst the 'spirit of Roman law' should be celebrated, legal science should cease to regard it as a source of law. For Jhering, the time had come for the modern science of law to absorb the methodological essence of Roman law but end the 'slavish adherence to its substance'.[40] Legal science should in other words develop 'through Roman law, but over and beyond it'.[41]

Secondly, Jhering had ambitions to develop a 'natural science' of law. By natural legal science, Jhering did not mean a return to the natural law tradition. On the contrary, he wished to develop a legal science that possessed the same status and formal attributes of certainty, coherence and unity as 'pure' or 'exact' sciences. Jhering wrote at a time when the natural sciences were gaining a great deal of intellectual and academic prestige, due mostly to a series of spectacular breakthroughs (theory of evolution, laws of thermodynamics, germ theory and so forth). In these circumstances, the temptation was great for those outside the natural sciences to present their work as a 'real' science, to give it some form of intellectual legitimacy. Marx presented his materialist philosophy as a 'scientific explanation' of history. Freud built a new 'science of dreams'. Jhering, for his

[36] Georg Friedrich Puchta, *Cursus der Institutionen* (Leipzig, Breitkopf und Härtel) 100 ('das Recht selbst ein System ist').

[37] Reimann, 'Nineteenth Century German Legal Science', above n 23 at 860.

[38] Georg Friedrich Puchta, *Vorlesungen über das heutige römische Recht* (Leipzig, Tauchnitz, 1852) 39.

[39] Jean-Louis Halpérin, 'L'histoire du droit constituée en discipline: consécration ou repli identitaire?' (2001) 4 *Revue d'Histoire des Sciences Humaines* 9, 12–14.

[40] Reimann, 'Nineteenth Century German Legal Science', above n 23 at 862.

[41] Rudolf von Jhering, *L'esprit du droit romain dans les différentes phases de son développement, vol I* (Paris, Librairie Marescq, 1886) 14 ('par le droit romain, mais outre et au-delà').

part, called for the development of pure science of law, capable of producing 'objective truths' about the legal universe, just as the natural sciences are producing objective truths about the natural universe.[42]

For Jhering, law should be studied as a living organism. The task of legal science is to dissect law's 'anatomy' and to reveal its 'physiology', that is, to identify the various components of the organism as well as their function and interaction.[43] Legal science, in this perspective, becomes a sort of normative biology, which seeks to show how rules can be grouped into larger systematic wholes – legal concepts and institutions – and how these concepts and institutions surround the rules, 'just as the muscles surround the bones'.[44] Jurisprudence becomes something more than the mere interpretation and organisation of historical data. Jurisprudence turns into 'an art and a free science; an art which gives the material a form, an artistic aspect, and which breathes life into it; a science which, despite the positive character of its subject, can be called a natural science in the realm of the intellect'.[45] Whether artistic or scientific, the defining feature of Jhering's jurisprudence is that it turns law into a game of induction and deduction, in which rules are reduced to the role of logical building blocks: 'law – says Jhering – is a logical organism of juridical institutions and definitions'.[46] The validity and authority of a rule no longer depend on history, practical sense or social utility but on the rule's logical connection with the totality of the overall system. As one commentator puts it, the law is no longer a product of history; with Jhering, it becomes a pure 'creature of logic'.[47]

D. Intermediate conclusion

By the end of the nineteenth century, German legal science was far from unified. There were still tensions between the Romanists and the Germanists, historicism and reformism, the proponents of the 'law of jurists' and the advocates of 'popular law'. But however complex and multi-faceted, *Rechtswissenschaft* was structured around three overarching ideas which have subsequently remained remarkably constant and have become key tenets of German legal culture. The first idea is that legal science only has one legitimate object: positive law. Everything else belongs to metaphysical speculation and must be left to philosophers. The second idea is that, despite its phenomenal diversity, the law always contains organic principles, general laws of organisation that govern the mutual

[42] Ibid at 24.

[43] Ibid at 26–27.

[44] Ibid at 36.

[45] Rudolf von Jhering, *L'esprit du droit romain dans les différentes phases de son développement, vol III* (Paris, Librairie Marescq, 1886) 52: ('un art, une science libre; un art qui donne à la matière une forme, un aspect artistique, qui lui insuffle la vie; une science, qui malgré le caractère positif de son objet, peut être désignée comme une science naturelle en matière intellectuelle').

[46] Jhering, *L'esprit du droit romain – vol I*, above n 41 at 43.

[47] Reimann, 'Nineteenth Century German Legal Science', above n 23 at 864.

relations of its parts. The third idea is that legal science, in order to be a 'true' science – comparable in dignity and respectability to the natural sciences – must seek to show that these laws of organisation form together a complete and coherent logical system. In other words, the German legal culture inherited from the nineteenth century is characterised by the notion that, *by definition*, a positive science of law must be a science of the unity of law.

This basic notion or hypothesis was soon exported abroad by German jurists. It was exported, first of all, to other domestic jurisdictions, and in particular in the Anglo-American world, where law had just begun to emerge as an academic discipline. John Austin, for example, following a residence at the University of Bonn in 1827–28, declared his admiration for German legal science and said that it had represented a direct source of inspiration for his *Province of Jurisprudence* and for other works in which he had sought to provide a universal and scientific explanation of the law.[48] Similarly, in the United States, most common lawyers of the 'classical period' of Anglo-American jurisprudence (1851–1914) explicitly referred to German *Rechtswissenschaft* as a model.[49]

The discipline of international law also came under the influence of the aims and methods of German legal science. In fact, the predominance of German legal thought in the development of international law in the nineteenth century is striking. One reason for this, as noted by Koskenniemi, may have been the realisation that many of the techniques developed by German public lawyers to deal with the fragmentation of the Holy Roman Empire were well suited to deal with the problems of European organisation after the Napoleonic wars.[50] Whatever the reasons, what is clear is that the methods and techniques of the *Rechtswissenschaft* served as a direct source of inspiration for early German international lawyers like Martens, Heffter or Bluntschli and that the German science of international law in the nineteenth century was at its core a science of the unity of international law, that is, a rational, synthetic and systemic *Völkerrechtswissenschaft*.[51]

This international law tradition, however, was not confined to Germany. During the first half of the twentieth century, it rapidly became paradigmatic of the international law discipline as a whole. In this regard, the influence of the German-Speaking émigré lawyers was decisive. Scholars like Lieber, Oppenheim, Lauterpacht, Friedmann, Schwarzenberger, Kelsen and many others after them were instrumental in disseminating the precepts and methods of the German

[48] See the preface in John Austin, *The Province of Jurisprudence Determined* (London, John Murray, 1861) xviii.

[49] See, on this point, Stefan Riesenfeld, 'The Influence of German Legal Theory on American Law: The Heritage of Savigny and His Disciples' (1989) 37 *American Journal of Comparative Law* 1; MH Hoeflich, 'Transatlantic Friendships and the German Influence on American Law in the First Half of the Nineteenth Century' (1987) 35 *American Journal of Comparative Law* 599.

[50] Martti Koskenniemi, 'The Fate of Public International Law: Between Technique and Politics' (2007) 70 *Modern Law Review* 1, 2.

[51] See, on this point: Pierre-Marie Dupuy, 'Taking International Law Seriously - On the German Approach to International Law' (2007) *EUI Working Papers* 1, 6–8.

Völkerrechtswissenschaft. Despite different political and intellectual sensibilities, these émigré lawyers shared a similar vision of international law *as a system* and a common conviction that the task of the science of international law should be to identify and envision the various rules of international law as arranged within a hierarchy, and composing together a coherent logical order.[52]

The pervasive presence of systemic thinking in the discipline of international law can certainly be explained by other factors. Yet there is little doubt that the 'law-as-unity' postulate, about which the ILC says that there is 'seldom disagreement' today, owes much to the combined influence of Kantian critique and German legal science. What should be remembered is that this type of unity is not an empirical fact, a juridical reality that is given by experience. It is above all a transcendental and logical condition of interpretation, an *a priori* form of judgement *projected* onto international law as a scientific object of knowledge. This is what, in the first chapter of this book, I called unity 'in idea' or 'in spirit' as opposed to unity 'in flesh'.

II. AXIO-LOGICAL UNITY

Although complexity lies at the heart of this book, the present section will address what is arguably the most complex of all perspectives on unity, that is, that which conceives of unity in terms of values. At the outset, this approach may seem odd. For is it not strange to conceptualise unity by appealing to values? Are values not by definition multiple, volatile, relative and changing? The stock exchange, where the concept of value originated, demonstrates to perfection that values, by nature, fluctuate according to market forces, investor attitudes, the political environment and so forth.

Likewise, many would argue that law is very much the opposite of the world of values: a confined space within which subjects deal with one another on an equal footing, with no regard for special interests, and on the basis of neutral, objective and *a priori* rules of the game. Isn't law a domain of objectivity, order and reason, created to escape the clash of passions, cultures and subjective values? In other words, doesn't law's main contribution lie in standing beyond values?

One might ask, then, if the world of law and the world of values are not by definition two alien and impervious worlds and if, by speaking of values, one does not automatically situate oneself outside the realm of law. This is what 'pure' positivists would have us believe. But of course, things are not that simple. There is not simply law on one side and values on the other. There are many lines of communication and complex relations between these two universes.

[52] On the influence of German-speaking émigré lawyers on the systemic vision of international law, see Benvenisti, 'The Conception of International Law as a Legal System', above n 6 at 1–4.

These lines of communication may be discreet or concealed. But they are real and manifold.[53]

For one thing, speaking of order, neutrality or predictability is already speaking of values. These, as we shall see below, are essentially 'formal' values. But they are values all the same. More importantly perhaps, a legal order is always a theatre of exchanges, negotiations and re-negotiations between positive law and values. This mutual relationship can take a number of forms:

- *The articulation and implementation of values through law*. Consider for instance three seemingly unrelated rules. The first rule sets a speed limit on motorways. The second rule makes it mandatory for vehicles to undergo a roadworthiness test once a year. The third rule requires all motorists to be insured against their liability for injuries to others. At first sight, the three rules have little in common: they apply to different objects and subjects. Yet we might say that this set of rules is somewhat coherent – that it makes sense – by reason of the fact that a common value – the safety of road users – is at issue in all three rules.[54] In this scenario, the law can be said to *express* or *realise* a given social value.
- *Law's mediation between competing values*. There are a number of ways in which the law can mediate between different values. This mediation can be achieved, first of all, by way of balancing. For example, a rule that sets a drink driving limit of 80mg of alcohol per 100ml of blood strikes a balance between the freedom of drivers to consume alcohol and the safety of road users. But the mediation between competing values can also be achieved by a more direct and forthright prioritisation of one or the other value. For example, a law that bans smoking in public places ranks public health above the freedom of smokers. In both cases, the law organises and *arbitrates* the relationship between values or value-systems.
- *The sublimation of values by the law*. Law is not simply a technique of ad hoc mediation between sets of values. In any legal order, law also serves to single out and elevate certain superior or mandatory values deemed to be essential to social order, coherence, peace or justice. These are, for instance, the great 'founding prohibitions' of criminal law, fundamental rights and freedoms, or 'public policy' rules. In these instances, law can be said to *magnify* social values.
- *The anticipation of values by the law*. If social values generally precede the law, there are occasions where the opposite is true. Sometimes, the law formalises values that have not yet been socially recognised or constituted.

[53] On the interaction between law and values, see John Tasioulas (ed), *Law, Values and Social Practices* (Aldershot, Darmouth, 1997); Andrei Marmor, *Positive Law and Objective Values* (Oxford, Oxford University Press, 2001); Gordon Anthony et al (eds), *Values in Global Administrative Law* (Oxford, Hart Publishing, 2011); Robert Kolb, 'Droit et valeurs: la réception de valeurs en droit' (2002) 21 *Refugee Survey Quarterly* 248.

[54] See Neil MacCormick, 'Coherence in Legal Justification' in Aleksander Peczenik and Lars Lindhal (eds), *Theory of Legal Science* (Dordrecht, Reidel, 1984) 237–38.

> Consider, for example, the notion of crimes against humanity. When crimes against humanity were first introduced in the 1945 Statute of the Nuremberg Tribunal, international law established a new 'founding prohibition' at a time when the notion of humanity had not yet been recognised or defined as a universal value worthy of protection. International law, in other words, *constructed* humanity as a value.[55]

This list is of course not exhaustive. It shows, however, that law and values are in a dialectical relation to one another, a relation of co-determination. Law, on the one hand, expresses, consolidates, formalises and implements value-choices or value-judgements. On the other hand, law's legitimacy and efficacy as a mechanism of social control largely depends on values. A legal system that produces or reproduces an unjust order, that is regarded as unfair by the majority of its subjects, or that disregards dominant social values is likely to be met with disobedience, resistance and, in the most extreme of cases, revolution. Thus values need law, and law needs values. Such is the meaning of Georges Scelle's famous assertion that law always exists 'at the junction of power and ethics'.[56]

This does not mean, of course, that all law can be reduced to values, or that all values can be expressed in legal terms. The twelve-mile rule in the law of the sea expresses no particular value. It merely reflects a political compromise reached by the contracting parties at the UN Conference on the law of the sea. Conversely, values like love or compassion are not directly or easily translatable into positive law. The fact remains, however, that the legal universe is saturated with references to values, both explicit and implicit.

One might ask, then, whether unity and coherence in law might not be conceptualised by reference to the legal values that are expressed in a system, rather than by reference to logical, normative or formal consistency.[57] The question is of particular interest in the field of international law, for international law, as discussed earlier, is formally ill defined and largely indeterminate. Rather than looking for unity in international law's rules and institutions, might one instead look for unity in the values that international law seeks to uphold or realise? In other words, might one envision unity as something which involves, not so much the immediate substance of rules or their logical links to one another, but rather

[55] See Mireille Delmas-Marty, 'Le paradigme du crime contre l'humanité: construire l'humanité comme valeur' in Pierre Robert Baduel (ed), *Construire un monde? Mondialisation, pluralisme et universalisme* (Paris, Maisonneuve & Larose, 2007).

[56] Georges Scelle, *Manuel de droit international public* (Paris, Domat-Montchrestien, 1948) 9.

[57] For an early argument in this direction, see Claus-Wilhelm Canaris, *Systemdenken und Systembegriff in der Jurisprudenz: entwickelt am Beispiel des deutschen Privatrechts* (Berlin, Duncker & Humblot, 1969) 21: 'the attempt to conceptualize the system of a particular legal order as a formal one or as an axiomatic-deductive one is doomed to failure from the very beginning. For the inner unity of meaning of the law, which is supposed to be grasped in the system, is – in accordance with its derivation from the notion of justice – not of a logical kind but rather of a value-driven, i.e. axiolgocial kind' (translated by Bruno Simma and Dirk Pulkowski, 'Of Planets and the Universe: Self-Contained Regimes in International Law' (2006) 17 *European Journal of International Law* 483, 497).

what Gérard Timsit calls the 'super-determination' of norms by juridical values?[58]

This notion of value-driven or axio-logical unity has seldom been considered in the literature. The rise of human rights since 1945, however, gives it a new resonance today, in both domestic and international law. In Canada, for example, the adoption of the *Charter of Rights and Freedoms* and a number of recent decisions by the Supreme Court have led some to speak of a new form of unity in public law, grounded in fundamental social values.[59] The *Baker* case, in particular, seems to have established a new form of axio-logical order in Canadian law.[60] This case concerned, among other things, the long-established dichotomy between discretionary and non-discretionary decisions in administrative law. Traditionally, Common Law courts have taken the view that decisions of public authorities in 'sensitive' areas (immigration, foreign relations, national security and so forth) are not subject to the same standards of procedural fairness and judicial scrutiny as ordinary decisions. The rule has been that, in these sensitive areas, considerable deference should be given to decision-makers and that discretionary decisions may only be reviewed on limited grounds such as the bad faith of decision-makers, the improper use of discretionary powers or the use of irrelevant considerations. Implicit in this traditional approach is the notion that the rule of law is somewhat flexible or variable, and that the duty of procedural fairness depends on the type of decision and the rights concerned.[61]

On this particular issue, the *Baker* case seems to have introduced a new element of transcendence in Canadian law. Whilst maintaining the principled distinction between discretionary and non-discretionary decisions, and restating that discretionary decisions will generally be given considerable respect,[62] the Court held that discretion must nonetheless be exercised within the limits contemplated by the legislature and, more importantly for our purposes, in accordance with 'the fundamental values of Canadian society', as expressed in the *Charter* and international law instruments.[63] This means that all branches of Canadian public law – whether constitutional or administrative law, and regardless of whether they apply to Canadians or to aliens – are now subject to a common axio-logical core of validity. Differences may of course exist between these various branches, but these differences are in a sense sublimated – or

[58] Gérard Timsit, *Les noms de la loi* (Paris, PUF, 1991) 151–53. For a general reflection on the possibility of theorising international law's unity from the point of view of values, see Erika De Wet, 'The Emergence of International and Regional Value Systems as a Manifestation of the Emerging International Constitutional Order' (2006) 19 *Leiden Journal of International Law* 611; Carol Harlow, 'Global Administrative Law: The Quest for Principles and Values' (2006) 17 *European Journal of International Law* 187.

[59] See David Dyzenhaus (ed), *The Unity of Public Law* (Oxford, Hart Publishing, 2004) 1–6.

[60] *Baker v Canada (Minister of Citizenship and Immigration)* [1999] 2 SCR 817 (hereafter *Baker*).

[61] See Paul Craig, 'The Common Law, Reasons and Administrative Justice' (1994) 53 *Cambridge Law Journal* 282.

[62] Baker, above n 60 at para 53.

[63] Ibid at para 56.

'super-determined' – by their common subjection to a single code of fundamental humanitarian values.

In international law too, some have started speaking of a process of 'humanisation' of the international legal order. According to these authors, human rights law and humanitarian law have become the new normative foundation of international law as a whole, from the law of treaties to the law of state responsibility, the law of the sea or the law of consular relations. Human rights and humanitarian law, they argue, are no longer discrete branches of the law. They have become a sort of axio-logical core, a superior code of values that possesses a distinct juridical status (*erga omnes* and *jus cogens*) and affects all other fields of public international law.[64] This new 'humanity's law', as one author puts it, 'cross-cuts' the differentiated functions of specialised regimes and may well represent an anti-fragmentation tendency, a form of 'unwritten constitution' that reconstitutes the structure, subjects and core values of the international order.[65] Implicit in this argument is, once again, the notion of 'super-determination' of material norms by a more or less coherent and formalised set of values.

The purpose of the present section is not to establish if – or to what extent – international law does indeed revolve around a stable and coherent axio-logical core. As in the rest of this book, I am primarily interested in the conditions of possibility of discourse on unity (in this case, axio-logical unity). My purpose in what follows is twofold. The first is to identify and recognise the axio-logical perspective as a possibility of discourse, as a valid theoretical perspective, as worthy of consideration as the material, formal, cultural or epistemo-logical perspectives. Starting from that position, however, my second purpose is to show that, once again, the unity question is far more complex than what might appear at first glance, and raises a whole range of difficult and largely unexplored theoretical questions.

At first glance, the concept of 'super-determination' of material norms by values looks rather simple and explicit: legal relations always express or reflect certain values and these values act as the 'centre of gravity' of the legal order. Just as the nucleus represents the focal point of the atom, the point around which the rest of the atom is gathered and organised, fundamental legal values represent the focal point from which the unity of the legal order emanates. But two questions immediately arise: what *are* these fundamental legal values, and what is the nature of the link that unites rules and values? Each of these questions can be answered from a great many perspectives, and the 'axiology' of international law can be conceptualised from a great many points of view,

[64] On 'humanisation' in international law, see especially Theodor Meron, *The Humanization of International Law* (Leiden, Martinus Nijhoff, 2006); Antonio Augusto Cançado Trindade, 'International Law for Humankind: Towards a New Jus Gentium' (2005) 316 *Collected Courses of the Hague Academy of International Law* 9.

[65] See Ruti Teitel, *Humanity's Law* (Oxford, Oxford University Press, 2011); Ruti Teitel and Robert Howse, 'Cross-Judging: Tribunalization in a Fragmented But Interconnected Global Order' (2009) 41 *New York University Journal of International Law and Politics* 959.

which as we shall see raises the additional question of the articulation between these different approaches.

That said, it may be useful to begin by considering the different meanings of the concept of 'legal value'. I shall do so by exploring a series of dialectical oppositions between substantive and formal values (A), individual and collective values (B), and patrimonial and programmatic values (C).

A. Substantive and formal values

A first distinction concerns the difference between substantive and formal legal values.[66] These two types of values have very little in common. Substantive values, on the one hand, refer to certain ways of being and acting, certain conditions, qualities or behaviours, which are regarded as socially desirable and thus represent legitimate ends for the law to promote. Freedom, justice, equity, order, security, dignity or welfare are examples of substantive values. Formal values, on the other hand, refer to certain intrinsic attributes or properties deemed necessary for the law itself to operate effectively and realise its (substantive) goals. Characteristics like generality, publicity, predictability, certainty or coherence are examples of formal values. This distinction between substantive and formal values more or less coincides with Fuller's dichotomy between law's 'external' and 'internal' morality. External morality, according to Fuller, is the repository of values and substantive conceptions of justice and fairness against which the 'goodness' of a rule can be assessed. A law that authorises torture, from this point of view, is bad, and a law that bans torture is good. Internal morality, on the other hand, concerns the formal or procedural attributes – that is, the formal criteria of legality – which the law must possess to be recognised and to operate as law.[67]

There is no necessary contradiction between formal and substantive values, between internal and external morality. Often, these two orders of legitimacy go hand in hand. One can say, for example, that the constancy and the predictability of the law (two of Fuller's eight formal 'markers' of legality) are likely to contribute to social order (a substantive value). There are situations, however, where obvious tensions exist between formal and substantive values. At certain moments, the requirements of constancy and predictability may very well be obstacles to justice or fairness.

Let us consider, for instance, the question of 'odious debt', which has taken on a new legal and political significance in recent years, following the removal from

[66] See generally Van de Kerchove and Ost, *The Legal System Between Order and Disorder*, above n 2 at 56–57; Duncan Kennedy, 'Form and Substance in Private Law Adjudication' (1975) 89 *Harvard Law Review* 1685, 1710–13.

[67] Lon Fuller, *The Morality of Law* (Yale, Yale University Press, 1969).

office of a number of former dictators.[68] The odious debt doctrine provides that where a debt has been contracted by a despotic regime in ways that are not beneficial or are harmful to the interest of the population, this debt should not be regarded as a public debt, but as a personal debt of the power. As a result, when an odious regime falls, its odious debt falls with it, and it need not be repaid by the successor state or government. According to this doctrine, populations that have been the victim of violent and oppressive regimes are therefore not bound by the obligations undertaken by these regimes for their own benefit.

The odious debt doctrine has traditionally been met with two types of criticism. One argument against the doctrine is that it compromises the fundamental principles of the sanctity of contracts (*pacta sunt servanda*) and the continuity of the state. Another argument is that the concepts of 'odious debt' and 'oppressive regime' are indeterminate and, as a result, that they risk being abused by debtors who are either unwilling or unable to repay their debt. In both cases, the odious debt doctrine is criticised for introducing too large an element of uncertainty and instability in international legal relations.[69] Advocates of the doctrine, for their part, argue that therein lies precisely the value of the doctrine: faced with the risk of non-repayment, lenders will simply stop doing business with corrupt or despotic regimes. They will be forced to act with diligence and take positive steps to ensure that a loan is not likely to be used to reinforce an authoritarian regime.[70]

The example of the odious debt doctrine demonstrates how formal and substantive values can, on a given question, take law in two radically opposite directions. Considerations of equity and the welfare of populations (substantive values) call for the annulment of odious international obligations. The constancy and predictability of legal relations (formal values), on the other hand, call for these obligations to be upheld and enforced. A rule or doctrine can thus be at once legitimate from an external point of view and illegitimate from an internal point of view (or vice versa). This represents a first line of tension in the axiology of law.

B. Individual and collective values

Every legal order also contains tensions between individual and collective values.[71] In a sense, this tension is consubstantial to law itself, since the very

[68] See, eg, James Feinerman, 'Odious Debt, Old and New: the Legal Intellectual History of an Idea' (2007) 70 *Law and Contemporary Problems* 192; Christiana Ochoa, 'From Odious Debt to Odious Finance: Avoiding the Externalities of a Functional Odious Debt Doctrine' (2008) 49 *Harvard International Law Journal* 109; Jeff King, 'Odious Debt: The Terms of the Debate' (2006) 32 *North Carolina Journal of International Law and Commercial Regulation* 605.

[69] See, eg, Christoph Paulus, 'Odious Debts vs. Debt Trap: A Realistic Help' (2005) 31 *Brooklyn Journal of International Law* 83, 88–90.

[70] See, eg, Jonathan Shafter, 'The Due Diligence Model: An Executive Approach to Odious Debt Reform' (2007) 32 *North Carolina Journal of International Law and Commercial Regulation* 75.

[71] See Christophe Grzegorczyk, *Théorie générale des valeurs et le droit* (Paris, LGDJ, 1982) 110–12; Aleksander Peczenick, *On Law and Reason* (Dordrecht, Kluwer, 1989) 75–76.

purpose of law is to organise and regulate the association (that is, the act of forming a society) between individuals or groups of individuals. On the one hand, then, are individual or private values, which can be attributed to a single individual. Values like freedom of choice, dignity or physical integrity are examples of individual values. On the other hand are collective or social values, which cannot be attributed to a single individual and instead concern collectively the members of a group or society. Classical examples of this type of values are peace, security, solidarity or progress.

Here again, individual and collective values are not necessarily contradictory. More often than not, these two axio-logical orders are compatible, and even mutually supportive. Solidarity, for instance, is often a condition *sine qua non* to achieve freedom or dignity (for example, solidarity through taxes allows the building of roads, schools, hospitals and other social services which, in turn, promote freedom of movement and conscience, access to health and education and so forth). From the social viewpoint, as Proudhon once said, 'freedom and solidarity are but different expressions of the same concept . . . the freest man is the one who has the most relations with his fellow men'.[72] Equally, the protection of individual freedoms is often a vital element in the establishment of a fair and peaceful society.

Inevitably, however, individual and collective values are bound to collide in certain situations, unless of course one believes in 'invisible hand' theories, according to which private interests, values and appetites spontaneously get along and, by reason of a sort of virtuous providence, promote the interests of society at large. If indeed individual and collective values got along spontaneously, there would be no need for law. All we would need to do is *laisser faire*.

But things do not work this way. Every human community is riddled with tensions between the individual and the collective: tension between freedom of religion and secularism, the free use of natural resources and protection of the environment, freedom of expression and public order, etc. And the same is true of the international community. Similar tensions arise between individual state values (sovereign autonomy, territorial integrity, state immunities and so on) and universal values (international peace and security, protection of the environment, human rights, development and so forth).

The issue of anticipatory or preemptive self-defence illustrates this point well. May a state use self-defence against an attack that is neither actual nor imminent, but is nonetheless plausible? In other words, may a state *strike first* to prevent a threat from materialising? On this issue, international law is largely indeterminate. There is no definitive answer to this question, whether in practice, in doctrine or in the case law of international tribunals.[73] This indeter-

[72] Pierre-Joseph Proudhon, *Oeuvres complètes* (Paris, Librairie des sciences politiques et sociales, 1938) 138.

[73] See, on this point, Matthew Flynn, *First Strike: Preemptive War in Modern History* (New York, Routledge, 2008); Michael Reisman and Andrea Armstrong, 'The Past and Future of the Claim of Preemptive Self-Defense' (2006) 100 *American Journal of International Law* 525; Michael

minacy, however, is not due to a defect or an anomaly in the system. Rather, it springs from the inevitable tension between two sets of values: the right of the state to protect itself, on the one hand, and the maintenance of international peace and security, on the other.

The safeguard of sovereignty (an individual value *par excellence*) calls for the use of preventive actions as soon as a state possesses evidence that it may be the object of an attack. States cannot be expected to await the attack like 'sitting ducks', but should be allowed to take all necessary measures to prevent the aggression to occur in the first place. The maintenance of international peace and security (a collective value), on the other hand, calls for the most stringent restriction on the use of force and for a narrow interpretation of the right of self-defence – allowing force to be used only where peace has *already* been compromised by an act of aggression. We are thus in a situation where two *universally recognised* imperatives pull international law in opposite directions.

The challenge for law in general, and international law in particular, is to negotiate and organise the coexistence of these two axio-logical orders, without renouncing either individual or collective values. This represents one of the most fundamental dilemmas of law. Law must limit and constrain the freedom of each so as to guarantee the freedom of all – alienate the one to better liberate the many. International law is asked to preserve the sovereign autonomy of states and, at the same time, to reach beyond their sovereignty to promote certain universal values. Should international law work toward perpetual peace without safeguarding sovereignty, it would become something other than international law, that is, something like the public law of a cosmopolitan state which, short of warranting the right of each people to constitute itself in a state, would unavoidably be perceived as despotic. Conversely, should international law only concern itself with maintaining state sovereignty, it would be useless as an instrument to tackle the great ills of the world – wars, genocides, economic and environmental crises and so on. Here again, international law seems to be 'super-determined' by value-systems that are not always compatible and between which there is no *a priori* hierarchy.

C. Patrimonial and programmatic values

The third line of axio-logical tension concerns what I shall call patrimonial values (*valeurs-patrimoine*) and programmatic values (*valeurs-programme*). The first type of values involves values that are 'already there', an established *acquis* that needs protecting or preserving, a condition that must be maintained and perpetuated. Legal values like dignity, autonomy, security, integrity (whether physical or territorial), culture or biodiversity are examples of patrimonial

Byers, 'Preemptive Self-defense: Hegemony, Equality and Strategies of Legal Change' (2003) 11 *The Journal of Political Philosophy* 171.

values. The second type of values, on the other hand, concerns conditions regarded as desirable but which have not yet been achieved or realised. Values such as intergenerational equity, distributive justice, well-being or development are typical examples of programmatic values.

The difference between these two axio-logical orders lies primarily in the sort of legal response or measures they require. Patrimonial values call for protective measures: protection against foreign interference, preservation of ecosystems, maintenance of biodiversity or cultural diversity, etc. We are here in a conservative logic of safeguarding a desirable or necessary state or condition. Programmatic values, for their part, call for change, transformation, new ways of being, acting or thinking: the redistribution of wealth, transfer of technologies, humanitarian intervention and so on. We are here in a reformist or interventionist logic.

Patrimonial and programmatic values, almost by definition, are in tension with one another. One need only think about the intrinsic and somewhat unavoidable tension between the principle of territorial integrity (patrimonial value) and the right to self-determination (programmatic value), between which there is no real margin of compatibility. An ethnic or religious minority that declares independence and sets up its own structures of governance *necessarily* affects the territorial integrity of the state concerned.[74] This contradiction can be managed peacefully if self-determination is negotiated and ratified by the different parties. Yet the fact remains that, once again, two values that are firmly recognised in positive international law point in different directions, not to unity.

D. Axiology of orientation and axiology of validation: super-determination 'hard' and 'soft'

The great diversity of juridical values represents a first element of complexity in the axiology of international law. Whilst international law can certainly be said to express certain values, unavoidable tensions exist between different axio-logical orders. Thinking about unity in terms of values thus raises the question of how to resolve these tensions. Who should decide? Are states the only legitimate arbitrators? Or should judges, whether domestic or international, be allowed to resolve axio-logical conflicts on a case-by-case basis? According to which criteria should axio-logical conflicts be resolved? Do lawyers have a role to play in this process and, if so, what role? It becomes clear that speaking of axio-logical unity involves more than listing the values expressed in positive law. One is

[74] On the inherent tension between self-determination and territorial sovereignty, see eg, Joshua Castellino, *International Law and Self-determination* (Boston, Martinus Nijhoff, 2000) 75; and Hurst Hannum, *Autonomy, Sovereignty, and Self-Determination: The Accommodation of Conflicting Rights* (Philadelphia, University of Pennsylvania Press, 1996).

immediately confronted with other problematics, both institutional (who decides?) and hermeneutic (how to interpret values in relation to one another?).

That said, the pluralism of values is but one element of complexity in the axiology of international law. Just as there are different ways of conceiving of legal values, so too are there different ways of conceptualising the link that unites rules and values. Earlier, I spoke of the 'super-determination' of rules by values. But what does 'super-determination' actually mean? To what sort of interaction does this notion refer? On this issue, at least two perspectives can be considered, which I shall call 'hard' and 'soft' super-determination.

'Soft' super-determination follows a logic of *orientation* of legal norms or activities through values. The idea here is that values act as a sort of ideal horizon toward which rules and institutions converge. This can mean two different things.

First, values can act as a form of interpretative focal point, that is, a point of meaning and reference towards which the law-applier – and in particular the judge – directs the rules it is called upon to interpret. A historical example might help to clarify this point. The 1917 Bolshevik Revolution caused a major problem of legal fragmentation in Russia. Following the October Revolution, imperial institutions were dismantled; Lenin granted the right of self-determination to the component nationalities of the Soviet states; he offered a large degree of regional autonomy to nations that did not secede from Russia; 'people's tribunals' were established in each and every province, but no provision was made for an appellate tribunal or a supreme court within the new Russian Republic to unify the practice of these courts. The post-revolutionary legal order was thus chaotic, and remained so until the formation of the USSR in 1922. Besides the obvious constitutional problems posed by the breakdown of the Empire and the various secessions, the new Russian legal order was marked by considerable variations in the application of civil and criminal standards from province to province.[75]

However, in an attempt to bring some order into this chaotic system, a decree was adopted in 1917 that instructed the newly created people's courts to decide the cases brought before them on the basis of Tsarist laws, but only to the extent that they had not been revoked and that they did not contradict 'revolutionary conscience and revolutionary legal consciousness'.[76] The new Russian Republic was well aware that appealing to the judges' revolutionary consciousness would result in some instability and uncertainty in the law. But the dominant idea at the time was that the organs of government would eventually identify a desirable approach and promulgate it in new laws. Meanwhile, the only unifying force in the post-revolution soviet system was the reference to common concepts of socialist justice and morality. What was at play from 1917 to 1922 was thus a

[75] See FJM Feldbrugge, *Russian Law* (Dordrecht, Martinus Nijhoff, 1993) 90–95.

[76] See Piotr Stucka, Robert Sharlet, Peter Maggs and Piers Beirne (eds), *Selected Writings on Soviet Law and Marxism* (New York, Sharpe, 1988) 184; Lewis Siegelbaum, *Soviet State and Society Between Revolutions, 1918–1929* (Cambridge, Cambridge University Press, 1992) 15.

form of 'soft' super-determination of the practice of people's courts through common hermeneutic circles of interpretation. This common reference to revolutionary values, this soft axiologisation, did not ensure strict unity in the law. It did, however, maintain a minimal degree of judicial consistency across the Russian Republic.[77]

'Soft' super-determination, however, can be understood from another point of view, which refers to values as principles of *narrative* coherence. Values provide orientation, in this perspective, not so much by acting as interpretative guidelines for the judge but by representing a repository of meaning from which to explain and analyse – in other words to *evaluate* – the law. Some have argued, for example, that the unity of a discipline like contract law can be understood through the single notion of the autonomy of the parties, which acts as a sort of constituent value from which everything else follows.[78] Others disagree and argue instead that the normative foundation of the law of contract lies in the moral force of promise. According to them, promise-keeping is the key value that helps understand the underlying nature of, and justification for, the rules that make up contract law.[79] In both cases, however, the unity of contract law is constructed by reference to a fundamental value that helps *make sense* of all the rest.

Some authors have made similar arguments about international law. Louis Henkin, for instance, has taken the view that nearly everything in international law can be explained by reference to the three fundamental 'axioms' of statehood, what he regards as the three fundamental 'state values': independence, equality and autonomy.[80] To be sure, this type of argument is largely contested today, in particular by authors who consider that human rights, not state values, represent the normative foundation or the axio-logical core of modern international law.[81] But in both cases, the integrity and the unity of international law are explained by reference to a set of cardinal values that act as principles of orientation or, as Kant puts it in his essay on 'orientation in thinking', as 'signposts' or a 'compass' by means of which the observing subject can find his way in the field of (legal) objects.[82] The reference to values, in this perspective, allows us to reduce the diversity of empirical data (the rules and institutions of the system) to a form of temporary unity of meaning. Values can be understood, in other words, to 'give the A', that is, the note or the tone from which all legal rules and institutions can be brought to (semantic) harmony, like instruments in an orchestra.

[77] See John Hazard, 'Unity and Diversity in Socialist Law' (1965) 30 *Law and Contemporary Problems* 270, 270–72.

[78] See, eg, Charles Fried, *Contract as Promise: A Theory of Contractual Obligation* (Cambridge, Harvard University Press, 1981).

[79] See, eg, Stephen Smith, *Contract Theory* (Oxford, Oxford University Press, 2004).

[80] Louis Henkin, *International Law: Politics, Values and Functions* (Dordrecht, Martinus Nijhoff, 1990) 130–31.

[81] See, eg, Fernando Teson, *A Philosophy of International Law* (Boulder, Westview Press, 1998).

[82] Immanuel Kant, *Political Writings* (Cambridge, Cambridge University Press, 1970) 245.

'Hard' super-determination, on the other hand, refers to a slightly different logic of orientation. It involves cases in which values are recognised as authentic criteria of validity of legal norms.[83] This scenario involves a legal order emphasising certain values among the fundamental norms of the system, and regarding these superior values as criteria of legality proper. Axio-logical unity, in this perspective, refers to the existence of a core of peremptory values, that is, values from which no valid rule can derogate.

The existence of this type of axio-logical core of peremptory values is well established in most domestic legal systems. These peremptory values typically take the form of fundamental rights and rules of public order or public policy. More often than not, this 'higher law' is crystallised or codified in constitutional or quasi-constitutional instruments (written or unwritten constitutions, bills of rights, charters of fundamental freedoms and so forth).

The situation in international law, needless to say, is significantly more complex. We know that international law is devoid of a constitution or, rather, that it is endowed with a plurality of constitution-like instruments – UN Charter, European Constitution, Constitution of the ILO, Agreement Establishing the WTO, etc – between which there is no clear line of demarcation or hierarchy. This does not mean that there is no element of 'hard' super-determination in international law. On the contrary, there is wide consensus today that certain fundamental principles of international law – those known as *jus cogens* principles – enjoy a preferential or privileged status in the international legal order. All of this is well known and does not warrant in-depth discussion here. It is sufficient to recall that, despite marginal doctrinal controversies,[84] *jus cogens* norms are recognised as part of positive international law and form a sort of 'superior law' in at least two respects. *Jus cogens* obligations, to begin with, are all *erga omnes* obligations, that is, obligations owed to the international community as a whole.[85] In practice, this means that all states have a legal interest in their fulfilment and that any state – whether injured or not – may therefore take action to see that these obligations are enforced.[86] More importantly for our purpose, *jus cogens* obligations are 'intransgressible' norms, that is, norms from which no derogation is ever permitted, by way of treaty or otherwise. An act or

[83] On values as criteria of axiological validity, see François Ost and Michel Van de Kerchove, *De la pyramide au réseau? Pour une théorie dialectique du droit* (Bruxelles, Publications des Facultés universitaires Saint-Louis, 2002) 337–39.

[84] See, eg, Michael Glennon, 'De l'absurdité du droit impératif (Jus cogens)' (2006) 110 *Revue Générale de Droit International Public* 529; Ulf Linderfalk, 'The Effect of Jus Cogens Norms: Whoever Opened Pandora's Box, Did You Ever Think About the Consequences?' (2007) 18 *European Journal of International Law* 853.

[85] Whilst *jus cogens* norms are all *erga omnes* obligations, the reverse is not true. On this point, see Michael Byers, 'Conceptualising the Relationship between Jus Cogens and Erga Omnes Rules' (1997) 66 *Nordic Journal of International Law* 211.

[86] *Case Concerning the Barcelona Traction, Light and Power Company, Limited (Belgium v Spain)* 5 February 1970, ICJ Reports (1970) 3, para 33: 'the obligations of a State towards the international community as a whole . . . by their very nature are the concern of all States. In view of the importance of the rights involved, all States can be held to have a legal interest in their protection; they are obligations *erga omnes*'.

behaviour that contravenes *jus cogens* is automatically regarded as invalid or unlawful.[87]

Jus cogens norms thus represent a body of higher rules of public policy, which take precedence over ordinary norms and form a sort of common international public order (*ordre public international*).[88] This, without a doubt, represents an embryonic element of 'hard' super-determination in international law. It constitutes 'hard' super-determination, first of all, since conformity to the cardinal values expressed in *jus cogens* is regarded as a criterion of validity of international (treaty) norms. But this axiologisation, at the same time, is embryonic, since *jus cogens* is made up of universal humanitarian values (human rights, prohibition of torture and slavery, war crimes) *as well as* individual state values (non-intervention, sovereign immunities, prohibition of the use of force), and these axiological orders or 'layers' often clash or contradict each other.[89]

III. INTERMEDIATE CONCLUSIONS: THE HESITANT FETTERING OF THE THOUSAND NECKS

> to create new values – not even the lion is capable of that: but to create freedom for itself for new creation – that is the power of the lion
>
> . . .

[87] *Vienna Convention on the Law of Treaties*, 23 May 1969, art 53: 'a treaty is void if, at the time of its conclusion, it conflicts with a peremptory norm of general international law'; *Legality of the Threat or Use of Nuclear Weapons*, advisory opinion, 8 July 1996, ICJ Reports (1996) 226, para 79: 'these fundamental rules are to be observed by all States whether or not they have ratified the conventions that contain them, because they constitute intransgressible principles of international customary law'.

[88] Case T-306/01 *Ahmed Ali Yusuf and Al Barakaat International Foundation v Council of the European Union and Commission of the European Communities* [2005] ECR II-03533, para 277: 'the Court is empowered to check, indirectly, the lawfulness of the resolutions of the Security Council in question with regard to *jus cogens*, understood as a body of higher rules of public international law . . . from which no derogation is possible'.

[89] For an example of conflict between norms of *jus cogens*, see *Al-Adsani v UK*, Series A no 11 (2002) 34 EHRR 11. In this case, the European Court of Human Rights was asked to resolve the conflict between the right to obtain reparation for acts of torture and the principles of state immunity. Whilst recognising that the prohibition of torture counts among the norms of *jus cogens*, the Court took the view that state immunities are an absolute procedural bar to civil actions regarding acts of torture: 'while the Court accepts . . . that the prohibition of torture has achieved the status of a peremptory norm in international law . . . the Court is unable to discern in the international instruments, judicial authorities or other materials before it any firm basis for concluding that . . . a State no longer enjoys immunity from civil suit in the courts of another State where acts of torture are alleged . . . The Court, while noting the growing recognition of the overriding importance of the prohibition of torture, does not accordingly find it established that there is yet acceptance in international law of the proposition that States are not entitled to immunity in respect of civil claims for damages for alleged torture committed outside the forum State' (paras 61–66). On the inherent tension between these two 'layers' of international law (the humanitarian and the sovereign layer), see Marco Sassoli, 'L'arrêt Yerodia: Quelques remarques sur une affaire au point de collision entre les deux couches du droit international' (2002) 106 *Revue Générale de Droit International Public* 791.

> Indeed, humans gave themselves all of their good and evil. Indeed, they did not take it, they did not find it, it did not fall to them as a voice from heaven
>
> . . .
>
> a thousand goals there have been until now, for there have been a thousand peoples. Only the fetters for the thousand necks are still missing, the one goal is missing. But tell me, my brothers: if humanity still lacks a goal, does it not also still lack – humanity itself?
>
> Friedrich Nietzsche, *Thus Spoke Zarathustra*[90]

In the present section, I have sought to show two things: that it is theoretically possible to think of unity by reference to the values that are expressed in positive law; and that, at the same time, this notion of axio-logical unity is far from simple or self-evident. In fact, what becomes apparent is that any attempt to transcend the multiplicity of rules by appealing to values is likely to move the analysis from one level of complexity to another. This is true, first of all, by reason of the absence of a stable or well-grounded value-system in international law. There are, instead, 'a thousand goals', as Zarathustra would say, and not simply because there are a thousand peoples, but also because, where common values do exist, these values are not always compatible. The second element of complexity follows from the fact that the 'super-determination' of norms by values can mean different things in different contexts, all answering to different 'logics of axiologisation': logic of interpretative focalisation, logic of narrative orientation, logic of peremptory validation and so forth. There are, in other words, many different levels and models of axio-logical unity.

To speak of axio-logical unity is thus not an easy thing to do. The axiology of international law is not a given that is simply 'there', once and for all, and is available for description and analysis. No table of values is given to us 'as a voice from heaven'. This does not mean, however, that the axio-logical perspective is a dead-end, or that we should not speak of values. Zarathustra, who was an early internationalist, observed that humanity lacks a single order of values. Yet he immediately added: if humanity still lacks a goal, is it not because 'it still lacks humanity itself'? The important point here is of course the adverb 'still'. It suggests that, whilst humanity remains axio-logically underdeveloped, it is nonetheless in the making.

The axio-logical perspective is thus a possibility of discourse, provided however that we use it '*à tâtons*', as Delmas-Marty puts it, that is, carefully, gradually, with prudence, and always keeping in mind that no community of values is given to us at the outset and that things develop slowly, step by step, and often in a disorderly fashion.[91] Different value orders (state values, humanitarian values,

[90] Friedrich Nietzsche, *Thus Spoke Zarathustra* (Cambridge, Cambridge University Press, 2006) 17, 43–44.

[91] 2007–08 lectures at the Collège de France, *Les forces imaginantes du droit (IV) – Vers une communauté de valeurs*, general conclusion, 20 May 2008, online (audio): www.college-de-france.fr/default/EN/all/int_dro/contenu_coursbrseminaires_ante.htm.

mercantile and non-mercantile values, etc) emerge simultaneously at the national, regional and international levels and the articulation between these different orders follows no coherent blueprint. The ordering of values often takes place on an ad hoc basis, almost by improvisation. International law lacks a single, central authority with the power to resolve tensions between competing values or value systems. As a result, the 'fettering of the thousand necks', which Zarathustra calls for, takes place haphazardly. A few 'founding prohibitions' are laid down (war crimes and crimes against humanity). Juridical techniques are developed to seek and reconcile the universality of human rights and the diversity of national cultures (national margin of appreciation). New concepts and vocabularies are invented to promote greater integration of economic and non-economic values (sustainable development). The realm of values is in the process of being developed. And one can imagine or, like Delmas-Marty, hope that it is through values that humanity will eventually be constituted. The important thing here is to accept axio-logical unity for what it is: not a ready-made catalogue of values, which is already there for us to use and build upon, but rather a complex and gradual construct.

8

General Conclusion: *Unitas Multiplex*

Un à un
les Huns
passent l'Aisne.
Nos aines confondent nos haines,
Henri Heine.
Un à un
les Huns
deviennent des nains.
Perdez-vous dans l'Ain
et non dans l'Aisne.

Hein?

Robert Desnos, *Corps et biens*[1]

HUMAN BEINGS ARE metaphysical animals.[2] By nature, we desire to know. By nature, we therefore demand unity. For if we desire to make sense of the world, in spite of its immense complexity, we must presuppose that the world unfolds in a systematic pattern of which we can gain knowledge. Albert Camus once called this natural – and in his view absurd – appetite for unity, clarity and familiarity '*la nostalgie d'unité*'.[3]

Human beings are also body-minded animals.[4] We are innately disposed to interpret our existence and the world around us in terms of bodily unity. Our sensory fields are naturally and spontaneously organised in terms of distinctive kinds of units. Unity, in a sense, is the condition *sine qua non* for the operation of human intelligence. This, too, is part of our inborn constitution and controls the interpretation of our experience, be it individual or collective.

This book began with a rather simple observation. Since the end of the Second World War, and more so still since the end of the Cold War, the discipline of international law has been seized by a sort of postmodern anxiety. Faced with

1 Robert Desnos, *Corps et biens* (Paris, Gallimard, 1968) 58.

2 Arthur Schopenhauer, *Le monde comme volonté et comme représentation* (Paris, PUF, 1996) 294.

3 Albert Camus, *Le mythe de Sisyphe* (Paris, Gallimard, 1942) 34–35.

4 Willard Quine, *The Roots of Reference* (La Salle, Open Court, 1990) 54: 'Bodies, bodily identity and bodily persistence, are the mainstay of ontology. Bodies, for the common man, are basically what there are; and even for the esoteric ontologist bodies are the point of departure. Man is a body-minded animal'.

technical, social and cultural change, the acceleration of historical time, the seemingly exponential widening and deepening of the juridical field, the multiplication of rules and institutions, the emergence of legal monsters, many international lawyers have started feeling like the playthings of a capricious history, advancing at full speed toward an unknown destination. The fragmentation angst was born out of this feeling that international law is involved in a sort of headlong rush whose trajectory and rhythm lawyers are no longer able to control. To be sure, not all international lawyers experience or comprehend this evolution in the same way. What is certain, however, is that fragmentation fascinates and impassions large numbers of international lawyers.

Yet *because* it is the object of fear and passion, what was at first a simple nostalgia for unity became a somewhat compulsive, almost obsessive concern. Unity became something of an empty formula, used and abused by international lawyers as if to slow down history and contain international law's outbursts and overflowings, but without ever being rationalised, justified or explained. It is as if unity had always been there, or as if the concept of unity was so plain and self-evident that it needed no elucidating or theorising.

In response to this rather chaotic, undefined and simplifying use of the concept of unity, the main purpose of this book has been to suspend the fragmentation discourse, to put it on hold. The goal is not so much to take sides, to argue for or against the proliferation of regimes and institutions in international law, but rather to ask a preliminary question without which everything else makes little sense: what does it mean to say that international law is – or was – 'one'? Whilst international lawyers often speak of the unity of their law, and of the dangers to which this unity is exposed, what do we really know about this taken-for-granted concept?

Though the question may appear simple or elementary at first sight, I have sought to show throughout this book that it is in fact infinitely complex. This complexity stems, first of all, from the multiplicity of the levels of analysis, of the theoretical doors through which unity can be examined and conceptualised. The conventional discourse on unity/fragmentation tends to reduce unity to issues of compatibility and formal arrangement between rules. I have tried to pluralise and complicate the analysis by showing that unity can be approached from at least three other perspectives: the cultural, the epistemo-logical and the axio-logical perspectives.

But the aforementioned complexity also stems from the fact that each level of analysis gives rise to a great diversity of possible theories. Material unity, as we have seen, refers to the absence of conflicts in the law. Yet there are at least three ways of defining normative conflicts. Formal unity concerns the orderly arrangement of norms into a system. But this formal arrangement can be of an institutional, inter-normative or hermeneutic nature. Cultural unity involves the internal structures of international law as an intellectual and a professional discipline, and these structures can be either mental or discursive. Axio-logical unity refers to the super-determination of norms by juridical values, but super-determination can follow a logic of supralegality or a mere logic of normative orientation.

Finally, there is complexity in the unity question simply because international law is a very peculiar type of law. International law is a disembodied legal order, a law without a clearly identified head or backbone. This raises a number of specific difficulties regarding, for instance, the determinacy and acceptance of secondary rules, the 'invisibility' of the college of international lawyers, or the interaction between different value orders (the 'fettering of the thousand necks').

Upon reaching the general conclusion of this book, we are thus confronted with a sort of paradox. The initial purpose of this book was to elucidate the rather vague and fuzzy concept of unity, which is often used instinctively, without further explanation. Yet in the end, we are left with a three-layered complexity. One might say, to paraphrase Desnos, that we are getting lost in unity – *on se perd dans l'un*!

This semantic dispersal and disruption is fully intentional. To be sure, there is always something reassuring in the sameness and stability of knowledge. And keeping things in the theoretical dark does sometimes make it possible to reach some form of consensus or surface unanimity. As Francis Bacon once said: 'all colours agree in the dark'![5] Yet Bacon immediately added that these forms of superficial unanimities are 'false peaces or unities'. They are grounded in 'implicit ignorance' and lead to confusion, rather than truth or progress.[6]

This book, in a sense, begins to unpack the sort of 'implicit ignorance' which has thus far dominated the fragmentation debate in international law. By doing so, and deconstructing the sort of floating notion of unity generally found in the literature, it does of course raise more questions than it answers. Two things, however, have been firmly established. The first is that there are many ways for international law to be 'one'. The second is that, depending on the point of view from which it is considered, unity will mean different things in different contexts. Objects, criteria and dynamics of unity vary from one level of analysis to another. In the end, unity presents itself as a complex assemblage of forces and dynamics that may complement or contradict each other. The notion of *Unitas Multiplex* denotes this complex and plural reality of unity.[7]

That being said, and instead of simply reformulating the arguments developed in the book, I shall bring this exploratory philosophy of unity to a close by developing a general conclusion in the form of a prolongation and of an opening. A prolongation, first of all, in which I shall seek to show through a concrete

[5] Francis Bacon, *Essays* (Oxford, Oxford University Press, 1955) 8: 'there be also two false peaces, or unities: the one, when the peace is grounded, but upon an implicit ignorance; for all colors will agree in the dark: the other, when it is pieced up, upon a direct admission of contraries, in fundamental points. For truth and falsehood, in such things, are like the iron and clay, in the toes of Nebuchadnezzar's image; they may cleave, but they will not incorporate'.

[6] Ibid.

[7] On this notion, see Edgard Morin and Jean-Louis Le Moigne, *L'intelligence de la complexité* (Paris, L'Harmattan, 1999) 224–26.

example that what this book suggests about the concept of unity is not only interesting on a philosophical level, but also has practical implications for our vision and our interpretation of international law. And an opening, lastly, on some of the sociological and professional considerations that lie in the shadow of the fragmentation debate and that might begin to explain why the question of unity has remained so largely under-theorised.

I. CHANGING LENSES: *TADIC* REVISITED

Throughout this book, I have attempted to show that concepts of unity and fragmentation are elusive, contested, and multi-faceted. Unity can be conceptualised at many different levels and from many different perspectives, each possessing its own underlying logic. Although one can express preference for one or the other perspective, no perspective is self-evident, objectively 'truer' or logically superior to the others. As a result, arguments about fragmentation are inevitably contingent. They mirror a particular perspective on unity and, ultimately, certain preferences regarding the nature of law and its function in the international community. What appears fragmented from one point of view might very well look united from another. A recent example should help illustrate this point.

The decision of the International Criminal Tribunal for the former Yugoslavia (ICTY) Appeals Chamber in the *Tadic* case[8] is widely regarded in the literature as an instance of fragmentation *par excellence*, an 'obvious and dramatic flash-point' for the fragmentation anxiety.[9] The ICTY in this case had to decide, among other things, whether the armed conflict in Bosnia was an international or a non-international armed conflict, in order to establish if, and to what extent, the Fourth Geneva Convention relative to the protection of civilian persons in time of war applied to the crimes committed by the accused. To do so, the Appeals Chamber had to decide whether the acts perpetrated in Bosnia by the Bosnian Serb Army (BSA) could be attributed to the Federal Republic of Yugoslavia (FRY), which would result in the conflict being 'internationalised'.

In a deliberate move to increase individual accountability for international crimes, the Appeals Chamber opted for the wide criterion of 'overall control' in lieu of the long-established test of 'effective control' developed by the ICJ in the *Nicaragua* case.[10] Under the effective control test, a state may only be held accountable for acts committed by individuals or groups of individuals if it has issued direct and specific instructions concerning the perpetuation of the

[8] *Prosecutor v Dusko Tadić*, Case No IT-94-1-A, ICTY Appeals Chamber, Judgment (15 July 1999) (hereafter *Tadić*).

[9] Ruti Teitel and Robert Howse, 'Cross-Judging: Tribunalization in a Fragmented but Interconnected Global Order' (2009) 41 *New York University Journal of International Law and Politics* 959, 962.

[10] *Case Concerning Military and Paramilitary Activities In and Against Nicaragua (Nicaragua v United States of America)* 27 June 1986, ICJ Reports (1986) 14.

unlawful acts in question.[11] The Appeals Chamber, for its part, took the view that this test was not relevant, at least not when dealing with highly organised and structured groups such as the BSA. For the Appeals Chamber, the control required by international law for attributing the acts of armed groups to a foreign state arises when a state 'has a role in organising, coordinating or planning' the acts in question. This requirement, however, does not go so far as to include the issuing of specific orders or instructions by the state.[12]

The vast majority of international lawyers have interpreted the *Tadic* decision as an event that compromises the unity of international law. Gilbert Guillaume, who was elected President of the ICJ a few months after the Appeals Chamber issued its judgment, spoke of it as a decision that 'breaks up' the law and warned against the risk of 'chaos' in public international law.[13] The International Law Commission, whose approach to fragmentation is more nuanced, described the consequences of *Tadic* as 'particularly problematic' for legal security and the equality of legal subjects.[14] Even authors who see fragmentation in a positive light, or take the view that the phenomenon is rather benign or marginal, seem to agree that *Tadic* constitutes an instance of fragmentation, albeit an isolated one.[15] There seems to be widespread agreement, in other words, on the fact that *Tadic* – for better or for worse – challenges the unity of international law.

This book tests this unanimous assumption, or at least sheds new light on it. If one interprets *Tadic* within the conceptual framework developed in this book, one quickly realises that the notion that *Tadic* constitutes fragmentation is in fact premised on a very specific vision of unity, and that other perspectives on unity may lead to very different interpretations. Let us consider, successively, the material, the cultural, and the axio-logical perspectives.

The notion that *Tadic* constitutes fragmentation is predicated upon a material conception of unity. The general view is that the decisions of the ICJ and ICTY are normatively incompatible and that this incompatibility is a source of incoherence and inconsistency in the law. *Tadic* and *Nicaragua*, in others words, conflict with one another, and this conflict compromises the unity of international law. What chapter four teaches us, however, is that the notion of conflict can be defined in a number of ways, some of which seem to suggest different interpretations.

[11] Ibid at para 115.

[12] *Tadic* above n 8 at para 137.

[13] Gilbert Guillaume, 'La Cour international de Justice – Quelques propositions concrètes à l'occasion du cinquantenaire' (1996) 100 *Revue Générale de Droit International Public* 323, 331.

[14] *Fragmentation of International Law: Difficulties Arising from the Diversification and Expansion of International Law – Report of the Study Group of the International Law Commission* (finalised by Martti Koskenniemi), UN Doc A/CN.4/L.682 (2006) paras 51–52.

[15] See, eg, Rosalyn Higgins, 'A Babel of Judicial Voices? Ruminations from the Bench' (2006) 55 *International and Comparative Law Quarterly* 791, 794; Pemmaraju Sreenivasa Rao, 'Multiple International Judicial Forums: A Reflection of the Growing Strength of International Law or Its Fragmentation?' (2004) 25 *Michigan Journal of International Law* 929, 955–57.

Leaving aside the question of whether conflicts between judicial decisions are conflicts of norms proper, it is important to recall that the existence of a conflict, under the narrow definition, presupposes some form of material overlap between the conflicting norms or decisions. For two norms to be in a conflict, they must deal with the same subject matter. Whether such overalap exists between *Tadic* and *Nicaragua* is not as obvious as might appear at first glance. According to one view, *Tadic* and *Nicaragua* deal with the same question: the conditions under which under international law an individual may be held to act as a *de facto* organ of a state. This was the view taken by the ICTY in *Tadic*. The Appeals Chamber found Nicaragua to be a relevant – though ultimately unpersuasive – precedent for the purpose of determining the nature of the armed conflict in Bosnia.[16] Under another view, however, *Tadic* and *Nicaragua* deal with two very different questions: individual criminal responsibility, on the one hand, and state responsibility on the other. This was the view taken by the Prosecution in *Tadic*, who contended that *Nicaragua* was immaterial and inapplicable to the issue of individual responsibility for grave breaches of the laws of war.[17] This was also the position taken by the ICJ in the 2007 *Bosnian Genocide Case*, in which the Court found that, logically speaking, *Tadic* and *Nicaragua* should not be put on the same plane. The two decisions, in the Court's view, deal with two issues which are 'very different in nature': *Tadic* is concerned with the degree and nature of a state's involvement in an armed conflict on another state's territory required for the conflict to be characterised as international; *Nicaragua*, on the other hand, deals with the degree and nature of involvement required to give rise to that state's responsibility for a specific act committed in the course of the conflict.[18]

Even assuming, as the ICTY does, that *Tadic* and *Nicaragua* apply to the same question or subject matter, the existence of a conflict under the narrow definition presupposes the existence of a deontic antinomy. *Stricto sensu* conflicts, it will be recalled, refer to situations where two norms are genuinely, mechanically and mutually exclusive, in other words, where there is no window of compatibility between them. Compliance with one norm automatically gives rise to a violation of the other. Here again, whether a true antinomy exists between *Tadic* and *Nicaragua* is largely open to question. Indeed, and contrary to what is generally reported, the ICTY in *Tadic* did not utterly reject the effective control test. The Appeals Chamber's decision is in fact more complex and nuanced than appearances might suggest. The Chamber does agree with the ICJ that the acts committed by private individuals may only be attributed to a state if the individuals have in effect acted under the control of that state. Yet the Chamber takes the view that the *degree of control* required for the purpose of

[16] *Tadic* above n 8 at paras 102–05.

[17] Ibid at paras 69–72.

[18] *Case Concerning the Application of the Convention on the Prevention and Punishment of the Crime of Genocide (Bosnia and Herzegovina v Serbia and Montenegro)* 26 February 2007, ICJ Reports (2007) 1, para 405.

attribution may vary according to circumstances.[19] According to the Appeals Chamber, two situations must be distinguished: the situation where the acts have been committed by a single private individual or a group that is not militarily organised, and the situation where the acts have been committed by organised and hierarchically structured groups such as militias or paramilitary units. In the Chamber's view, the first situation should undoubtedly be governed by the *Nicaragua* test, and the issuing of specific instructions by the state is therefore required.[20] By contrast, the second situation calls for a different, more flexible criterion of attribution. An organised group, according to the Chamber, differs from an individual in that it has a structure, a chain of command, a set of rules and the outward symbols of authority.[21] Members of an organised group do not act on their own. They are subject to the authority of the group leader and conform to the standards prevailing in the group. As a result, the issuance of specific and direct instructions to individual members of the group is not required for the purpose of attribution. It is sufficient, according to the Chamber, that the group as a whole be under the overall control of the state.[22]

It becomes apparent that there is no strict or necessary incompatibility between *Tadic* and *Nicaragua*. There is, between the two decisions, a margin of compatibility. One way of interpreting the relationship between *Tadic* and *Nicaragua* is to think of the two decisions as being in a relationship of accumulation: the *Nicaragua* test, on the one hand, governs situations where acts are committed by single individuals; the *Tadic* test, on the other hand, governs situations where acts are committed by organised groups. Under this interpretation, both tests are valid and applicable simultaneously. They do not exclude each other.[23]

In reality, only a wide definition of conflict allows us to speak of *Tadic* as an instance of fragmentation. In its widest definition, the concept of conflict refers to situations where two norms get in each other's way, that is, situations where norms, although not strictly incompatible, follow diverging normative trajectories and point in different directions. From this perspective, there is a little doubt that a conflict exists between *Tadic* and *Nicaragua*.

[19] *Tadic* above n 8 at para 137: 'international law rules do not always require the same degree of control over armed groups or private individuals for the purpose of determining whether an individual not having the status of a State official under internal legislation can be regarded as a de facto organ of the state. The extent of the requisite State control varies'.

[20] Ibid: 'Where the question at issue is whether a single private individual or a group that is not militarily organized has acted as a de facto State organ when performing a specific act, it is necessary to ascertain whether specific instructions concerning the commission of that particular act had been issued by that State to the individual or group in question'.

[21] Ibid at para 120.

[22] Ibid at para 137: 'acts performed by the group or members thereof may be regarded as acts of de facto State organs regardless of any specific instruction by the controlling State concerning the commission of each of those acts'.

[23] For a similar interpretation, see Antonio Cassese, 'The Nicaragua and Tadic Tests Revisited in Light of the ICJ Judgment on Genocide in Bosnia' (2007) 18 *European Journal of International Law* 649, 655–63.

Nicaragua follows a Westphalian logic centered on the sovereign autonomy of states. In the ICJ's view, states should not be held accountable for acts committed by non-state actors like militias or paramilitary groups. States are responsible for their own behaviour only. A clear distinction must be maintained between state and non-state violence. Attribution should only take place in the most extreme circumstances, where individuals depend on the state to such an extent that their actions are, for legal purposes, comparable the actions of *de facto* organs of the state.[24] Hence the narrow criterion of effective control.

Tadic, for its part, follows a post-Westphalian logic aimed at maximising accountability for international crimes. What matters to the ICTY is not preserving the sovereign autonomy of states or maintaining the canonical distinction between state and non-state violence. Rather, the ICTY seeks to ensure maximum protection for civilian populations and as wide an application of the laws of war as possible. From this point of view, it becomes important to ensure that states do not escape international responsibility simply by having private individuals carry out unlawful tasks and then arguing that these individuals are not classified as state organs under their domestic legislation.[25] Hence the wider criterion of 'overall control'.

On this particular question, *Nicaragua* and *Tadic*, it seems, 'point in different directions'. The two decisions work at cross-purposes. One decision seeks to undo that which the other seeks to sustain. In this wide sense, and in this wide sense only, a normative conflict can be said to exist.

This interpretation of *Tadic*, however, remains grounded in a material conception of unity, in which the focus is placed on issues of normative coherence among rules and institutions. Viewed from other perspectives, the *Tadic* decision takes on a whole new meaning. Let us consider, for example, the cultural perspective addressed in chapter six of this book. Cultural unity, as previously argued, does not refer to considerations of normative consistency among individual rules, but rather to the stability of international law's grammatical forms and intellectual structures. In this respect, it is doubtful whether *Tadic* can be read as a signal of fragmentation.

[24] *Nicaragua*, above n 10 at para 116: 'the Court does not consider that the assistance given by the United States to the contras warrants the conclusion that these forces are subject to the United States to such an extent that any acts they have committed are imputable to that State. It takes the view that the contras remain responsible for their acts, and that the United States is . . . responsible for its own conduct'. See also *Bosnian Genocide Case*, above n 18 at para 406: 'a State is responsible only for its own conduct, that is to say the conduct of persons acting, on whatever basis, on its behalf . . . the "overall control" test is unsuitable, for it stretches too far, almost to breaking point, the connection which must exist between the conduct of a State's organs and its international responsibility'.

[25] *Tadic* above n 8 at para 117: 'if it is proved that individuals who are not regarded as organs of a State by its legislation nevertheless do in fact act on behalf of that State, their acts are attributable to the State. The rationale behind this rule is to prevent States from escaping international responsibility by having private individuals carry out tasks that may not or should not be performed by State officials, or by claiming that individuals actually participating in governmental authority are not classified as State organs under national legislation and therefore do not engage State responsibility'.

The ICTY, to begin with, is not a hyper-specialised institution that stands clinically isolated from the rest of international law. Although the ICTY is an ad hoc tribunal, it was established under the auspices of the UN Security Council and sits in The Hague, the capital (some might say the Mecca) of international law, alongside the Academy of International Law, the International Court of Justice and the Permanent Court of Arbitration. The ICTY is also composed primarily (though not exclusively) of 'generalist' international lawyers. Behind the *Tadic* judgment, for instance, was Antonio Cassese, a world-renowned academic in the field of public international law and a member of the *Institut de Droit International*.[26]

This pedigree has a clear impact on the work of the ICTY, and the judgment in *Tadic* is typical in this respect. When discussing the legal grounds on which armed forces engaged in an internal conflict can be regarded as acting on behalf of a foreign power, the ICTY unquestionably speaks the language of public international law. In fact, the tribunal goes so far as to explicitly acknowledge the need for the laws of war to be read, interpreted and – where necessary – supplemented by or in light of 'general' international law:

> International humanitarian law does not contain any criteria unique to this body of law for establishing when a group of individuals may be regarded as being under the control of a State . . . Consequently, it is necessary to examine the notion of control by a State over individuals, laid down in general international law, for the purpose of establishing whether those individuals may be regarded as acting as de facto State officials. This notion can be found in the general international rules on State responsibility[27]

In a sense, the Appeals Chamber situates its legal reasoning within the confines – one might say under the authority – of public international law. Far from reading its branch of the law (humanitarian law) hermetically, as a self-contained and fully autonomous regime, it seeks the solution to a specific problem of humanitarian law (the nature of the armed conflict) in the general rules on state responsibility.

Furthermore, the ICTY refers extensively to the ICJ findings in the *Nicaragua* case when ascertaining and interpreting these general rules on state responsibility, and this in spite of the Prosecution's objection that *Nicaragua* is entirely immaterial to the issue of individual criminal responsibility. To be sure, the Appeals Chamber ultimately finds the *Nicaragua* test unpersuasive. Yet it recognises the 'authority' of the ICJ on matters pertaining to general international law and only discards the effective control test after a careful and lengthy analysis of case law, state practice and the spirit of the law on state responsibility, with which the Chamber finds *Nicaragua* to be at variance. Whereas the ICJ in

[26] The other four judges were: Mohamed Shahabuddeen (former ICJ judge and member of the *Institut*); Wang Tieya (professor of public international law for 55 years and member of the *Institut*); Rafael Nieto-Navia (professor of public international law for 35 years and former President of the Inter-American Court of Human Rights) and Florence Ndepele Mzachande Mumba (member of the Permanent Court of Arbitration).

[27] *Tadic* above n 8 at para 98.

Nicaragua laid down the criterion of effective control without ever truly justifying it, the Appeals Chamber grounds its decision in a detailed examination of the practice of the US-Mexico Claims Commission, the Iran-US Claims Tribunal, the European Court of Human Rights, the Düsseldorf Court of Appeal, the Dutch Court of Cassation, the UN Security Council and, of course, the ICJ and the ILC. Only after this thorough analysis does the ICTY eventually conclude that the *Nicaragua* test is at variance with the letter and spirit of the law on international responsibility.[28]

Lastly, the ICTY's rejection of the effective control test tends to obscure the fact that the Appeals Chamber accepts that *some degree* of direction or control is always necessary to engage a state's responsibility. The Chamber, far from dismissing *Nicaragua* altogether, simply holds the view that international law need not require the same degree of control in all situations. In the presence of an organised and hierarchically structured group (with a chain of command, sets of rules and symbols of authority), the Chamber decides that the overall control test should apply. At the same time, however, it accepts that the effective control test should remain the rule in the case of crimes or acts committed by single private individuals.

In sum, in spite of what is admittedly a direct critique of the ICJ's reasoning in *Nicaragua*, and notwithstanding what appears to be a result that is inconsistent with general international law, the ICTY's decision essentially endorses the general principles and rules of international law. The decision of the Appeals Chamber rests on well-established grammatical forms and lines of argument. It mobilises the sources rhetoric and, to justify its rejection of the effective control test, moves back and forth between 'hard' arguments – treaties, state practice and international case law' – and 'soft' arguments – the 'spirit' of humanitarian law and the 'logic' of the law on state responsibility. The *Tadic* decision, in other words, follows discursive policies, an aesthetic of argument and enunciative protocols that are all characteristic of international law. *Tadic* is 'within the true' of the international law discourse. It is a 'disciplined' decision which, from a cultural point of view, can hardly be said to represent a breaking point. *Tadic* respects and maintains the structures of international law as a generative language and as a collective system of production and reproduction of legal arguments.

The move from the material to the cultural perspective significantly transforms our interpretation of *Tadic*. What appeared fragmented from one point of view now looks regular and consistent. The demonstration, however, can be taken a step further by looking at the axio-logical perspective. *Tadic*, in this perspective, takes on yet another meaning. Value-driven unity rests on the idea of a common denominator of fundamental values that transcend individual rules and provide the legal order with a general sense of direction. Fragmentation, in this perspective, does not stem from conflicts of norms. It occurs where a

[28] Ibid at paras 115–45.

regime, a government, or a tribunal undermines the axio-logical core of international law, whether this core is already well established or simply in the making.

On this particular point, *Tadic* seems to be doing precisely the opposite. By replacing the effective control test by the much more relaxed overall control test, the ICTY does, to be sure, deviate from a pre-existing ruling and creates normative friction with ICJ case law. Yet at the same time, the ICTY removes a significant barrier to the application of certain parts of international humanitarian law to the crimes committed by the Bosnian Serb Army in Bosnia. Had the Appeals Chamber applied the *Nicaragua* test, the crimes perpetrated by the Bosnian Serb Army would not have been attributed to Yugoslavia, resulting in the conflict being characterised as a non-international conflict and the Fourth Geneva Convention being inapplicable.[29]

By putting forward a more relaxed attribution test, applicable to the acts committed by organised and structured groups, *Tadic* offers a response to the problem posed by the rigidity of *Nicaragua*'s one-size-fits-all formula. The ICTY, in effect, considerably expands the material scope of application of international humanitarian law, and its justiciability. From this point of view, one might say that, by re-interpreting existing standards of general international law in light of new humanitarian considerations, the ICTY contributes to the progressive 'humanisation' of international law. This seems to be the ICTY's own view, as evidenced by a decision issued a few months only after *Tadic*, in which the Appeals Chamber held that:

> to the extent that it provides for greater protection of civilian victims of armed conflicts, this different and less rigorous standard is wholly consistent with the fundamental purpose of Geneva Convention IV, which is to ensure protection of civilians to the maximum extent possible[30]

Tadic can thus be interpreted as a decision that consolidates, not undermines, the emerging humanitarian core of the international legal order. Therefore, if *Tadic* can be seen as a decision that causes fragmentation from a strict material point of view, it can *also* be seen as a decision that *engenders* unity from an axio-logical point of view.

II. TERRITORIAL BATTLES AND MERCHANTS OF UNITY

> most of a philosopher's conscious thinking is secretly guided and channelled into particular tracks by his instincts. Behind all logic, too, and its apparent tyranny of

[29] Convention relative to the Protection of Civilian Persons in Time of War, 12 August 1949, art 2: 'the present Convention shall apply to all cases of declared war or of any other armed conflict which may arise between two or more . . . Parties'.

[30] *Prosecutor v Zlatko Aleksovski*, Case No IT-95-14/1-A, ICTY Appeals Chamber, Judgment (24 March 2000), para 146.

movement there are value judgements, or to speak more clearly, physiological demands for the preservation of a particular kind of life

Nietzsche, *Beyond Good and Evil*[31]

We have now reached the end of this study, with one key conviction and many new questions. The conviction is that there is no evident, objective or neutral approach to issues of fragmentation. What the previous section on *Tadic* has demonstrated is that, depending on one's point of view, the same norm or decision can be interpreted as fragmentation, continuity or unity. Any discourse on fragmentation, in other words, is predetermined by certain preferences regarding the nature and the function of international law as consisting of rules, language or values. It follows that unity, whether as a regulative idea or as a concept, must always be justified and substantiated. For unity is not a given, but rather a theoretical construct of which no facet is logically more rational or self-evident than another. Unless unity is justified, conceptualised and theorised, the debate on unity/fragmentation risks degenerating into a cacophony of competing voices in which arguments operate at different semantic levels and never really speak to one another. Some might be speaking of material unity whilst others are interested in formal, grammatical, ethical or axiological principles of unity. Debating unity and fragmentation in international law will serve little purpose if there is no shared understanding of, or at least some form of conversation on what the terms of the debate actually are.

This conviction, needless to say, implies no certainty. It merely opens up a new field of investigation about fragmentation and leads to further questioning. By way of conclusion, I shall briefly consider one of these further questions, which follows directly from the above discussion: given unity's highly ambiguous and multidimensional nature, why has the debate on fragmentation in international law remained so remarkably under-theorised? Why such intellectual reductionism in the face of complexity? This is a broad question which, alone, could be the topic of an entirely different book. I shall therefore only offer the beginning of an answer, a mere intuition, to open up the debate and initiate a different type of conversation about fragmentation issues.

This intuition concerns the territorial battles which, secretly, anonymously, almost clandestinely, guide and channel the fragmentation debate. What do I mean by 'territorial battles'? It is generally said that fragmentation involves conflicts between rules and institutions. Undoubtedly, this represents one aspect of the fragmentation phenomenon. International law today develops in diverse areas, at different speeds and in different directions, and this creates normative friction. Yet at the same time, one might ask if the fragmentation debate is perhaps also guided and determined by slightly different considerations, which concern not so much international law *per se* as its reconfiguration and its transformation as a professional field.

[31] Friedrich Nietzsche, *Beyond Good and Evil* (Oxford, Oxford University Press, 1998) 7.

Like any other professional field, international law represents a battleground where interests, power and prestige operate. International law professionals, like other legal professionals, struggle to secure a legitimate position for themselves within the legal field, and compete to conquer new markets for their legal expertise and services. Recent developments in international law have not only engendered normative friction. They have also led to a new distribution of knowledge, power and labour in the international law profession. One might ask, then, whether the fragmentation debate, or at least part of it, is also perhaps the mirror of a sort of hegemonic struggle between different classes of international lawyers fighting for the appropriation or re-appropriation of certain forms of social capital.

The fragmentation debate, it must be recalled, unfolded against the background of *specialisation*. Since 1945, international law has developed a series of autonomous branches or regimes, each generating its own norms and institutions to deal with increasingly complex and specific problems (trade, war, human rights, investments, telecommunications, environment and so forth). This progressive specialisation of international law – the 'splitting up' of law into functionally defined regimes and institutions – has far-reaching consequences for the sociology of the international law profession. Alongside these new regimes, new networks of professionals tend to develop, with technical expertise in specific domains of regulation and an authoritative claim to policy-relevant knowledge within these issue-areas. Inevitably, the rise of these 'epistemic communities' – with their own system of knowledge and communication, their own mindset, normative values and practices – challenges existing professional hierarchies.[32]

One important aspect of this evolution is the progressive marginalisation of the *Einheitsjurist* – the generalist, uniform and versatile lawyer – as the ideal-type professional model of classical international lawyer.[33] The ever-widening range of issues considered on the international agenda; the growing complexity of the international system in terms of the number of actors and the extent of interactions; and the expansion of the global economy lead many to regard all-encompassing or academic knowledge of the law as somewhat superfluous. Increasingly, the general feeling is that, in order to manage problems such as the trade of GMO food, the implementation of technical environmental standards, the management of pandemics or telecommunications, what is needed is no longer comprehensive wisdom but concrete, material and practical skills.[34]

This new deference to special/technical forms of legal expertise is also nourished by the sense that, unlike traditional or general international law, the new branches of international law are more like 'real' law: norms are thicker, harder

[32] On the role of epistemic communities in international regimes, see Peter Haas, 'Epistemic Communities and International Policy Coordination' (1992) 46 *International Organization* 1.

[33] On the figure of the Einheitsjurist, see Annette Keilmann, 'The Einheitsjurist: A German Phenomenon' (2006) 7 *German Law Journal* 293.

[34] Haas, 'Epistemic Communities', above n 32 at 12–13.

and more determinate (European law); they are enforced by judicial institutions, whose jurisdiction is compulsory and whose decisions are fully binding (WTO law). The voices of victims are heard (human rights). Remedies are available (investment law). Criminals are prosecuted and sent to prison (international criminal law). These new forms of regulation, in a sense, are not only deemed more useful. They are also regarded as more legitimate.[35]

All this leads to a progressive marginalisation of 'general' international law and its nineteenth-century categories (territory, statehood, treaties, state responsibility) as something that is merely doctrinal and theoretical, that is, something that is 'interesting but not essential'.[36] This is evidenced, for instance, by recent trends in legal education. Whilst interest in international law matters is growing among students, faculty and administrators, specialised courses (human rights, international criminal law, international environmental law, EU law) tend to vastly outnumber traditional international law courses (public international law, international organisations, use of force, etc). Equally revealing is the tendency in an increasing number of law schools to offer advanced or specialised international law courses without public international law serving as a prerequisite.[37] Even in institutions offering a rich curriculum in international law, general/public international law tends to become optional. As one commentator puts it, the feeling within law schools is that general/public international law is intellectually or 'academically valuable', but cannot be justified as preparation for what goes on in real-life practice (that is, in war crimes tribunals, human rights courts, trade negotiations or investment arbitrations).[38]

These developments, needless to say, considerably undermine the occupational power of 'generalist' international lawyers. Their *raison d'être*, credibility and utility as lawyers 'properly-so-called' becomes disputed, even *within* the international law discipline. With their social capital declining, prospects are dimming for the 'general practitioners' of international law and their know-how. Fewer universities, for instance, will hire generalists unless they are able and willing to teach 'real' law courses (constitutional law, EU law, international commercial law, etc).[39] Bureaucracies, whether domestic or international law,

[35] See Frédéric Mégret, 'Three Dangers for the International Criminal Court: A Critical Look at a Consensual Project' (2001) 12 *Finnish Yearbook of International Law* 193, 241–47.

[36] Gerry Simpson, 'On the Magic Mountain: Teaching Public International Law' (1999) 10 *European Journal of International Law* 70, 73.

[37] See the latest survey of international law in American and Canadian Law Schools by John K Gamble, *Teaching International Law in the 1990s* (Washington, American Society of International Law, 1992).

[38] See 'Roundtable on the Teaching of International Law' (1991) 85 *American Society of International Law Proceedings* 102, 109.

[39] For a view of what this situation implies for career advancement, see the provocative thoughts of Mary Ellen O'Connell in 'Roundtable on the Teaching of International Law', above n 38 at 111–13: 'within the ivory tower of the law school, there is a sense of inadequacy, a sense that international law is a lower priority, that it is an elective, that it is not as important as other courses . . . When I first started teaching at Indiana, my dean said to me: "After ten years we finally hired a public international law teacher. That's very nice. We would like, however, for you to teach a real law course in addition to international law. The students will take international law more seriously

seem to offer no better prospects for the generalist lawyer. There, too, functional specialisation is the *mot d'ordre*.[40] And finally, in the field of research, funding and publications – two critical forms of social capital in academia – clearly prioritise the special, the technical and the practical over the general, the doctrinal and the theoretical.

These transformations have led to the emergence of a new professional economy in which the dominant figure is no longer the *Einheitsjurist* but the specialist practitioner, with her concrete, technical and pragmatic expertise in a given area of the law. In this new professional hierarchy, old hierarchies are broken down and social capital is redistributed among new classes of international lawyers. With most of the legal business now going to the specialists, the generalist lawyers might be becoming the poor relative of international law. In these circumstances, it is not surprising that the generalists – who once held a monopoly over meaning and interpretation in international law – would experience and express a certain existential malaise, an 'anxiety of influence'.[41] When ICJ judges speak of the 'evisceration of the docket of the Court' and of the risk that the Court be 'cut off from a growing and very important part of the international law system', they clearly express this fear of professional exclusion and irrelevance.[42] If trade law goes to trade tribunals, human rights law to human rights tribunals, and investment law to investment tribunals – they seem to say – what function or purpose is there left for *me* and my expertise?

This phenomenon, it should be noted, is not confined to international law. Nearly every profession in which functional differentiation and specialisation have occurred has experienced similar tensions between the old cadres of the system and the new professionals. The medical field, to give but one example, has had its own fragmentation debate at the turn of the twentieth century, as medical and surgical specialities were proliferating. Faced with the rapidly growing – and often more lucrative – speciality practices, general medical practitioners (GPs) experienced an identity crisis not unlike that of the *Einheitsjurists* in today's international law profession. GPs, too, spoke against the compartmentalisation of professional knowledge and practice, denounced the loss of an

if they see you're teaching a real law course" . . . Public international law is where I do my research, where I have had years of graduate work, where I have practised. But I am encouraged to teach in an area where I have not had those kinds of rich experiences in order to display my capableness to my students . . . Thus, the vast majority of the evaluations say that I am a pretty good teacher, but not great . . . Of course, tenure is based upon the ability to teach, and that is taken almost entirely from the teaching evaluations. So, teaching international law has some down sides in the career of a law school academic'.

[40] At the time of writing this book, 21 out of 31 advertised UN legal jobs required specialisation or significant field experience in human rights, humanitarian affairs or international criminal law. See www.jobs.un.org/Galaxy/Release3/vacancy/vacancy.aspx.

[41] Susan Marks, 'State-Centrism, International Law, and the Anxieties of Influence' (2006) 19 *Leiden Journal of International Law* 339.

[42] Address to the Plenary Session of the General Assembly of the United Session by Judge Stephen M Schwebel, President of the International Court of Justice, 26 October 1999, available at: www.icj-cij.org/court/index.php?pr=87&pt=3&p1=1&p2=3&p3=1; Robert Jennings, 'The Role of the International Court of Justice' (1997) 68 *British Yearbook of International Law* 1, 57.

overall vision of the patient, and claimed that there is but one science and one art of medicine, against which all specialties must be tested and evaluated. And GPs, too, cloaked their opposition to specialisation in the morally superior vocabulary of 'patient interest', much like today's anxious generalist lawyers oppose fragmentation because of the risk it poses to the 'operation of justice'.[43]

In this new professional economy, several strategies are available to the general/public international lawyer to fight the prospect of professional *déclassement*. One such strategy is reconversion, that is, the repositioning of the generalist lawyer within the legal field.[44] To avoid being confined to the periphery of the discipline and being labelled 'romantic' or 'kitsch', generalists may become specialists themselves and find a new clientele for their legal services. Generalists may start writing, teaching or practising in special areas of the law, such as human rights, environmental law or the WTO (or, better yet, WTO *and* human rights/the environment). The most determined jurists might even attempt to create a new field of law of which they, if successful, may become pioneers. Viewed from this perspective, the 'sustainable development law' movement can be seen as a strategy of conversion of symbolic capital, in which a small group of lawyers is making 'new law' with old concepts and principles. By calling sustainable development law an 'area of international law in its own right'[45] – where, in fact, most would agree that sustainable development is merely a 'conceptual matrix' or an 'interstitial norm'[46] – these lawyers create a new 'brand' of international law of which (only) they can claim to be the legitimate specialists.[47]

Strategic reconversion, however, comes at a cost. Professional reconversion is more than a mere 'hat-changing' exercise. One does not proclaim oneself a trade or environmental law specialist from one day to the next. Reconversion demands significant personal investment to acquire new expertise and become a credible professional. Generalists may also have good reasons – personal, political or otherwise – not to want to become specialists. For these reasons, general-

[43] See, eg, William Welch, 'The Unity of the Medical Sciences' (1906) 155 *Boston Medical Surgery Journal* 367; Joseph Arkwright, 'The Unity of Medicine' (1931) 25 *Proceedings of the Royal Society of Medicine* 179.

[44] On strategic reconversion, see Yves Dezalay, 'Professional Competition and the Social Reconstruction of Transnational Markets' in Yves Dezalay and David Sugarman (eds), *Professional Competition and Professional Power: Lawyers, Accountants and the Social Construction of Markets* (London, Routledge, 1995) 4.

[45] See, eg, Marie-Claire Cordonnier Segger and Ashfaq Khalfan, *Sustainable Development Law: Principles, Practices and Prospects* (Oxford, Oxford University Press, 2004) 368.

[46] On sustainable development as a conceptual matrix, see Pierre-Marie Dupuy, 'Où en est le droit international de l'environnement à la fin du siècle?' (1997) 101 *Revue Générale de Droit International Public* 873, 878. On sustainable development as an interstitial norm, see Vaughan Lowe, 'Sustainable Development and Unsustainable Arguments' in Alan Boyle and David Freestone (eds), *International Law and Sustainable Development: Past Achievements and Future Challenges* (Oxford, Oxford University Press, 1999) 31.

[47] This claim to (exclusive) fame is most evident in Cordonnier Segger and Khalfan, *Sustainable Development Law*, above n 45 at 369. After having defined international sustainable development law as a legal field 'in its own right', the two authors add that 'very few lawyers can realistically develop expertise in all of the diverse areas of law related to sustainable development'.

ists will often prefer to fight marginalisation by engaging in what Bourdieu calls 'strategies of self-representation' (*strategies de présentation de soi*), that is, strategies that aim to portray the social universe in a way that is most favourable to one's social being.[48] Rather than – or in addition to – investing in regulatory niches, this type of strategy aims at defining international law in terms that privilege the skills and attributes of generalist lawyers themselves. Self-representation, for the (anxious) generalist, will typically consist of describing international law as a fully integrated – in other words unified – system; defending that unity not only as an epistemological imperative but as an empirically verifiable fact; and characterising diversification, proliferation and complexification as threats to the legitimacy and the efficacy of the legal order.[49]

The point, of course, is not to deny the existence or the importance of special regimes, but rather to insist that public international law, far from being optional or peripheral, is the systemic background from which no regime, however autonomous or sophisticated, is totally disconnected. In this perspective, regimes are reduced to 'sub-disciplines' (and, at times, legal specialists to second-rate 'sub-professionals').[50] They never operate outside public international law, but inevitably 'fall back' on its general principles of interpretation and application.[51] Trade law, human rights or EU law might represent the most advanced and sophisticated forms of international regulation. But they remain *subordinated* to general international law, of which they are but one segment or chapter.[52]

To speak of the unity of international law, from this point of view, is to define international law as a territory over which generalists have natural and necessary

[48] Pierre Bourdieu, *Méditations pascaliennes* (Paris, Seuil, 1997) 223.

[49] See, eg, Gilbert Guillaume, 'L'unité du droit international public est-elle aujourd'hui en danger?' (2003) 55 *Revue Internationale de Droit Comparé* 23; Pierre-Marie Dupuy, 'L'unité de l'ordre juridique international' (2002) 297 *Collected Courses of the Hague Academy of International Law* 9, 38–41.

[50] See, eg, Ian Brownlie, 'Problems Concerning the Unity of International Law' in *International Law in the Time of its Codification: Essays in Honor of Roberto Ago* (Milan, Giuffrè, 1987) 160:

> There is one remaining issue, and that is the problem of specialization and the consequent threat to the coherence of the law. Since the Second World War certain aspects of international law have received much attention from publicists and teachers, some with little grounding in general international law, who have focused on the particular field of interest . . . with no sense of the place of the subject-matter within the matrix of rules of general international law . . . Certain of the writers . . . on specialist subjects are not in fact qualified lawyers, and some of the literature shows a lack of analytical rigour.

[51] Bruno Simma and Dirk Pulkowski, 'Of Planets and the Universe: Self-Contained Regimes in International Law' (2006) 17 *European Journal of International Law* 483, 507–12.

[52] For a representative example, see Alain Pellet, 'Human Rightism and International Law' (2000) *Gilberto Amado Memorial Lecture Series*, at: www.alainpellet.fr/Documents/PELLET%20-%20 2000%20-%20Human%20rightism%20and%20international%20law%20%28G.%20 Amado%29.pdf. Pellet criticises human rights lawyers for their 'secessionist' tendencies and argues that human rights law remains 'firmly rooted in international law'. He warns that human rights specialists 'should be careful to avoid cutting the branch from the tree, for it would wither'. See also Prosper Weil, 'Le droit international économique, mythe ou réalité?' in SFDI (ed), *Aspects du droit international économique* (Paris, Pedone, 1972) 34: 'from a scientific point of view, international economic law is but one chapter of general international law' (author's translation).

jurisdiction. And to diagnose fragmentation as a pathological development is to create a social need, which calls for the kind of treatment that generalists alone can provide. The communication of former ICJ Presidents in the 1990s on the issue of proliferation is once again revealing. For not only did the ICJ Presidents speak of the risk of 'chaos' in international law, at a time when no genuine conflict had occurred between regimes or tribunals. They went on to suggest that, in order to preserve the coherence of international law, recourse should be had to the ICJ's advisory jurisdiction to arbitrate conflicts of norms or jurisdiction.[53] The subtext is clear: proliferation has created a need that (only) *I* can legitimately address.

The expansion, specialisation and increased complexity of international law have prompted new territorial battles in which different classes of lawyers compete to gain control over contested areas of work and specialisation.[54] Central to these territorial battles are what Bourdieu calls 'classification struggles' (*luttes de classement*), that is, cognitive quarrels between different groups of social agents ('ancients' versus 'moderns', 'generalists' versus 'specialists', 'old cadres' versus 'new technocrats') regarding the legitimate definition of the social space and of their role within it.[55] In this context, one quickly comes to realise, 'fragmentation' often constitutes a rhetorical device used by generalist/public international lawyers as an instrument of symbolic legitimisation in their ongoing struggle for professional recognition and dominance.

If this strategy of self-representation is to be successful, however, it must not say its name. Indeed, the key to winning the competition is having the symbolic hierarchies and interpretive procedures advocated by generalist lawyers deemed acceptable and legitimate by the rest of the legal profession and by their audience (states, international organisations, transnational corporations, universities and so forth). The unity/fragmentation rhetoric must therefore be couched in language that is sufficiently neutral, objective and universal to be perceived as a public policy issue, not as the defensive strategy of a particular class of lawyers competing for business. When ICJ President Guillaume, for instance, expressed his concern about forum shopping before the General Assembly, his claim was that conflicting judgments would generate confusion which, in turn, would 'distort the operation of justice'.[56] Before the Sixth Committee, he confirmed that overlapping jurisdictions and conflicting jurisprudence 'would be profoundly damaging to international justice'.[57] The vocabulary is both

[53] See 'The proliferation of international judicial bodies: The outlook for the international legal order', Speech by His Excellency Judge Gilbert Guillaume, President of the International Court of Justice, to the Sixth Committee of the General Assembly of the United Nations, 27 October 2000, available at: www.icj-cij.org/presscom/index.php?p1=6&p2=1&pr=85&search=%22nagymaros%22.

[54] See Yves Dezalay, 'Territorial Battles and Tribal Disputes' (1991) 54 *Modern Law Review* 792.

[55] Pierre Bourdieu, 'Classement, déclassement, reclassement' (1978) 24 *Actes de la recherche en sciences sociales* 2.

[56] Speech by HE Judge Gilbert Guillaume, President of the International Court of Justice, to the General Assembly of the United Nations, 30 October 2001, available at: www.icj-cij.org/court/index.php?pr=82&pt=3&p1=1&p2=3&p3=1.

[57] Above n 53.

impersonal (conflict of norms) and universal (operation of justice). This is not – the argument seems to say – *my* problem as a professional losing influence over the discipline. Instead, fragmentation concerns us all: it endangers the very legitimacy and efficacy of international law as a whole.

This, in the end, explains why the discourse on fragmentation has remained one-dimensional, rather technical and under-theorised. To operate as a rhetorical instrument of symbolic legitimisation, unity/fragmentation must be given the appearance of historical inevitability and absolute necessity. This requires emptying fragmentation of its ideological and political content. Unity is therefore assumed, not explained. Fragmentation, for its part, is defined as an apolitical – quasi-accidental – problem. The vocabulary – overlapping jurisdiction, conflict of norms, conflict-resolution techniques, source hierarchy, treaty interpretation – is for the most part neutral. And, at the end of the day, subjective anxieties are turned into universal concerns.

To think of unity and fragmentation solely as a substantive/technical problem of normative conflicts, as the above makes clear, is to conduct the analysis on the basis of conceptual categories created by and for the merchants of unity themselves. It is perfectly understandable that generalists, like every other social agent, are guided by a demand for preservation and that they seek to promote certain types of knowledge and representations that favour their social relevance. The point here is not to stigmatise a particular class of international law professionals or to reduce the semantic-conceptual complexity of unity to these tribal disputes. The point is simply that these dynamics exist, that they matter, and that they tend to channel thinking into tracks and directions that *precisely* do not do justice to the multi-dimensional nature of unity and fragmentation. I do not mean to suggest that fragmentation does not exist or that normative conflicts do not pose any real, practical problems. Neither am I suggesting that *all there is* to fragmentation are these hegemonic struggles. On the contrary, my argument is that only after revealing these professional dynamics can the debate 'take off' and develop beyond the narrow limits within which it is currently held. Explicating these territorial battles is also, in a sense, liberating discourse from them and opening up the debate to a series of questions which, to date, have remained largely unexplored.

International lawyers, by and large, favour the unity of their law, but what type of unity does international law need today? Should one be content with a form of aesthetic or formal unity? Or should we move beyond the mere management of normative frictions and rethink international law as a blueprint for society? Which rationality and which values should make up that project: state sovereignty or human dignity? Human rights or security? Trade or the environment? Should lawyers be in charge of deciding and arbitrating between different value-systems? If so, how can we ensure that their decisions are legitimate, that is, reflective of the needs and aspirations of the international community as a whole, and not simply of a handful of privileged nations (or, worse, of privileged lawyers)?

The discourse on fragmentation should be taken with a pinch of salt and with some critical distance. Our traditional concern for doctrinal purity should not distract us from more meaningful conversations about the substance and direction of the law. Instead of asking whether *Tadic* is 'fragmenting' international law, we ought perhaps to be debating the actual merits of the ICTY decision and what it says about the state, the individual, the humanitarian project and so forth. I shall not engage in this kind of conversation here. As stated in the introduction, this book only aims to make a start, to bring some light to bear on the conditions of possibility of discourse about unity in international law, and to open the door to complexity. This door has been opened. The debate can now head through the doorway.

For my part, I shall head through the door of complexity by going back, one last time, to Deleuze – a fellow traveller throughout this philosophical journey – and his *Anti-Oedipus*.[58] Why conclude with the *Anti-Oedipus*, a book on desire? The first reason lies in Deleuze's general approach, which is directed against the 'technicians of desire' who subjugate the multiplicity of desire to the twofold law of structure and lack. Deleuze wants to move beyond Freud, beyond the psychoanalysts and the semiologists, in order to study desire in all its diversity, its flux and reflux, its fluid dynamics and its lines of flight. This book, in a sense, represents a very modest attempt at duplicating this approach and applying it to the field of international law, against the 'technicians of unity', who want to reduce international law's unity to the twofold law of rule and conflict, and in favour of a more complex analysis that thinks of unity in terms of movement, cross-flows, overlaps and mobile arrangements between a plurality of principles and dynamics of unity.

The Anti-Oedipus is interesting for another reason, however. Halfway through their examination of 'desiring machines', Deleuze and Guattari put forward an idea that is a simple as it is correct: 'no one – they observe – has ever died from contradictions'.[59] The present book explores the concept of unity through a series of juxtapositions, proliferations and super-impositions. By doing so, it opens the door to new and unsuspected contradictions. But contradictions are not the death of thought. International law – and we as international lawyers – are not facing possible death by contradiction. If all unities are not worth preserving, neither are all fragmentations worth rejecting. Making good law or good justice sometimes demands breaking old norms and institutions. We, as theoreticians, need to think about international law's complex unity without complexes, in a dispassionate way, by seeking to achieve greater coherence where possible, but also by being prepared to welcome legal advances in their spontaneous and disorderly irruption, in the play of their differences and immediacy, even if contradictory or conflictual. Kant himself, who was anything but an advocate of fragmentation, conceded that good can come out of friction, opposition or conflict:

[58] Gilles Deleuze and Felix Guattari, *Anti-Oedipus: Capitalism and Schizophrenia* (London, Continuum, 2004).

[59] Ibid at 166.

> [I]t is resistance that awakens all human powers . . . [Without] the resistance that each person necessarily encounters in his selfish presumptuousness, human beings would live the arcadian life of shepherds, in full harmony, contentment, and mutual love. But all human talents would thus lie eternally dormant . . . all of the excellent natural human predispositions would lie in eternal slumber, undeveloped. Humans desire harmony, but nature knows better what is good for their species: it wills discord . . . continual resistance drive one to the renewed exertion of one's energies, and hence to the further development of the natural predispositions'[60]

Concord may thus be established through discord. Or better yet: there can be no progress without discord, no new developments without a new exertion of forces and energies. Complex thinking, in international law, must thus be able to integrate and absorb conflicts and competition between norms, regimes and institutions as normal, perhaps even desirable, elements in the life of the law. This is a challenge to legal reason, which tends to despise emptiness, randomness and multiplicity. This may also be the source of new anxieties. The mix is unstable. It makes the juridical machine more difficult to comprehend and operate. But what matters, in the end, is for the machine to function. On this point, let us find comfort one last time in the work of Deleuze and Guattari:

> The more [the social machine] breaks down, the more it schizophrenizes, the better it works . . .[61]

[60] Immanuel Kant, 'Idea for a Universal History From a Cosmopolitan Perspective' in *Toward Perpetual Peace and Other Writings on Politics, Peace, and History* (New Have, Yale University Press, 2006) 7–8.

[61] Deleuze and Guattari, *Anti-Oedipus*, above n 58 at 8.

Index

www.ingramcontent.com/pod-product-compliance
Ingram Content Group UK Ltd.
Pitfield, Milton Keynes, MK11 3LW, UK
UKHW020812290926
15470UKWH00003B/1105

9 781849 460439